Green Politics in Japan

A breakthrough into the political mainstream seems unlikely for Japan's Green political parties. Increasing concern about the environment has yet to manifest itself in a fashion similar to the rise of Green parties in Europe. In Japan the well-oiled party machines of the established political groupings continue to dominate the social networks that are crucial for electoral success.

Lam Peng-Er examines the strengths and organizations of Japan's "Greenest" party, NET (The Network Movement), as well as the older parties such as the LDP (Liberal Democratic Party) and the JCP (Japan Communist Party). He looks at the strong grassroots support for the LDP and the JCP, and the ways in which they are able to undermine NET through the adoption of certain Green policies. The ideology, support and sponsors of NET are also closely analyzed, as is the role of women.

Green Politics in Japan reveals that urban politics in post-industrial Japan is still dominated by the old parties and the conservative values of hierarchy and deference that bind voters to the likes of the LDP. Lam Peng-Er demonstrates that until such ties and attitudes change, any Green political force in Japan is likely to remain a minor one.

Lam Peng-Er is a lecturer in the Department of Political Science, National University of Singapore.

The Nissan Institute/Routledge Japanese Studies Series

Editorial Board

Other titles in the series:

Biotechnology in Japan
Malcolm Brock

Britain's Educational Reform: a Comparison with Japan
Michael Howarth

Language and the Modern State: the Reform of Written Japanese
Nanette Twine

Industrial Harmony in Modern Japan: the Intervention of a Tradition
W. Dean Kinzley

Japanese Science Fiction: a View of a Changing Society
Robert Matthew

The Japanese Numbers Game: the Use and Understanding of Numbers in Modern Japan
Thomas Crump

Ideology and Practice in Modern Japan
Roger Goodman and Kirsten Refsing

Technology and Industrial Development in pre-War Japan
Yukiko Fukasaku

Japan's Early Parliaments 1890–1905
Andrew Fraser, R.H.P. Mason and Philip Mitchell

Japan's Foreign Aid Challenge
Alan Rix

Emperor Hirohito and Shōwa Japan
Stephen S. Large

Japan: Beyond the End of History
David Williams

Ceremony and Ritual in Japan: Religious Practices in an Industrialized Society
Jan van Bremen and D.P. Martinez

Understanding Japanese Society: Second Edition
Joy Hendry

The Fantastic in Modern Japanese Literature: The Subversion of Modernity
Susan J. Napier

Militarization and Demilitarization in Contemporary Japan
Glenn D. Hook

Growing a Japanese Science City: Communication in Scientific Research
James W. Dearing

Green Politics in Japan

Lam Peng-Er

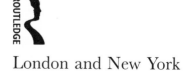

London and New York

First published 1999
by Routledge
11 New Fetter Lane, London EC4P 4EE

Simultaneously published in the USA and Canada
by Routledge
29 West 35th Street, New York, NY 10001

© 1999 Lam Peng-Er

Typeset in Baskerville by
J&L Composition Ltd, Filey, North Yorkshire
Printed and bound in Great Britain by
Biddles Ltd, Guildford and King's Lynn

British Library Cataloguing in Publication Data
A catalogue record for this book is available
from the British Library

Library of Congress Cataloging in Publication Data
A catalog record for this book has been requested

ISBN 0–415–19938–7

Contents

List of figures

List of tables

Series editor's preface

Japan, as the new century approaches, is going through a turbulent period in which some of her most entrenched institutions and practices are being increasingly questioned. The financial crisis which began in the latter half of 1997 – but whose origins go back several years earlier – gravely affected Japan, as well as other Asian countries. Quite apart from the economic and political implications of recession, widespread bankruptcies, increasing unemployment and a falling yen, the crisis is having a considerable impact on the psychology of ordinary Japanese people. They had been accustomed to steadily increasing prosperity and the international respect generated by the successes of their politico-economic model. Now, however, they were coming to wonder whether attitudes and ways of doing things that had been central to their lives and outlook over several decades were still appropriate to the disturbingly unstable world in which they now found themselves.

One straw in the wind was a hugely popular soap opera aired on Fuji Television in the spring of 1998, entitled *Shōmu 2* (General Affairs Section 2), in which a group of women office workers egotistically assert their rights as individuals and challenge time-honoured working practices. By challenging the prevailing atmosphere of ineffeciency, refusal to face up to responsibilities, conformism, sexual harassment of women and mindless deference to hierarchy, this feisty group of 'office ladies' succeeds in saving the company from bankruptcy.

However much of a caricature the Fuji TV soap opera may be, it is symptomatic of a spreading sense that not all is right in what used to be seen as an unbeatable set of methods for running society. Grave though the crisis being faced by Japan was as the century approached its close, the impressive human and material resources that the country was still able to command were advantageous in the struggle to overcome the crisis. Whatever might be the outcome at the economic level, however, a troubling intellectual problem remained. Few could doubt that radical reform was needed, but if this reform was simply to be a case of conformity with the norms of an

America-centred global economy (following the principles of the free market and egotistical individualism), where did that leave the status of Japanese values? History suggested that simple acceptance of foreign models was an unlikely outcome, and that ultimately a creative solution might emerge, mixing external with indigenous elements. To follow this process over the coming years should be an intriguing task.

The Nissan Institute/Routledge Japanese Studies Series seeks to foster an informed and balanced, but not uncritical, understanding of Japan. One aim of the series is to show the depth and variety of Japanese institutions, practices and ideas. Another is, by using comparisons, to see what lessons, positive or negative, may be drawn for other countries. The tendency in commentary on Japan to resort to outdated, ill-informed or sensational stereotypes still remains, and needs to be combated.

There are many studies of party politics in Japan, and it is widely thought of as being strongly embedded in the more traditional structures of Japanese society. Thus personal connections, local loyalties, pork-barrel politics, personal support machines, factionalism and the playing down of national policy issues are widely see as salient aspects of the way Japanese parties actually work. During the 1990s the party scene has been unusually turbulent, but although the Liberal Democrats, who have dominated politics for almost the entire period since the Second World War, were put into opposition for a period, they were eventually successful in clawing their way back to power. The Socialists, who were the largest party of opposition from the 1950s to the 1990s, have been reduced to a shadow of their former selves and in their place a progressive party called the Democratic Party has come into existence. Meanwhile the Communists, semi-dormant for many years, have been experiencing a limited resurgence.

Dr Lam's book, however, examines the development of a social movement party called the Network Movement (NET), which has had some recent success in urban local elections. It is very different from most other political parties in Japan. For one thing, it is dominated by women in a male-dominated society. It also emphasises the rights of consumers, hitherto much ignored in the Japanese system in the interests of producers. Third, it is deeply concerned with ecology and has much in common with Green parties in Europe and elsewhere.

This is a new sort of politics in Japan, and those involved in the NET are a radically new kind of politician. Dr Lam gives to the reader a perceptive analysis of the significance and future possibilities of this movement.

J. A. A. Stockwin
Director, Nissan Institute of Japanese Studies
University of Oxford

Acknowledgments

The origin of this book was a doctoral dissertation submitted to Columbia University. Completing the dissertion and converting it into a book was indeed a marathon of faith and hope, and a labor of love. In this trial of endurance, I was never alone. Along the route I had unstinting support, encouragement and understanding from family, teachers, and friends.

First, I would like to thank my Lord Jesus Christ for His love, joy, and protection. Next, I am very thankful to my supervisor Professor Gerald L. Curtis for his inspiring intellectual and moral support. He always had time for me and made my training at Columbia worthwhile and an experience to be cherished always. I am also grateful to Professor James Morley who encouraged me to study at Columbia when I first met him in Singapore. Not once did I regret taking his advice. Especially useful were his comments on the draft of my dissertation which helped me to crystallize my ideas. Learning the Japanese language was indeed an uphill climb. Fortunately, I had good and patient language teachers at Columbia and the Inter-University Center in Yokohama. Heartfelt thanks to them, especially Mrs Ito Watt who first introduced the language to me. In Japan, I enjoyed a one year homestay with the family of Dr Hayashi Akimune. I also benefited as a Visiting Scholar at the law faculty of Keio University, thanks to Professor Horie Fukashi. Professor Igarashi Akio, and Professor Watanabe Noboru also assisted me when I was in Japan. Ohta Hiroshi, my classmate at Columbia and fellow researcher at Keio, provided comradeship and help in preparing a questionnaire in Japanese. He also painstakingly checked and corrected my Japanese translations.

I am also thankful to Umezawa Kenji, Secretary General of the Kanagawa Liberal Democratic Party (LDP), for allowing me to follow his political campaign in the 1991 Local Election. In addition, the Seikatsu Club consumer co-operative members, the LDP, the Network Movement, and Japanese Communist Party assembly members, party officials, and ordinary members were extremely helpful, generous, and co-operative during my research and interviews. Also appreciated was the tremendous response from NET assembly women to my 1992–93 questionnaire survey about the Network Movement.

Many thanks to Professor T. J. Pempel, Dr Kevin Tan, Dr Huang Jianli, and Dr James Jesudason who commented on various sections of my dissertation. I would also like to thank my referees from Routledge for their critique of my manuscript. It has been a pleasure to work with Ms Victoria Smith, Senior Editor, Routledge, on this and other academic projects. Thanks also to Ms Elizabeth Gant, Ms Diane Stafford, Mr Malcolm Henson, and Mr Joe Whiting for their able assistance in bringing this book into fruition. Though I have benefited tremendously from the comments of teachers, friends and reviewers, responsibility for errors of fact and judgment (which are inevitable in all human enterprise) are mine alone.

Three chapters of this book have already been published in academic journals. Earlier versions of chapters 2, 3, and 4 appeared in the *Asian Journal of Political Science*, the *Japan Forum*, and *Pacific Affairs*. Thanks to these journals for granting permission to reprint my articles.

Many thanks to the following institutions and people who provided me with generous financial support to bring this project into fruition: the National University of Singapore and Singapore tax payers for my salary, overseas stipend, and the cost of my education; Columbia University for a dissertation write-up scholarship, and the Lee Foundation for a round-trip ticket for my dissertation defense.

Love and gratitude to Janet for her unfailing love, unflinching support, and technical assistance. The latter included Japanese word processing for the NET questionnaire and formatting the manuscript to meet Routledge's stylistic requirements. In appreciation, for the boundless joy that she has given me, this book is dedicated to Janet and our daughter Karis Lam Xinyue.

A note on names

Japanese names are presented in the style of that language, that is, family name first and given name second. The bibliography is listed by family name for all authors.

1 Introduction

The advent of industrialism led to a burgeoning working class and the development of labor unions. In twentieth-century Europe, workers and their unions provided mass membership, funds, organizational support, and votes to labor-based parties.[1] Bourgeois parties responded by building mass organizations to compete against the working-class parties.[2] West European party politics in the industrial era were divided along class lines. In some European countries, class cleavages were further complicated by other social cleavages based on ethnicity, linguistics, religion, and regionalism.[3]

By the 1970s, post-war years of unprecedented affluence had led to the "embourgeoisement" of the working class, and the rise of the white-collar occupational sector had diminished the ranks of the blue-collar workers. This dilution of class consciousness and the transformation of occupational structures contributed to the decline in voting based on class lines.[4] As one commentator put it: "[T]he prospects of the labor-based political parties that emerged in most industrial countries a century ago and then grew to become major contenders for power, have faded."[5]

In contrast to the decline of the labor parties, Green parties have proliferated in many West European countries.[6] The rise of the Greens has been heralded as "one of the most important political developments within West European societies in the last two decades."[7] The excitement generated by the Greens can, in part, be attributed to their allegedly different style of politics, organizational principles, a "new" agenda that promotes ecology, gender equality, pacifism, an anti-nuclear platform, the practice of an alternative economy and an egalitarian and participatory ethos that sets them apart from the traditional parties. Scholarly fascination with them also lies in the Greens' efforts to defy expectations that political parties, regardless of their democratic pretensions, will succumb to the "iron law of oligarchy": all organizations are dominated inevitably by a small elite.[8]

Attempts to classify the Greens and distinguish them from the established parties are reflected in various terms: "Left-libertarian party,"[9] a "new type of party,"[10] "New Politics party,"[11] "Anti-Party party,"[12] and "movement party."[13] The term "movement party" suggests the duality and the internal tension faced by Green parties. On the one hand, they desire to remain as anti-hierarchical social movements challenging the norms of the old political order and seeking to change various aspects of that establishment to reflect their agenda. On the other, they are forced to adopt a modicum of party organization despite its inherent dangers of oligarchy in order to contest elections to secure those goals.

A Green party has dual features: it is a social movement and a political party.[14] It is necessary at this juncture to clarify the two terms. Sidney Tarrow, in his review of the literature on social movements, points out that the term "social movements" has been used loosely in many different ways. He writes: "The only common denominator on the variety of definitions employed is that social movements are uninstitutionalized groups in some insurgent relationship to existing society involving unmediated bonds between leaders and followers."[15] The defining characteristic of a political party is an agency that offers labels to candidates who compete in elections. Leon Epstein writes: "[P]olitical parties are all the otherwise varied groups that provide the labels under which candidates seek election to governmental office . . . [T]he defining characteristic is the provision of labels for candidates seeking elective office."[16]

A social movement can abstain from the electoral arena; it attempts to challenge the status quo and redefine some aspects of the social order without a direct involvement in electoral politics and hence remains strictly a social movement. A political party need not have the features of a social movement; it endorses its own candidates running under the party's labels but upholds the status quo. A movement party has overlapping features: a social movement and a political party. In the real world, the boundaries between social movements, movement parties and conventional political parties may be blurred. It is possible for a group of people to begin as a social movement to challenge the social order, and then change into a movement party by acquiring a parliamentary arm to complement and promote that movement's goals, and finally to evolve into an established party with a stake in the status quo. Conceivably, a social movement need not follow such a teleological path. Alternatively, a movement party can abandon electoral politics and concentrate on its role as a social movement.

Significance of Green parties

At the outset of the 1980s, the national electoral results of the Greens were negligible; their electoral support hovered around 1 percent. Barely a decade later, many West European Green parties have secured between 5 and 10 percent of the popular votes (Table 1.1). Some of the Green parties chalked up even more impressive voter support at the local and European Community elections (Table 1.2). Nevertheless, Green parties are relatively weak in terms of mass membership and electoral successes compared to the old, established parties. Green parties everywhere suffer from the weakness that theirs is only a partial agenda. In many or most cases they fail to address economic and other issues that vitally affect voters, so that everywhere they are a minority movement. This is true even in Germany, but even more so elsewhere in Western Europe where they made less of an impact than in Germany.

Yet the Greens have attracted attention because they may have an impact that is out of proportion to their size. Thus, their significance cannot be viewed solely from the narrow criterion of electoral performance at the national level. They may influence the political agenda by stimulating the established parties to co-opt the new issues that were raised by the Green parties. The Greens may also join ruling coalitions in local governments.[17] If the Greens succeed in expanding their political support, they may help accelerate the "decomposition" of electoral alignment based on class fissures, and forge a new realignment in the party system with the added dimension of New Politics issues.[18] The significance of the Greens lies in their role of adding a new conflict dimension to old social cleavages. More importantly, this movement reflects the changing structures and the values of a post-modern or post-industrial society.

A theory of value change

While the rise of mass parties is associated with an industrial democracy, the emergence of Green parties is connected to a democratic, *post*-industrial society (Figure 1.1). In a technologically advanced and knowledge-intensive, democratic, post-industrial society, the bulk of its population is relatively well-educated and affluent. Ordinary citizens have more resources, including information, that enable them to participate in politics. A hallmark of a post-industrial society is the prevalence of the white-collar, service sector rather than the blue-collar, industrial sector in its economy.[19]

A number of theories have been offered to explain the decline of class voting, but few suggest what new patterns might develop in its place.[20] The theory of value change proposed by Ronald Inglehart[21] seeks to explain not only the decline of class voting but also the rise of New Politics, Green parties and social movements in advanced industrial democracies. Inglehart argues that a younger generation of voters who grew up in an affluent, post-industrial society will place less value on such material issues as food and security once basic needs are met. They will emphasize such quality of life

Table 1.1 Electoral results of selected Green parties in national parliamentary elections (percent)

	1979	1980	1981	1982	1983	1984	1985	1986	1987	1988	1989	1990	1991	1992	1993
Australia												1.2			
Austria					3.2			4.8				6.8			
Belgium			4.5				6.2		7.1						10.0
Denmark												0.9			
Finland					1.5				4.0				6.8		
France	0.1		1.1					1.2		0.4					10.7*
Germany															
(Former East)												6.0			
(Former West)		1.5			5.6				8.3			4.8			
Ireland														1.4	
Italy									2.6					3.0	
Luxembourg	1.0					5.8					8.4				
New Zealand												6.8			
Sweden				1.6			1.5			5.5			3.4		
Switzerland	0.8				6.4								6.1		
U.K.														1.3	

Source: Kaelberer, "The Emergence of Green Parties in Western Europe", p. 230; *Electoral Studies* and *European Journal of Political Research*, various issues.

Note:
* First ballot votes (France)

Table 1.2 The 1989 and 1994 European Community electoral results of Green parties (percent of voter support)

	Green parties	
	1989	*1994*
Belgium	13.9	11.5
Denmark	–	–
France	10.6	2.9
Germany	8.4	10.1
Greece	2.6	–
Ireland	7.9	3.7
Italy	8.7	3.2
Luxembourg	10.4	10.9
Netherlands	7.0	3.7
Portugal	–	–
Spain	2.8	–
U.K.	14.5	3.2

Source: *Electoral Studies*, Vol. 8, No. 3, December 1989, p. 222 and *The Economist*, June 18, 1994, p. 52.

issues or post-material values as ecology, self-expression, gender equality and direct participation by ordinary citizens in politics.[22] This value change among younger voters gives rise to a new political cleavage in advanced, industrial societies: a new material–post-material conflict dimension in addition to old social cleavages. Social movements and New Politics parties are underpinned by the value change in post-industrial societies.[23]

The emergence of New Politics parties is associated with a democratic post-industrial society. It does not imply that New Politics parties will

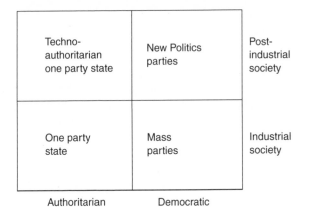

Figure 1.1 Regime type, society, and political parties.

Table 1.3 Occupational sectors of Japan, the U.S., West Germany, France, Italy, and the U.K.

Sectors	Japan (1990)	U.S. (1990)	U.K. (1987)	West Germany (1989)	France (1987)	Italy (1989)
Primary	7.2	2.9	2.4	3.7	7.5	9.2
Industrial	34.1	26.8	30.2	40.2	30.5	32.0
Tertiary	58.7	59.5	67.4	56.1	62.0	58.8

Source: *Nihon kokusei zue*, 1992, p. 90.

displace the mass, established parties, but will coexist and interact with them. Post-industrial society still retains important primary and secondary sectors (Table 1.3), and they will continue to underpin Old Politics parties. Moreover, these parties are not necessarily confined to their traditional social bases of political support: adaptable Old Politics parties with an attractive mix of policies and organizations may even win new social bases of support in a society with a large tertiary sector.

A precondition for the rise of Green parties is a democratic polity. Conceivably, a darker, alternative outcome of a post-industrial society in its extreme will be an authoritarian, single party that can marshal computer technology and other surveillance techniques to penetrate society, compile dossiers on individuals and control its populace. New Politics parties will not be found in such a hostile Orwellian environment. The typology also points out that an industrial society did not necessarily lead to mass parties. An industrial society coupled with extreme authoritarianism is best exemplified by the one-party states of Hitler or Stalin, wherein mass parties were crushed in a totalitarian, industrial society.

Significance of Japan as a case study

The literature on social movements and New Politics parties focuses on Western Europe.[24] This neglect of non-European case studies poses theoretical problems for the literature. It is unclear whether the phenomenon of social movements and New Politics parties in post-industrial societies is peculiar to Western Europe, with its common historical, religious and cultural heritage, or whether it is universal in nature. Are generalizations about this phenomenon applicable only to Western Europe and its cultural offspring in North America, Australia and New Zealand or do they apply to all examples of post-industrial democracies, including Japan? An examination of Japan will help to avoid ethnocentricity in the literature of New Politics. Hitherto, the models of New Politics parties and social movements have been based on the European experience. Instead of adopting the West as the universal model and then trying to fit the Japanese experience onto a Procrustean bed, we will synthesize the Japanese case with literature on European Greens and reconsider our current understanding of New Politics. In his review of the literature on New Politics parties, Robert Harmel points out that "research on new parties has tended to be confined to Western Party systems; more study of new parties elsewhere would both enrich and extend the generality of theory on party development."[25]

Japan is too important to be ignored. It is the world's second-largest economy, the largest creditor nation and a member of the Group of Seven (G-7); Japan is at the vanguard of technological innovation and has a sizeable population of 124 million. A society is said to have crossed the threshold to post-industrialism when its tertiary sector is larger than the industrial and the agrarian sectors.[26] Japan attained its post-industrial status sometime in the 1970s[27] (Table 1.4). Notwithstanding its post-industrial status, Japan continues to retain significant agrarian and industrial sectors. These sectors will continue to underpin the established Japanese parties.

A Green party in Japan?

Japan has undergone a post-material transformation in which its structures and values have changed substantially.[28] Theoretically, this social transformation leads to political change in which social movements and New Politics parties become the mode. The rise of Green parties in many West European countries suggests that this hypothesis is borne out in varying degrees in different advanced industrial democracies. If we rank the post-industrial societies along a "Green spectrum" that indicates the relative strength of the Green parties according to their representation in national parliamentary elections, Germany, Belgium, Luxembourg, Switzerland, Austria, and Finland would be placed near the top; France, New Zealand and Sweden would be situated along the middle of the continuum; Japan is located at the bottom along with the U.S., Britain, Canada, and Australia. In the last group, Green parties, if they exist at all, lack representation in national parliaments. Generally, Green parties are relatively weak, even in

Table 1.4 Japan's changing occupational sectors (percent)

Sectors	1950	1960	1970	1980	1990
Primary	48.3	32.6	19.4	10.9	7.1
Secondary	21.9	29.2	34.0	33.5	33.2
Tertiary	29.7	38.2	46.6	55.3	59.1

Source: *Nihon kokusei zue*, 1992, p. 89.

Germany, when compared with the Old Politics parties. Thus, Japan is not wholly exceptional in having a Green movement that is weak. On the other hand, it is clearly exceptionally weak in Japan.

Japan is especially interesting as a case study because, unlike most countries in the bottom group, it did not have a first-past-the-post electoral system at the national level until the 1996 Lower House Election.[29] Instead, it had a non-transferable, single-ballot, medium-sized, multi-member electoral district in the Lower House and proportional representation by party list as a component in the Upper House electoral system. The first-past-the-post system, unlike proportional representation, often discriminates against smaller parties (including the Greens) since a plurality of votes must be won in an electoral district. Thus, the first-past-the-post system discourages the growth of Green parties even in advanced industrial countries with post-material values. But post-war Japan did not have a first-past-the-post system. Hence, the Japanese electoral system is not a key reason why there are no significant Green parties in that country despite substantial changes to its structures and values.

Scholars have discounted the presence of Green Parties in Japan.[30] However from the 1980s onwards an ecology party known as the Network Movement (NET)[31] has launched challenges in local elections in half of the largest cities of Japan, including Tokyo, Yokohama, Kawasaki, Fukuoka, Sapporo, and Chiba City. With the exception of the national capital, the other five cities are "special designated cities" (*seirei shitei toshi*) with powers equivalent to a prefectural government. NET is a social movement party whose formal members and candidates for elections are women; it operates in a male-dominated political system. NET's parent organization is the Seikatsu Club (Livelihood Club) (SC), a consumer co-operative (co-op) which espouses Green values. (In the case of Fukuoka NET, the parent organization is Fukuoka Green Co-op, North Block.) The Japanese press considers NET a practitioner of New Politics,[32] and suggests that it may play the role of the German Green Party in the political system.[33]

By 1996, NET successfully obtained 123 seats in prefecture, city, ward and village assemblies (Table 1.5).[34] The party was a ruling coalition partner in the local governments of Kamakura, Kawasaki, Fujisawa, Zushi, and Machida cities. It reflects the voters' shifting concerns towards New Politics issues, the increasing ability of Japanese women to participate in politics, and rising demands from consumers at the periphery of local politics that challenge the producer-oriented, corporatist structure of national politics to place greater emphasis on livelihood issues. NET appears therefore as a harbinger of political change.

Table 1.5 Electoral record of NET

Year	Number of Candidates					Candidates elected					Cumulative *
	Tokyo	Kanagawa	Chiba	Others	Total	Tokyo	Kanagawa	Chiba	Others	Total	
1977	1				1	0				0	0
1978											
1979	1				1	1				1	1
1980											1
1981											1
1982	1				1	1				1	2
1983	5	1			6	5	1			6	7
1984		1			1		0			0	7
1985	1	2			3	1	2			3	10
1986	2	4	1		7	1	3	1		5	14
1987	14	16	2		32	14	10	2		26	32
1988											32
1989	5	2		1(F)	8	3	2		1(F)	6	36
1990	4	6	2	1(F)	13	4	4	2	1(F)	11	42
1991	28	35	8	1(S),1(N) 6(F),4(H)	83	24	21	7	1(S),1(N) 4(F),4(H)	62	77
1992			1		1			1		1	78
1993	4	2		2(F)	8	4	2		2 (F)	8	86
1994	3	5	4		12	3	4	2		9	95
1995	45	40	14	9(H),1(I) 1(Y)1(S), 6 (F), 3(N)	120	42	33	12	5(H),1(I), 1(S) 6(F),2(N)	102	120
1996			1	2(S)	3			1	2(S)	3	123

Key:
F = Fukuoka, S = Saitama, N = Nagano, H = Hokkaidô, I = Iwate, Y = Yamanashi

Sources: Statistics from Social Movement Center and various issues of *Shakai undô*.

Note:
* Cumulative number of NET assembly women

A model of a New Politics party

To answer whether there is a Japanese Green party, we need, first, to construct ideal-type models of the Old and the New Politics parties. Let us lay out the characteristics of an ideal-type, New Politics party (Table 1.6).[35] Such a party is a gender-inclusionary organization. Not only must a substantial number of its rank and file activists be women, there must be a significant female leadership that exercises real influence on the decision-making process of the party. Formal or ceremonial party positions occupied by women reflects mere tokenism if these posts are unaccompanied by real power. A New Politics party promotes egalitarianism in its structure and processes; it is different from established parties that are marked by oligarchic tendencies. Instead of an organization where a few leaders dominate the majority, ordinary members exercise real control over office holders.

Table 1.6 Models of Old and New Politics parties

Characteristics	Old Politics party	New Politics party
Leadership	a) Professionals	Amateurs
	b) Males	Females and males
Organizational principles	a) Vertical	Horizontal
	b) Centralized	Decentralized
Organizational strength	Strong	Weak
Motivation of activists	a) Material incentives	Purposive incentives
	b) Purposive incentives (e.g. class ideology)	Solidaristic incentives
	c) Solidaristic incentives	
Social bases of support	a) Class	Post-materialists
	b) Ethnicity, religion, language	
	c) Patronage	
Issues	Economic growth, security, law and order, producer interests	Ecology, feminism, human rights, alternative economy, anti-nuclear facilities, pacifism, direct participation, consumer interests
Money and politics	Corrupt	Clean
Strategy	Catch-all party and vote maximization	Single-issue party and representation of constituency

Source: Synthesis from Offe, Kitschelt and author's conceptions.

Activists of a New Politics party are motivated by purposive and solidaristic incentives rather than by material incentives. They are usually amateurs who do not depend on politics as a career. There are no spoils or patronage to be won in Green politics because a New Politics party is not intertwined with the state bureaucracy or entrenched interest groups. The social base of a New Politics party does not rest on patronage, or on class and other traditional cleavages, but on an affluent, well-educated, white-collar, post-war generation which finds New Politics issues appealing. The new social cleavage represented in the politics of advanced industrial democracy is between those who support material values and those who support post-material values.

The issues raised by a New Politics party are universal in nature. Ecology, feminism, human rights, an alternative economy, anti-nuclear protests, pacifism, consumer interests, and direct participation by ordinary citizens are to be binding on the larger community[36] if the Greens succeed in implementing their agenda. However, the perceived benefits are not peculiar to a particular social class. While many Green activists come from the white-collar middle class, the policies they pursue are not class-specific; they are of-a-class but not on-behalf-of-a-class.[37] Social classes beyond the white-collar middle class will also benefit from clean air and water.

Not every political party that subscribes to ecological issues or gender equality does not automatically becomes a New Politics party (Figure 1.2). Stimulated by the challenge from the Green Party, the Social Democratic Party (SPD) of Germany has incorporated ecology issues as part of its

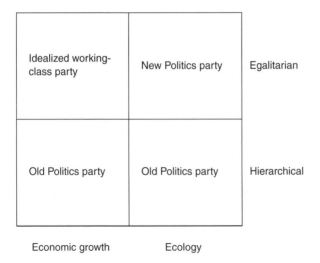

Idealized working-class party	New Politics party	Egalitarian
Old Politics party	Old Politics party	Hierarchical

Economic growth	Ecology

Figure 1.2 Political parties, issue orientation, and participatory style.

political agenda, but its oligarchic nature precludes the SPD from being considered a New Politics party. This typology raises the theoretical possibility of a party with a participatory ethos aiming for economic benefits. However, Robert Michels exploded this myth in his study of the SPD. He pointed out the inherent oligarchic tendencies even in a "democratic" proletarian party.[38]

Daniel Bell highlights pervasive political corruption as a disturbing feature of advanced industrial democracies that may lead to the alienation of voters from party politics and an erosion in the legitimacy of the political system.[39] Bell notes that political corruption is present in varying degrees in all advanced industrial societies. It is particularly endemic in established parties that are interlocked with big business, interest groups, and the bureaucracy. In contrast, we would expect a New Politics party to practise clean politics, since it is neither a partner of the establishment nor a peddler of pork-barrel politics.

The priority of a New Politics party is to represent its constituency and promote Green values rather than the electoral game of vote maximization at the expense of the party's ideological soul.[40] Nevertheless, it may become less radical in its rhetoric and actions in the quest for more votes. When a New Politics party joins the electoral process, it is confronted by a strategic dilemma: should it become less radical and embrace more pragmatic policies to win broader mass acceptance or should it stick firmly to its principles and face the prospect of remaining at the fringe of politics? A New Politics party may be transformed from the parliamentary arm of a social movement into a full-fledged, orthodox party if it concentrates on the electoral game.

Questions to be addressed

Social changes in metropolitan Japan have led to the emergence of New Politics. Various aspects of New Politics have appeared in the efforts by some political parties and social movements to experiment with the agenda and the organizational techniques of the European Green parties. But no significant Green parties have arisen in Japan. Green parties have not won any representation at the national level. Even NET, the "Greenest" party in Japan, lacks some of the credentials that would qualify it as an authentic Green party. The study of New Politics parties is important, even though they have not made a deep political impact in Japan. An examination of their limitations will highlight the nature of Japanese urban politics and society that hinders the growth of the Greens and perpetuates the strengths of the Old Politics parties.

What is perhaps more surprising than the sprouting of "Greenism" has been the persistence of oligarchic practices in the "Greenest" of these sprouts, the SC and NET, and the adoption and strengthening in all political parties of the local candidate support organization (*kōenkai*) thought to be characteristic of the "Old Politics." Why have significant Green parties not arisen in post-industrial Japan? Why have all political parties inclusive of NET adopted *kōenkai* as their urban political organization?

To what extent is Japan converging with the West in its post-industrial politics? Is NET similar to the West European Green parties, and to what extent does it approximate the model of a New Politics party? Is NET fundamentally different from the Old Politics parties of Japan? Why are Old Politics parties so resilient despite "post-modern" issues, especially rising ecological concerns, among a majority of the Japanese? What is the nature of urban politics in post-industrial Japan?

Explanations

Political organizations, oligarchic structures and strong local support groups are as necessary in a "post-industrial"[41] as in an "industrial" democratic polity. Green parties, regardless of their pretensions of establishing direct participatory structures and processes, inevitably succumb to oligarchic tendencies. The tyranny of Michel's iron law of oligarchy does not spare even the "New Politics parties" once they embark on the parliamentary road to seek social transformation. The logic of electoral competition transforms them because strong leadership and hierarchical structures are necessary to win elections. The Green parties are caught in a contradiction. If they repudiate strong grassroots organization, they will probably be politically ineffective; if they adopt strong organizations, oligarchic tendencies will set in and these parties will not be substantially different from the orthodox parties. Despite the organizational efforts of the SC and NET, they cannot match the strong grassroots organizations (*kōenkai*) owned by the candidates of the Old Politics parties.

Males conceived and established the SC and NET. The Founding Fathers' prestige, experiences in social movements, and continued dominance in shaping ideology, organization, and strategies have resulted in an enterprise populated by housewives but informally led by men. We can trace the organizations' oligarchic tendencies back to their male-directed origins. This pattern of male oligarchy is further reinforced by Japanese norms where women do not usually play top leadership roles in politics.[42] Despite the rhetoric and perhaps even the genuine belief in the values of direct democracy and equality among ordinary members, their actions belie their attachment to "traditional" values of "motherhood" rather than "modern" or "post-modern feminism." Participation in social movements and politics is often seen as an extension of the traditional role of a wife and mother to safeguard the health and well-being of her family. A narrow social base of urban housewives who pursue a narrow range of motherhood issues has limited political appeal in Japan.

This juxtaposition of "premodern," "modern" and "post-modern" elements even in metropolitan Japan suggests that post-industrialization does not represent a total transformation of society. These are not teleological, successive stages in societal change. First, post-industrial society continues to retain important agrarian and industrial sectors. Second, "post-industrial" sectors arising in society continue to embrace more profound "modern" or even "premodern" values and behavior that include small group loyalties, emotional attachment to neighborhood associations and "former villages," and female deference to male leadership. Thus, a Japanese who is sympathetic to ecological concerns may also abide in the norms of interpersonal ties and mutual obligations. Such a voter will not automatically support a Green party but may cast his vote on the basis of personal ties rather than policies. The Old Politics parties, especially the LDP, are successful in tapping local and group sentiments, and organizing them into formidable urban political machines.

The persistence of such patterns can be attributed partially to the fact that around half of Japan's population belonged to the primary sector at the end of the Second World War. Traditional values are unlikely to disappear within a single generation. Moreover, the sense of material well-being among the Japanese probably became much stronger only from the 1970s onwards, when it was apparent that Japan was experiencing an unprecedented "economic miracle." Thus, post-modernity and even modernity are recent phenomena in Japan.[43]

Japanese norms place a higher value on small-group, communal ties and personal loyalties, regardless of the attraction of "post-modernism," "modernism" or "premodernism." Political parties do have different images. The LDP has a traditional tinge, the Japan Communist Party (JCP) is a "modern" party, while NET has been called a New Politics party. Despite their different ideological hues, these parties and their mobilization approaches are not based purely on ideology. They are based on personal ties, the bonding of small groups and social networks. New Politics parties will face difficulties trying to appeal to voters outside its social web purely on the basis of Green issues.

"New Politics" is attractive in the peculiar situation of rapid urban migration, when communal ties are most disrupted, but its loses some of its attractiveness once new communal ties are forged. Rapid industrialization and urbanization brought along a host of problems that include pollution of the environment and the food-chain, social alienation, and a need for belonging. These were addressed by the JCP and NET, amongst other parties. The formation of small groups (*han*) by the SC to collectively order safe and inexpensive food provided avenues for housewives to seek companionship, mutual help, and fulfilment of their roles as concerned mothers who monitor their families' well-being. With the decline of rapid urbanization and the emergence of new urban communities, there is less need to join the "social clubs" provided by the JCP and NET in order to acquire a sense of belonging. However, political parties, regardless of their traditional, modern or even post-modern images, can attempt to mobilize political support from these budding urban communities, especially if some of their supporters belong to these urban networks. Supporters may obtain political support for their preferred candidates on the basis not purely of political ideology but also on personal relationships enmeshed within the group.

Comparison between Old and New Politics parties

We cannot, however, understand the New Politics party in Japan without understanding the Old Politics party; the Greens cannot be examined in isolation. Such a comparative approach has been advocated by scholars who pointed out the inadequacies of the present research on New Politics parties. Robert Harmel writes:

> What is clear is that a potentially fruitful line of research has been largely unexplored. More systemic comparison of new and older parties is needed before we can adequately answer the question of whether (and if so, in what ways), new parties, or some subset of them, are fundamentally different from other parties. . . . additional work is needed to assess more fully the distinctiveness of any of the new parties from their older counterparts; especially lacking are comparative studies of the organizational features of new and old parties.[44]

Since NET does not exist in a political vacuum, we must examine its interaction with the established parties. The Old Parties' strategies and their interest in or indifference to certain New Politics issues will have an impact on NET's strategies and future. The LDP, a party from the Right, and the JCP, a party from the Left, are picked as case studies. The former is also selected because it has been party-in-power at the national level since 1955. Even though the LDP fell from power in 1993, it rebounded, formed a coalition government the following year, and recovered the premiership in January 1996. In October the same year, the LDP further strengthened its position by capturing 239 out of 500 seats in the Lower House, an increase of 28 seats over its performance three years earlier. It exemplifies the Old Politics in Japan: machine politics, pork-barrel politics, political corruption, structural nepotism, intimate ties with big business, agriculture, and other interest groups – a pragmatic, catch-all party.

While some of these features are present in the Old Politics of the West, Old Politics cleavages in Japan were different from those in Western Europe. Rather than class cleavages, post-war Japanese politics was structured around profound disagreement over fundamental domestic and foreign policy principles.[45] The ruling LDP supported constitutional revision (especially the war-renouncing Article 9), the U.S.–Japan Security Treaty, and the legality of the Self-Defense Force (SDF), while the Japan Socialist Party, the main opposition party between 1955 and 1993, advocated just the opposite: protection of the Constitution, unarmed neutrality and dissolution of the SDF. This overriding ideological polarization that cut across class lines was termed "cultural politics" by Watanuki.[46] Instead of political mobilization on the basis of class, the LDP has garnered support from social networks based on patronage and camaraderie provided by political machines in exchange for votes. In this aspect, Old Politics in Japan is similar to the urban political machines of the U.S.

The choice of the JCP may come as a surprise. Yet it is the oldest party in Japan, having been founded in 1922. The JCP is included as a case study because it is a predominantly urban party and, among the established parties, has a historical involvement in social movement activities. In addition, the JCP is reputed to have the strongest party organization in Japan. Among the Japanese political parties, the JCP comes closest to Duverger's model of a programmatic, mass-based, hierarchical party. Indeed, the JCP is the largest non-ruling communist party in the world. Moreover the party has enjoyed an electoral upsurge since the mid-1990s and even superseded its traditional rival on the Left, the Japan Socialist Party (JSP).

The JSP is excluded as a case study because it has become increasingly a rural party. Historically, the JSP was a party of the Left but it can no longer be classified as such. In recent years the Marxist-leaning factions within the JSP became increasingly isolated. In 1993, the JSP joined an eight-party coalition which toppled the LDP from power. Barely a year later, the JSP abandoned the coalition and forged another ruling alliance with its erstwhile enemy, the LDP and Sakigake (Harbinger Party). To make itself acceptable to its coalition partners, the JSP expediently jettisoned its traditional policies of unarmed neutrality, the rejection of the military as unconstitutional, and opposition to nuclear power stations. By surrendering its traditional agenda, the JSP ceased to be a true party of the Left. Moreover, it desperately sought a facelift in 1996 by renaming itself the Social Democratic Party (SDP), but to no avail. In the Lower House Elections in the same year, the SDP was routed and marginalized at the polls and retained only a paltry 15 seats, a mere shadow of its historical status and mission as the most important opposition party in post-war Japan. The JSP does not warrant a special and separate treatment in our study. It will be dealt with only in the context of its interaction with NET.

Also excluded from our case studies are the traditional Center Parties, the Kōmeitō (Clean Government Party) and the Democratic Socialist Party (Minshatō). Although they formed important components in the eight-party ruling coalition in 1993, these Center Parties are not directly relevant to the theme of our study. Both parties relied on external sponsors for organizational support and had no local party organizations to boast of.[47] These two parties eventually merged with other "new" parties, including those established by LDP renegades, the Japan New Party (Nihonshintō) and the Japan Renewal Party (Shinseitō) to form the New Frontier Party (Shinshintō) as a conservative alternative to the LDP. However, the New Frontier Party splintered by 1997. Similarly, discontented politicians primarily from the JSP and the Sakigake formed the Democratic Party (Minshutō) as a "liberal third force" in Japanese politics. Thus, by the late 1990s, many political parties had proliferated and portrayed themselves as "new," reform-oriented parties. These parties, however, are oligarchic and do not qualify as New Politics parties according to our yardstick of direct participation by amateurs and an emphasis on ecology.

The approach

Ronald Inglehart interprets the rise of social movements and Green parties as a phenomenon underpinned by value change in advanced industrial democracies. Yet the rise of post-materialism does not necessarily lead to political activism and support for the Greens. That is but one possible outcome. If political support is not mobilized by a New Politics party with attractive policies, candidates, and a sound strategy, post-material values may be diverted to other non-material alternatives such as religious mysticism or the "privatized enjoyment of art and nature."[48] Between value change and the emergence of social movements and Green Parties in Inglehart's causal chain, there is a "black box;" we are not told how and why value change at the mass level is translated into political activism in the public sphere and not into hedonistic pursuit in the private realm.

Value change *per se* does not inevitably lead to the emergence of social movements and New Politics parties. It has to be mediated by a strategic mix of leadership, policies and organization. Instead of looking only at value change among the Japanese, we will also examine the *political* factors that have led to the emergence of the SC and NET. They include: charismatic leadership, mobilization issues, ideology, organization building, and the pooling of such resources as human talent, labor, money, time, and facilities.[49] Activists are faced with opportunities, uncertainties, and constraints in their quest to promote their movement. When we shift the focus from political culture to collective action, the dilemma and choices of leaders and activists over strategies will be highlighted. Political outcomes are open-ended since success or failure, in part, hinge on the strategies adopted by the Greens and their protagonists.

Political entrepreneurs and strong leadership are indispensable to the emergence of a New Politics party. Japanese leadership style is often stereotyped as weak,[50] while the more individualistic West has produced strong leaders. Hitherto, the literature on social movements and New Politics parties has concentrated on structures that include evolving industrial sectors and class composition, value changes among the masses, the impact of electoral systems and party organization. However, it has rarely singled out any individual who has made a substantial difference in Green politics. This vacuum would be addressed in our study of the SC and NET.

Chapter outline

The relative weakness of the Greens in Japan is also due to the strengths of the established parties: organizational power and responsiveness to voter concerns, including ecology. The next three chapters provide information and analysis about the competitive social and political setting in which the Green movement has to operate. Chapter 2 deals with the quintessential Old Politics party, the LDP in post-industrial Japan. LDP politicians have strong urban grassroots organizations and mass support based on patronage and interpersonal relationship between candidates and voters. This chapter provides a comparison between the political organizations of NET and LDP candidates. Conservative political machines and their insatiable demand for money are the main themes of the chapter. We will examine the paradox of why political machines have flourished in urban Japan despite predictions of their demise.

Chapter 2 proves that political practices associated with "modern" and even "premodern" Japan are still pervasive in the most urban constituencies. The social networks of political machines (*kōenkai*), old village (*kyū mura*) sentiments, and ubiquitous neighborhood associations (*chōnaikai*) are mobilized to rope in urban political support for the conservatives. The LDP has succeeded in expanding its urban political machines and even managed to tap support from emerging urban communities. The persistence of these patterns of behavior makes it difficult for NET to expand its political support by appealing purely to New Politics issues. Unlike the established parties, NET lacks powerful grassroots organizations, ties to neighborhood associations, and appeal to "village" sentiments in urban Japan.

New Politics parties may pose a challenge to the old political order.[51] However, the opposite is often true. Old Political parties can pose a serious challenge to New Politics parties by stealing some of the Green issues. In Chapter 3, we examine the attempt by the LDP Prefectural Chapter in Kanagawa to embark on a novel and bold attempt to launch policy-making party organizations at the prefectural level. In an attempt to refurbish its tattered image as an archaic and corrupt party devoid of policy initiatives at the local level, the Kanagawa Forum 21, a prefectural party organization with six policy divisions, was launched. Especially interesting is its attempt to woo urban voters by emphasizing the environmental divisions within the party's prefectural organization.

While *kōenkai* is a formidable organization even in urban Japan, it is not able to reach large numbers of urban voters who are outside its web. The LDP has tried to respond to environmental concerns among the public but has had limited success. We will examine the obstacles faced by the LDP in Kanagawa prefecture when it sought to co-opt the issue of ecology. If the Old Politics parties continue to devote more attention to ecology and urban consumer issues, they may even pre-empt the Green parties from gaining more political support.

The JCP is our case study in Chapter 4. Unlike the German Green Party which did not compete against a significant communist party, NET had to compete against two established parties on the Left, the JCP and the JSP. In a more crowded party system than Germany, NET has a tougher task to win political support. Both the JCP and NET are essentially urban-based parties that seek the support of new residents, run a large slate of women candidates to woo the female votes, espouse welfare and ecological concerns, and are active in the co-op movement. The communists' ambivalent relationship with the SC and NET will be examined. Driven by the necessity to compete against other parties in elections and to operate in a country whose political norms emphasize the social bonding of the group, the JCP has adopted *kōenkai* too. This is especially surprising for a party that prides itself for its "modernity" and yet ended up embracing an approach that it has castigated as "premodern." Such political organizations were not detected by Duverger when he examined the West European communist parties.

In the case of Western Europe, many young, well-educated and affluent voters who supported the Euro-communist parties in the 1970s eventually switched their support to the Green parties. However, in Japan, voters who flirted with the JCP may support other emerging "reformist" parties rather than NET. Conceivably, NET may not be a beneficiary of a hypothetical demise of Japanese communism. In actuality, the JCP is enjoying a resurgence in the mid-1990s. This chapter examines the puzzle: why is the JCP so resilient in the post-Cold War era despite the global crisis of communism as an ideology? A key reason is the JCP's sustained success in building *kōenkai*. This has implications for the post-industrial social movements in Japan. Given the persistent strength of the Old Left in that nation, it is difficult for these movements to have a stronger impact on Japanese politics.

Chapter 5 examines the permissive conditions of value change, an open, democratic political system, and rapid urbanization that have contributed to the SC's emergence. However, these are necessary but not sufficient conditions for its expansion. In Chapter 6, we study the SC's origins in order to comprehend its rise, its development as a male-led organization, and its narrow dependence on urban housewives. We also trace the story of Iwane Kunio, its Founding Father with a vision to launch a social movement, the choice of an appropriate mobilization issue and the recruitment of Japanese housewives.

No movement or political party can be understood without studying its founding moment, origins, and intent. As Angelo Panebianco puts it:

> The way in which the cards are dealt out in the formative phase of an organization, continues in many ways to condition the life of the organization even decades afterwards. The organization will certainly undergo modifications and even profound changes in interacting throughout its entire life cycle in the continually changing environment. However, the crucial political choices made by its founding fathers, the first struggle for organizational control and the way in which the organization was formed, will leave an indelible mark. Few aspects of an organization's function and current tensions appear comprehensible if not traced to its formative phase.[52]

Chapter 7 examines the decisive roles of Founding Fathers who left their imprints on the SC's ideology and organization. An eclectic ideology and a solid organization are mobilizing tools that paved the way for the co-op's expansion. Thus, this chapter focuses on its organization and ideology. The male-led, oligarchic nature of the SC and NET is, in part, a result of the Founding Fathers' critical roles in developing their ideology and organization. Paradoxically, the SC organization is a source both of strength and weakness for NET. Unlike the West European Greens, NET can rely on an external sponsor, its parent organization. Its dependence on a co-op comprising urban housewives has limited it to a narrow base of support. Its limited ability to reach out to other social groups is a source of weakness. In contrast, the European Greens derive broader support from well-educated, white-collar citizens and youths from both sexes. The ideological outlook of top SC leaders is inspired by Gramscian ideas, a variant of Marxism. Unlike the West European Greens, they are still wedded to a doctrine that has no appeal to most Japanese.

To what extent does NET approximate the ideal-type of a New Politics party? That is the central question of Chapter 8. Rather than taking its rhetoric at face value, we will observe the party's actual behaviour. Do women play a leading role in the party? Are its daily activities at the ward level, the selection of party leaders and candidates, election campaign strategies, policy formulation and committee meetings open to the "inputs" of ordinary members? Does the party implement rules and principles to prevent oligarchic tendencies from surfacing in its organization? How does NET raise funds for its daily activities and election campaigns? Is it distinctively cleaner than the Old Politics parties that practise money politics? Does NET preach and practise New Politics?

Despite sharing some of the organizational principles and practices of the German Green Party, NET has oligarchic tendencies and avoids a commitment to "feminism." Its members are also practitioners of certain aspects of "Old Politics." Besides deferring to male leadership and the acceptance of traditional norms of motherhood, many NET candidates have established *kōenkai* that are grassroots organizational structures associated with "Old Politics." NET does not have many of the defining characteristics of a New Politics party. At best, it qualifies only as a quasi-Green party. The New Politics party is supposed to be a political vehicle for those who subscribe to post-material values. Since it lacks some of the characteristics of a New Politics party, it is difficult for NET to appeal to those post-materialists who are beyond the SC's social web.

In Chapter 9, the problems and prospects faced by both parent and child organizations will be canvassed. Confronted by a constellation of problems, NET is relatively weaker than most of the West European Green parties. Their manifold problems include attempts by the ruling party, the LDP, to curb the co-op's participation in electoral politics. The LDP lambasted the SC for its involvement in politics. Social movements are challenged not only by the possibility of established parties stealing their issues but also the creation of a new legal regime to depoliticize the co-op movement. A crowded party system and an electoral system at the national level that does not favor small parties are other impediments to NET's growth.

The last chapter draws the following conclusions. Japan appears to converge with the West in certain aspects of its post-industrial politics: the rise of post-material values, social movements, and Green-like parties. Nevertheless, there are significant differences between Japan and the West, not only in the nature of their Green politics but also the societal values which underpin them. They differ because of the profound "value persistence" in post-industrial Japan. Such values (small-group loyalties, the norms of motherhood, deference to male leadership, and emotive ties to the place of residence and neighborhood association), which are usually associated with "traditionalism," are embraced even by many "post-industrial" elements. These norms continue to underpin both the Old Politics parties and NET. Political parties, regardless of their ideologies and social bases of support, continue to rely on *kōenkai* in post-industrial Japan. Electoral competition and the social norms of small-group loyalties are some factors that support the expansion of *kōenkai* in urban Japan. Unlike the West European Greens, many NET candidates have adopted *kōenkai* in order to win elections. Thus, the conservatives, the communists and the Greens in Japan share commonalties in their urban political organizations. The possession of strong local mass organizations, including *kōenkai*, is a key reason why the Old Politics parties, especially the LDP and the JCP, remain powerful in post-industrial Japan. All social movements and political parties in urban Japan rely on social networks to rope in support. Political support is often based on the social glue of interpersonal ties and obligations rather than an appeal to ideology *per se*, whether Red or Green.

What, then, is the nature of urban politics, the most "modern" or even "post-modern" sector in Japan? The nation's politics appears to be in a state of flux. This includes the fall and restoration of LDP one-party dominance, kaleidoscopic "new" political parties that emerge, the demise of many parties both old and "new," calls for political reforms, the adoption of a new electoral system for the Lower House, the increasing dealignment of voters from the established parties, and declining voter turnout. Yet there is profound continuity in Japanese politics. Values associated with "tradition" persist in underpinning political mobilization, recruitment, and behavior, even in metropolitan Japan. The ability of the Old Politics parties, the LDP and the JCP, to tap these social norms explains their resilience, even in a post-industrial society, while the inability of the NET to cast its social nets further and wider limits its mass support.

2 The Liberal Democratic Party and urban political machines

The relative weakness of the Greens in metropolitan Japan is due in part to the ability of the Old Politics parties to attract substantial voter support. The organization adopted to secure these loyalties is *kōenkai*. Unlike the Old Politics parties, NET lacks powerful political machines at the grassroots and ties to neighborhood associations, and it has difficulties tapping local support beyond the social web of the SC's *han*. The persistence of "traditional" values and the emergence of new urban communities permit even the Old Politics parties to mobilize political support on the basis of social networks. These phenomena make it difficult for NET substantially to increase its political support.

This chapter examines the puzzle: why has *kōenkai* expanded to metropolitan Japan despite predictions of its demise as a quasi-traditional organizational approach to mobilize electoral support? There are three key reasons why *kōenkai* has flourished even in the big cities. First, electoral competition compels politicians to develop their personal political machines in the absence of grassroots party organizations. Second, *kōenkai* has not withered away because "modern" and even "premodern" values and behavior are still pervasive even in post-industrial Japan. Moreover, the *kōenkai* approach of political mobilization that stresses personal ties and small-group loyalty is consonant with Japanese norms of social interaction. Indeed, the emphasis on social bonds is strong even in metropolitan Japan. The end of rapid urbanization and the rise of urban communities have created opportunities for politicians to tap social networks through political machines. Third, *kōenkai* persists because there is a constant demand for political patronage and services among a segment of the urban electorate.

Political machines in Yokohama

The choice of Yokohama has the following merits. It is the second-largest city in Japan and has the second highest rate of urbanization among the big cities.[1] Yokohama is the most unlikely case for an effective *kōenkai* approach because a large and mobile urban population is supposed to impose difficulties for *kōenkai*-style mobilization. Yokohama is a relatively young city compared with other metropolises, such as Osaka and Nagoya which have their origins as old castle towns.[2] Yokohama attained its post-industrial status about 10 years earlier than most cities when half of its working residents were engaged in the tertiary sector by 1965.[3] Large numbers of white-collar salary men work in Tokyo and sleep in Yokohama. The city was also led by the progressive mayor Asukata Ichio who was noted for his stringent regulations to curb industrial pollution in Yokohama. From the late 1980s, Yokohama became the bastion of the Kanagawa Network Movement. Thus, a post-industrial milieu, a history of progressive administration and environmental protection, and the advent of NET in Yokohama provide a challenging setting for conservative political machines to operate.

The origins of *kōenkai*

Although its antecedents can be traced to the *Taisho* democratic interlude of pre-war Japan, *kōenkai* is best seen as a post-war innovation by candidates to secure mass support in the absence of party organization at the grassroots level.[4] Personal candidate support organizations are one possible organizational device (especially when local party structures are weak or non-existent) in democracies, where it is necessary to obtain electoral mass support. Other approaches include the reliance on local party organizations to mobilize support and the use of media, especially television, to project carefully crafted candidate images and "sound bites" to sway the electorate.

The emergence of post-war *kōenkai* can be attributed to many factors.[5] First, land reforms introduced by the American Occupation of Japan eliminated the powerful landlord class. Since politicians could no longer rely on the landlords to collect bloc votes from their tenants, politicians built mass organizations whereby they could establish face-to-face contact with a large number of voters on a regular basis.

Second, rapid urbanization undermined the traditional community structure and its social networks dominated by local notables. Gerald L. Curtis argues that in rural Japan, where community bonds were relatively stronger, local notables were able to mobilize voters on behalf of their candidates who need not appeal directly to the voters. However, in small and medium cities, local notables exercised less clout on voters. The decline of the community as a result of migration and influx of newcomers untied to the neighborhood, have undermined the brokerage role of the local notables. Intermediaries' inability to deliver bloc votes forced the conservatives to establish *kōenkai* as a direct link to voters.

Third, electoral systems and laws have facilitated the *kōenkai's* emergence. Until 1996, Japan's unique single-ballot, multi-member constituency system in the Lower House, with an average of three to five seats, pitted two or three candidates from the same conservative party against each other. Conservative candidates must build up their personal candidate organizations because they cannot expect to receive help from the party chapter. This is similar to the reliance candidates in the U.S. placed on their personal support organization because candidates from the same party compete against each other in the primaries. A strait-jacket is placed on election campaigning in Japan. A ban on door-to-door canvassing and media advertisements, and a short campaign period, have resulted in an official campaign which tends to separate the candidate from voters. To overcome this problem, candidates rely on *kōenkai* to act as bridges between them and the voters even during non-election years.

Fourth, *kōenkai* emerged because it catered to many voters' demands for services and benefits. Even though the legendary U.S. urban political machine was notorious for corruption, it was also a social welfare institution that provided such benefits as employment, consultation, and help in daily living, especially to disoriented new immigrants, and integrated them into the community in exchange for their votes.[6] Similarly, *kōenkai* emerged, persisted, and expanded because it satisfied the demand for services, companionship, and entertainment among many Japanese voters. Inoguchi Takashi and Iwai Tomoaki have examined the extent voters perceive that they have benefited from the services offered by politicians.[7] Inoguchi and Iwai also argue that the provision of services by politicians to their constituencies is indispensable to creating a good image of effectiveness and dependability among voters.

Fifth, the need for *kōenkai* springs not only from factional competition between LDP candidates within the same electoral district but also from the need to face the challenge from the opposition parties. When the party on the Right is confronted by a mass-based, working-class party, it must transform itself into a mass-based party to compete with the Left. In Maurice Duverger's term, the conservatives contracted a "contagion from the left."[8] The JSP, unlike Duverger's party of the Left with a large membership, relied on labor unions as substitutes for mass-based, party organizations. The LDP, unlike Duverger's party on the Right, did not develop as a party with a large membership, but resorted to its Diet Members' personal candidate support organizations in response to the Left-leaning trade unions. Lacking an external sponsor with mass membership in the cities, such as *Nōkyō* (Agricultural Co-operative Association) in the cities, the conservatives must depend exclusively on *kōenkai*. The party cannot rely on local party organizations, trade unions, religious bodies, consumer co-operatives, or other mass organizations. Thus, LDP candidates must build strong *kōenkai*. In the face of the conservatives' organization-building, and the absence of socialist grassroots organizations, JSP candidates too developed their *kōenkai* to supplement the trade unions.

Masumi noted that by the 1958 General Elections *kōenkai* of LDP candidates had become conspicuous and widespread as an electoral organization. In the 1963 Local Elections, local politicians followed suit and adopted *kōenkai* as their mass organizations.[9] In the early years of *kōenkai*-building throughout Japan, both the LDP and JSP had reservations about the *kōenkai* approach because it was thought to stymie the growth of local party organizations.[10] Despite the desire to build a "modern," mass-based party organization, both the LDP and the JSP gave in to electoral logic and, with great ambivalence, accepted *kōenkai* as their grassroots organizations.[11] The rise of urban parties, the DSP, Kōmeitō and the JCP in the 1960s and 1970s, provided further incentives to LDP candidates to maintain and expand their *kōenkai* in the cities. In Duverger's idiom, the LDP contracted a "contagion from the center" given the presence of the DSP and Kōmeitō in the big cities.

The urban political machine

There are two arguments why *kōenkai* was not expected to flourish in metropolitan Japan. The first hypothesis suggests that *kōenkai* lacks the capacity to organize huge number of votes needed to win elections in the big cities.[12] In the metropolises, a mobile and transient population not integrated into the local community coupled with the enormous task of organizing a large number of voters needed to win office makes the *kōenkai*-style mobilization less effective.[13] The experience of Diet Member Kōno Yōhei, whose constituency in Kanagawa prefecture is a dormitory town of Tokyo, is offered as an illustration that the *kōenkai* approach would not work.[14] This was due to the large numbers of new residents and floating votes in Kōno's district. In 1967 Kōno claimed that he had to rely on a media approach to win support.[15] Revisiting Kōno's constituency, Kanagawa District Five, about two and a half decades later, we discovered that Kōno has built a large *kōenkai*, despite his constituency's location in the Tokyo metropolitan area.[16] Kōno's conservative rival in the same constituency, Kamei Yoshiyuki, also has a massive *kōenkai* with a membership list of around 160,000.[17] It is evident that *kōenkai* is neither a transitional organization nor one which is essentially limited to small and medium cities.

An LDP party official suggested that except for Diet Members with high media profiles, such as Ishihara Shintarō, most have to rely on *kōenkai* to win votes.[18] Ishihara gained tremendous domestic and international publicity when he called for a more assertive and nationalistic Japanese attitude toward the U.S. in his book *Japan That Can Say No*. Since Ishihara was a well-known novelist even before the book was published, he was an unlikely candidate to depend on *kōenkai* given his access to the media. Nevertheless, Ishihara maintained a large *kōenkai*. His political secretaries managed a large *kōenkai* and engaged in proxy home visits to cement the ties between Ishihara and *kōenkai* members.[19]

The second argument is based on the assumption that, as Japan enters the post-industrial era, modern values will increasingly displace the traditional values which underpin *kōenkai*. Tsurutani Taketsugu writes:

> [W]ith the growing valuational and attitudinal change taking place among people and the subsequent decline in conventional political and interpersonal referents and behavioral inhibitions, the traditional properties of personal and social relations that have been the organizing principles of MP's personal support clubs are likely to suffer further erosion.[20]

Contrary to these assumptions, statistics from the Akarui senkyo suishin kyōkai (ASSK), or Association to Promote Clean Elections, indicate the steady growth of *kōenkai* in terms of overall membership participation all along the rural–urban continuum. These organizations expanded steadily even in the big cities, the most modern sector of Japanese society throughout the 1970s, 1980s and into the 1990s. Most of their expansion was registered after Japan entered its post-industrial phase around 1970. *Kōenkai*-building in the 1970s and 1980s coincided with the post-industrial era which saw the rise of citizens' movements, New Politics issues, and value change among the Japanese. Indeed, the ascent of new values thus far has not precluded or stymied its growth. The organization's expansion is remarkable in the context of the diminution of farmers in Japan's social composition. Since the farmers are the most active social group in *kōenkai* participation, we might expect the relative and absolute decline of the farming community to depress the overall figures of *kōenkai* participation. On the contrary, despite the post-war long-term decline of the agrarian sector, participation soared in the 1970s and has remained stable into the 1980s and 1990s. According to the ASSK, which began tracking *kōenkai* in 1967, the rate of voters' participation in *kōenkai* leapt from 5.8 percent that year to 26.9 percent by the time of the 1995 Local Elections.[21] Within a span of nearly three decades, *kōenkai* membership growth has risen almost fivefold and has also registered strong growth in the big cities.

Let us examine three sets of statistics compiled by ASSK. The rate of *kōenkai* participation is different in the three sets because the questions about *kōenkai* membership were phrased differently. Table 2.1 shows *kōenkai* membership after each Lower House Election. Table 2.2 indicates membership after each Local Election. Voters were asked specifically to identify *kōenkai* membership of only local politicians in that particular election. Table 2.3 is from a survey which had been executed only twice. It asked the broader question: "Are you and your family *kōenkai* members?" Moreover, the question regarding membership is not confined to the local elections, but participation in national-level elections too. Table 2.3 indicates a much higher level of 35 percent in 1991 than the other two sets of statistics. Thus, slightly more than one-third of Japanese households have at least one *kōenkai* member. Undeniably, politicians have succeeded in organizing a large segment of the Japanese voters.

Some 36.4 percent of LDP supporters were *kōenkai* members in 1995

Table 2.1 Kōenkai membership: Lower House elections (percent)

Year	1967	1969	1972	1976	1979	1980	1983	1986	1990	1993
Metropolises	4.2	15.6	9.1	9.8	20.1	14.1	11.4	14.5	16.1	13.6
Small and medium cities	6.4	10.5	9.9	14.9	20.9	14.6	16.0	19.3	18.3	16.8
Villages	5.8	10.2	8.8	15.3	16.6	16.9	18.1	18.7	19.3	17.4
National average	5.8	11.5	9.5	14.0	19.7	15.1	15.6	18.2	18.2	16.3

Source: *ASSK*, various years.

Table 2.2 Kōenkai membership: local elections (percent)

Year	1971	1975	1979	1983	1987	1991	1995
Metropolises	14.3	24.3	22.4	20.4	26.1	21.7	18.7
Small and medium cities	15.3	25.8	30.7	34.0	35.6	30.0	30.9
Villages	10.1	15.0	27.0	25.8	22.0	24.7	24.2
National average	13.7	22.8	28.2	29.3	30.3	27.1	26.9

Source: *ASSK*, various years.

Table 2.3 Kōenkai membership: households (percent)

Year	1987	1991
Metropolises	28.1	30.4
Small and medium cities	39.6	37.9
Villages	40.4	32.4
National average	37.6	35.0

Source: *ASSK*, 1987 and 1991.

(Table 2.4). It is said that "the LDP is not a party of strong supporters but, rather, a strong party of weak supporters."[22] Perhaps it is more accurate to say that the LDP is a strong party of both weak and strong supporters. The LDP's weak supporters may be likened to Miyake Ichirō's "negative partisans [who] lack a positive affective tie with the party they regularly support."[23] *Kōenkai* members are "loyal partisans" or strong supporters who have positive, affective ties to individual conservative politicians.[24] Close to half of LDP supporters have been invited to join a political machine (Table 2.5).

The *kōenkai* is a necessary but not a sufficient condition for the electoral success and long-term LDP rule. Put simply, the LDP cannot stay in power without the political machines. Their importance goes beyond the collection

Table 2.4 *Kōenkai* membership and party support

Party supporters	Total numbers	*Join* Kōenkai (%)	*Not join* Kōenkai (%)	*Don't know* (%)
Sakigake	13	53.8	46.2	–
Shinshintō	74	33.8	66.2	–
JSP	133	33.8	66.2	–
LDP	552	36.4	63.2	0.4
Kōmeitō	70	28.6	71.4	–
JCP	39	23.1	76.9	–
Others	25	36.0	64.0	–
Non-party supporters	1,257	21.6	77.7	0.7
Don't know	111	22.5	74.8	2.7
Total	2,274	26.9	72.4	0.6

Source: *ASSK*, 1996, p. 369.

Table 2.5 Invitations to join *kōenkai*

Party supporters	Number	*Yes* (%)	*No* (%)	*Don't know* (%)
Sakigake	6	50.0	50.0	–
Shinshintō	49	44.9	55.1	–
JSP	88	46.6	53.4	–
LDP	349	44.4	54.2	1.4
Kōmeitō	50	34.0	66.0	–
JCP	30	53.3	46.7	–
Other parties	16	43.7	56.3	–
Non-party support	977	42.0	57.3	0.7
Don't know	83	32.5	66.6	1.2
Total	1,648	42.3	56.9	0.8

Source: *ASSK*, 1996, p. 389.

of votes from each member. The effectiveness of the election campaign lies in the involvement and enthusiasm of members to contact their families, relatives, friends, and colleagues, and other potential LDP supporters who are non-*kōenkai* members. Some of the non-*kōenkai* LDP supporters may be influenced by phone calls, postcards, distribution of pamphlets, and road-side speeches made on behalf of the candidate by *kōenkai* members to go out and vote.

Why is the LDP able to recruit *kōenkai* members even in metropolitan Japan? First, because the benefits of being a member outweigh the costs. The whole range of services, a sense of belonging, and the fun and enter-tainment enjoyed by a member are often free. Very few members pay membership fees, and those who do pay only token sums in exchange for a range of material and solidaristic benefits.[25] Second, voters also become members out of a sense of obligation (*giri*),[26] interpersonal relationship (*ningen kankei*), ties of blood (*ketsuen*) and soil (*chien*), and to further their economic self-interest related to work by rubbing shoulders with the power-ful. According to the 1996 ASSK survey, 49.3 percent of members joined a conservative political machine because of human relationship and obliga-tions. Only 17.8 percent did so for economic reasons.[27] The challenge to LDP candidates in metropolitan Japan is to organize those urban residents who are not related by blood and soil, and whose economic interests related to work and business are not enhanced by *kōenkai* membership. The orga-nizational mode is based on social networks, services and entertainment, and the personality and charisma of the candidate. It is certainly not based upon a set of ideas or policies.

The persistence of tradition in metropolitan Japan: "former village" mentality and *kōenkai*

The merger of villages to form new wards or cities does not necessarily obliterate the sentimentality of voters toward their "former villages."[28] Such attachment to one's "former village" is not an anachronism which belongs solely to rural Japan but is also present in metropolitan Japan in the 1990s. Conservative politicians are often skilled at tapping local sentiments and induct long-term residents with their extensive social networks into their political machines.

Although Midori ward in Yokohama is one of the most urban in Japan and the bastion of the Kanagawa SC, tradition, localism, and consciousness of old village boundaries persist among old residents. Midori ward com-prised five "former villages" which were amalgamated to form part of Yokohama city in 1939.[29] Thirty years later, the five "former villages" were detached from Kōhoku ward to form Midori ward. Even half a century after the merger of the five villages, support for conservative candidates is still structured along old village boundaries.[30] Each "former village" sends its champion running on the LDP label to Yokohama City Assembly. Although each LDP city assembly member in Midori ward seeks support beyond the boundaries of his or her own "former village," the core of the member's support and the bulk of his or her *kōenkai* members come from the "former village."

Voter support for a conservative candidate is often transfered to his or her successor, often the son or son-in-law, even in urban Japan. At the national level, about half of the LDP Diet Members belong to political families.[31] Even though Japanese voters are said to increasingly subscribe to modern values and New Politics issues, they are also electing more second-generation politicians to office. Old residents alone do not have sufficient numbers to elect second-generation conservatives.[32] Both LDP prefectural assembly members of Midori ward, Kojima Yukiyasu and Miyoshi Yoshikiyo, inherited their seats.[33] Kojima is the third generation of his family to secure a prefectural seat. The first Kojima won the seat in 1896. After marrying the daughter of his predecessor, Kojima Yukiyasu became an adopted son (*yōshi*) of the Kojima family. He then changed his original surname from Katō to Kojima after marrying into the family. Kojima Yukiyasu has three daughters and no sons. He intimated that he will adopt a son-in-law who marries into the Kojima family. The son-in-law will become a fourth-generation Kojima and carry on the family tradition of occupying a prefectural seat. Despite sweeping socio-economic and political changes in Japan during the past century, the ability to appeal to local sentiments and to serve local interests has helped to sustain three generations of Kojima politicians. Perhaps there may even be a fourth-generation Kojima politician in twenty-first-century Japan. The benefit of inheriting a seat from one's father or father-in-law is not only name recognition among voters, but also receiving a ready-made political machine. For a political newcomer, it takes time and money to build a support organization. A second-generation politician with an inherited *kōenkai* has an enormous advantage over a newcomer who has to build his own *kōenkai* from scratch.

Neighborhood association heads and *kōenkai* in metropolitan Japan

A unique feature of Japanese society is the extensiveness of the neighborhood association (*chōnaikai* or *jichikai*[34]). By 1980, *chōnaikai* had been organized in 3,256 out of 3,278 cities, wards and villages in Japan.[35] In Yokohama, 90 percent of households are organized into the neighborhood association.[36] The development of *chōnaikai* as an unique institution has been attributed to Japanese culture and society, since its counterpart cannot be found in the western advanced industrial societies.[37] In actuality, *chōnaikai* is not exclusively a spontaneous institution of civil society but an institution consciously supported by the state. During the Second World War, *chōnaikai* were mobilized by the military regime to support the war effort. Under the American Occupation, they were disbanded becuase of ties to Japanese militarism and alleged anti-democratic tendencies. *Chōnaikai* staged a come-back after the American Occupation as a result of the organizational efforts to build local communities by local residents with support from local governments.

The roles of *chōnaikai* include acting as a transmission belt between local governments and residents, and also functioning as the administrative tip of local governments.[38] In return, *chōnaikai* receive financial aid for their activities from city governments. *Chōnaikai* activities are supposed to be apolitical. They include the promotion of good neighborliness, recreational activities, culture, welfare, sports and other events for children, women, and the elderly, recycling of rubbish, bottles, and newspapers, night patrol of the neighborhood, the maintenance of street lamps and the spraying of insecti-cide.[39] Membership comprises households and not individuals.

In Yokohama city, close to 90 percent of *chōnaikai* federations' heads are males.[40] A disproportionate number of *chōnaikai* heads are shopkeepers, landlords, farmers, and self-managed businesses.[41] In Midori ward, although around 1 percent of the population are farmers, close to 12 percent of *chōnaikai* heads are farmers.[42] If we were to examine the occupa-tion, gender, and age of *chōnaikai* heads,[43] they tend to belong to social groups which lean toward the conservatives. A symbiotic relationship exists between many conservative politicians and *chōnaikai* heads, even in metro-politan Japan. In pre-war Yokohama, there was a history of close ties between local politicians and *chōnaikai* heads; many politicians were either ex-*chōnaikai* heads or were simultaneously holding an assembly seat and a *chōnaikai* headship. Between 1934 and 1942, 59 city assembly members in Yokohama were also *chōnaikai* heads.[44]

A neighborhood association acts in the following ways when it helps a politician.[45] First, it officially endorses a candidate in its own name. Second, a *chōnaikai* head would endorse a candidate personally, avoiding the use of the neighborhood association's name as a sponsor. Last, a *chōnaikai* head and his or her lieutenants do not officially endorse any candidate (to maintain the semblance of neutrality), but key *chōnaikai* members join a separate organization, especially a *kōenkai*, to campaign for the candidate. The last pattern is more common in urban Japan. If an urban neighborhood asso-ciation and its office holders were openly to endorse a candidate, that could incur the wrath of some *chōnaikai* members who may be supporters of other parties, and risk splitting the neighborhood association. The ASSK asked whether the respondent's neighborhood association had endorsed any candidates. The results show that official endorsement is more prevalent in rural than in urban Japan (Table 2.6).[46] Not captured in the survey was the extent to which key members of *chōnaikai* have acted on behalf of candidates without making an explicit endorsement.

It has been pointed out that official endorsement of politicians by *chōnaikai* has been declining gradually.[47] A decline of official endorsement is, however, no indication that the heads and office bearers of *chōnaikai* are abstaining from electoral politics in greater numbers. They may support a candidate without using the name of *chōnaikai*. When Japanese voters were asked whether it is a good thing for their neighborhood association to endorse a candidate, only 19.9 percent of those surveyed felt that it is bad for *chōnaikai* to do so.[48] Revulsion among voters against involvement in electoral politics by their *chōnaikai* appears to be low, and this is probably one reason why *chōnaikai* heads can persist in their involvement in electoral politics.

Neighborhood association, *kōenkai* and politics in Yokohama

All four LDP city assembly members in Midori ward have close ties with neighborhood associations.[49] In contrast, the NET prefectural and city assembly members from Midori ward have few ties to *chōnaikai*. The Kanagawa SC sought to build its own grassroots organization as a local substitute for the *chōnaikai* in order to challenge the conservatives. However, it is not easy for the co-op to fulfil that ambition because *chōnaikai* is an entrenched institution in Japanese society. Those neighborhood associations that support conservative politicians invariably aid the LDP candidate who comes from the "former village" territory where the associations are located.

While *chōnaikai* tend to support conservative candidates, there are

Table 2.6 Candidate endorsement by neighborhood association (percent)

	Yes	*No*	*Don't know*
12 big cities	21.6	61.9	16.5
Small and medium cities	32.9	57.9	9.2
Village	32.4	61.8	5.8
General	30.3	59.6	10.2

Source: *ASSK*, 1996, p. 358.

occasions when *chōnaikai* also help candidates from other parties and citizens' movements. JSP city assembly members in Midori ward claim that they too receive some support from neighborhood associations in their residential areas. The husband of a JSP city assembly member was the founding member of her *chōnaikai* and on the basis of interpersonal relationship was able to swing his *chōnaikai* behind his wife.[50] In Sakae ward, Yokohama, a number of the neighborhood associations supported a coalition of residents' movements against a highway project which cut across the ward.[51] In the 1991 Local Election, the anti-highway construction coalition of neighborhood association and residents' movement ran two candidates for the city and prefectural assembly on the single issue of opposing the highway construction plans. Since the conservatives supported the highway project, neighborhood associations that opposed the road construction did not endorse the LDP candidates. Only one of the NET assembly members in Yokohama received support from her neighborhood association, which comprises only 28 households.[52] Another NET representative receives support from some members of her *chōnaikai* because she was a newsletter editor of her *chōnaikai*.[53]

The interests of conservative politicians and *chōnaikai* heads often dovetail. The requests made by *chōnaikai* heads in Yokohama include are often for road repairs and improvement.[54] Most LDP assembly members, both local and national, are specialists in road repairs. The logical way to get quick results on infrastructure improvements is to contact the LDP representatives. LDP Diet Members and local assembly members often act as patrons to *chōnaikai* events such as sports meets and club sessions, and make financial contributions to such activities. A Diet Member from Yokohama noted that every summer, for *bon odori* (festive dances) alone he receives requests from at least 40 to 50 neighborhood associations. The Diet Member is not expected to come empty handed.[55] Politicians try to represent the interests of *chōnaikai* and, in return, politicians have the opportunity to make a good impression on *chōnaikai* leaders and members and win their votes.

Out of the 12 LDP city and prefectural assembly members from Yokohama interviewed by the author, only one politician, Fukuda Susumu, claimed to receive little support from neighborhood associations.[56] In his first attempt to secure a seat in Kanagawa ward in 1983, Fukuda tried but failed to obtain a candidate endorsement from the LDP. His conservative rival, the head of a *chōnaikai* federation, was also denied an LDP official endorsement. Not surprisingly, various *chōnaikai* heads backed one of their own rather than Fukuda. Since the LDP City Chapter was unable to choose between the two conservative candidates, Fukuda and his rival ran as independents with the expectation that the winner would subsequently be accepted as a LDP assembly member. Fukuda lost and ended as the runner-up (*jiten*). Luckily for Fukuda, he became an assembly member when his rival was disqualified and arrested along with four heads of *chōnaikai* federations for election bribery.[57] Upon investigation, it was discovered that Fukuda's rival secured support from half of the 20 heads of *chōnaikai* federations in Kanagawa ward. Money was handed to the heads to distribute ¥1,000 to each voter who attended the *kōenkai* meeting on the pretext of reimbursing them for transportation cost. The incident showed the deep involvement of *chōnaikai* heads in election campaigning even in metropolitan Japan.

In an account of an election campaign in semi-rural Japan, it was noted that those involved in the LDP candidate's organization "all have one thing in common: they are without exception, active members of their neighborhood association."[58] In the election campaign of Umezawa Kenji, a number of key campaign workers were active leaders in their neighborhood associations.[59] Neighborhood associations were tapped by conservatives to win support even in the *danchi* (public housing complexes). During the 1991 Local Elections the author followed a group of Umezawa's campaign workers to prepare for a speech at the premises of the neighborhood association in a *danchi* complex.[60] While the campaign workers were methodically setting up posters, banners, lanterns, and sound system, the author explored the premises of the *jichikai*. Decorating the walls of the main hall were pictures of festivals and various social activities held by the *jichikai*. Especially prominent were photographs of many children carrying the portable shrine (*mikoshi*) along the parameters of the *danchi* complex. Lifting the portable shrine may be interpreted by some to demarcate the spiritual boundaries of the community. To many, however, it holds little religious significance but is merely a fun activity for the children. Festivals such as parading the portable shrine reflect the emergence of a new urban community or possibly attempts to foster a sense of community among new residents where none existed before.[61]

An old resident and a key lieutenant of an LDP city assembly member remarked to the author that the portable shrines and festivals held by some of the new residents in Yokohama are cheap imitations of the authentic, traditional festivals. Whether the festival in the *danchi* is manufactured or not, it symbolizes the evolution of a new urban community which is, in part, consciously nurtured by some of the *danchi* residents. About 20 years ago in the same *danchi*, the sense of community was probably weak since strangers assembled almost overnight from different regions. After the passage of more than two decades, children of a *danchi* might have attended the same kindergartens and schools and parents would have served in the same PTA and *chōnaikai*. Some housewives would join social activities, including the co-ops, and discover a sense of belonging (Table 2.7). Thus,

Table 2.7 Participation in local activities: case of Yokohama residents (percent)

Activity	Participation
Office holder of neighborhood association	33.7
Physical education, livelihood, consumption	2.5
Office holder of children's association, women's association or old folks' club	15.9
PTA office holder	21.5
Welfare activities	5.1
Office holder of sports group	8.3
Office holder of cultural clubs, e.g., music, movies, study groups	5.0
Co-op movements and purchasing through *han*	7.2
Office holder of religious and political organization	2.4
Others	1.6
Do not participate in any local activities	46.7
Unclear	0.3

Source: Yokohama shi kikaku zaiseikyoku kikaku choseishitsu, 1992, p. 13.

Notes
N = 2,223, multiple answers

the picture of a disoriented, atomized urban Japan best fits in the 1950s and 1960s, when there was rapid economic growth and high urban migration, rather than the 1990s, where there is slower economic growth and less urban migration. A period of residential stability and the growth of social networks in the place of residence, especially among women, have led to the emergence of urban communities which facilitate political mobilization by candidates, both conservative and non-conservative, in metropolitan Japan.[62]

The ability to tap emerging social networks even in *danchi* is not limited to the LDP but is shown also by enterprising opposition parties and the NET movement. In the case of Umezawa, he won the support of a *jichikai* head at the *danchi*, who then assembled about 60 residents that night to meet and hear Umezawa for the very first time. The campaign workers systematically collected their names, addresses, and phone numbers to be placed on the *kōenkai*'s mailing list. Umezawa, for his part, had to work hard to break the ice with a pack of strangers with his well-worn one liners. He outlined things he desired to do for the community and, finally, to show his earnestness to win their support, wrote his home telephone number on the board and said, "If you have a problem, you can call me anytime, day or night. My eldest son will take your message if I am not in." Thus, Umezawa sought their support by tapping a pre-existing social network and also offering tangible services to his potential voters.

Kōenkai and new residents

The term "new resident" (*shin jūmin*) is rather ambiguous, but politicians in Yokohama usually use the term in reference to someone who has stayed in the city for less than 20 years. Attracting new residents to join *kōenkai* is not an easy task for the LDP politician. Salary men who only return to Yoko- hama only to sleep lack the time to be actively involved in politics. Other salary men who worked only for a few years in the Tokyo metropolitan region before being transferred to other parts of Japan or abroad are unlikely to sink roots in the locality.

In semi-rural Japan, a Diet Member's *kōenkai* members may be benefici- aries of employment benefits generated by such pork-barrel projects as roads, bridges and other construction work. In metropolitan Japan, where the infrastructure is relatively well developed, politicians have to resort to other strategies to build their *kōenkai*. Moreover, white-collar salary men from big corporations with the expectation of lifetime employment need not resort to *kōenkai* for welfare and employment opportunities. Rather than local development projects, conservative politicans in urban Japan have to emphasize cultural and recreational events to attract new residents.

Despite the difficulties involved in attracting new residents to join the *kōenkai*, there are indirect ways in which the conservative politicians woo them. The first strategy is to provide a range of services and entertainment which may attract some new residents and their children. The second strategy is to squeeze every possible social network to pull in the new residents. Neither of these strategies is unique to metropolitan Japan. A common approach is to organize sports teams, especially baseball teams, and sports meets for the local children. This is done in the hope that parents of children who enjoy such recreational services will support their LDP benefactor. One prefectural assembly member of Midori ward sponsored 155 baseball teams for both adults and children.[63] Since baseball appeals to some urban residents regardless of length of residence, conservative politi- cians in Yokohama have successfully attracted some support from new residents whose children enjoy recreational benefits. For adults, golf tourna- ments are held by a number of the local assembly members.

Concerts and vacation trips are other standard fare for *kōenkai*. Pop concerts and rock stars are appreciated by some new residents as it means they need not travel all the way to Tokyo and pay a hefty sum to attend a concert. Travel to hot springs, grape-gathering trips and package tours to Tokyo Disneyland are also part of *kōenkai*'s extensive range of services. As these services escalate, it is common for even local assembly members to organize overseas vacations for supporters to popular destinations like the U.S., Europe, and Australia. Local assembly members travel with a tour group of 50 to 200 *kōenkai* members for about a week, during which time they rub shoulders with their supporters and promote a sense of camaraderie.[64]

Since the costs of overseas vacations for supporters are too expensive to be borne by the assembly members, participants have to pay for their *kōenkai* trips abroad.[65] However, the cost of such trips is typically less than the market rate because of the ties between assembly members and travel agencies. Moreover, all the paperwork for a planned overseas trip is handled through the auspices of *kōenkai* and its favored travel agency. Thus, *kōenkai* members are spared the trouble of planning for an overseas vacation on their own. Trips abroad can also be a psychological strain on the assembly members. One LDP city assembly member intimated that he dreaded having to organize overseas trips for supporters. If a member of the tour group is involved in an accident, for example, he could be held morally responsible for the tragedy.[66] In the competition for political support, other assembly members are prepared to take risks and act as shepherds for *kōenkai* members in an unfamiliar, foreign country and to become embroiled in organizing an endless round of services and entertainment for supporters. To ensure that new residents are aware of *kōenkai*, the supporters of some assembly members will distribute invitation forms, newsletters, and pamphlets which report on the politician's assembly and the *kōenkai* activities to every single household in the ward.

The second strategy is to squeeze every possible social tie for political support. During Umezawa's election campaign, the author attended several small group meetings assembled by local notables such as postal masters, principals of kindergartens and other educational institutions. In Japan, a premium is placed on education for children. Both old and new residents send their children to cram schools (*juku*) to prepare them for tough entrance examinations which will decide their fate in life. Principals and teachers who support conservative candidates can tap their extensive networks of "education mamas." The PTA is also a popular hunting ground for political support. While white-collar salary men are usually too busy to serve as PTA leaders, conservative supporters often have the time and the desire to play active roles in the PTAs of their school districts. Through the PTA, conservative supporters establish personal relationship with the wives of salary men and other new residents who serve in the same PTA. The conservatives' ability to tap political support rests on a case-by-case basis because other PTA members may be supporters of NET or other non-conservative parties. Candidates also exploit the old boys' network, which often lasts a lifetime. LDP candidates who grow up in the constituency where they are running can count on the support of their kindergarten, primary- and high-school mates. Through the old boys' network, candidates can even reach out to new residents who graduated from the same university.[67]

A social network is assiduously cultivated and organized, and nothing is left to chance. The human circle which underpins *kōenkai* takes time to cultivate but, once established, its bonds are unlikely to dissipate rapidly.[68] Maintaining a *kōenkai* requires a great deal of routine, organizational work. Most LDP local assembly members in Yokohama have computerized their *kōenkai* membership list. An example of a meticulously maintained *kōenkai* is one which belongs to Iijima Tadayoshi of Sakae ward, Yokohama. He showed the author a computer printout of his *kōenkai* name list, which is divided into three groups: hard-core members (group A), strong supporters (group B), and those placed on the mailing list (group C). Besides the use of computers to keep track of members and their particulars, name cards of each member are also kept. Each time a member has attended an event, it is carefully recorded on the cards. In this way, Iijima can tell the degree to which each member is enmeshed in his *kōenkai*. To maintain the social bonds with his *kōenkai* members, Iijima, like other typical politicians, attends funerals and weddings of his supporters' families and also visits the homes of his supporters. Home visits are also meticulously planned and recorded. In various maps which indicate every household in Sakae ward, Iijima marks the homes of every *kōenkai* member of the A and B groups. After visiting the home of a supporter, he crosses that house in red on the map.

A less common approach to win support from new residents is through the landlords (*ōyasan*) who ask their tenants to vote for a particular candidate.[69] In land-scarce Tokyo metropolitan area, an apartment is often too expensive for an average salary man to purchase. If company housing is not provided, he will have to rent an apartment. There have been cases where landlords have felt comfortable enough to ask their tenants for their votes. However, it is a soft appeal and not a demand for votes, and is fundamentally different from the pre-war, rural social relations whereby a landlord might exercise coercive power over their agrarian tenants.

Included in the social networks of some LDP politicians are the *yakuza*, the Japanese version of the Mafia.[70] The LDP is a catch-all party which attracts support from almost all social groups, including the Mob. The overwhelming majority of the LDP's support is above board, but the underworld also forms part of the social networks of some LDP candidates. It has been reported that the *yakuza* participates in the fundraising parties of some senior prefectural assembly members in Kanagawa prefecture.[71]

A prominent personality in Yokohama with alleged Mob ties and close LDP connections is Fujiki Yukio[72] who runs one of the largest transport companies in the city. During election campaigns, workers from his company were despatched to help various LDP candidates and he also personally made speeches to endorse them. According to a four-part series on Fujiki by the *Asahi shinbun*, his father was a *yakuza* tied to leaders of the largest mob organizations in Japan. It was reported that there were instances when mobsters extorted money from small business in Yokohama by threatening "Don't you know the name of Fujiki?"[73]

Fujiki was a close friend of Okonogi Hikosaburo, Chairman of Kanagawa LDP Prefectural Chapter and ex-MITI Minister. The *Asahi Shinbun* reported that Fujiki is also the chairman of former Prime Minister Takeshita's fundraising organization in Kanagawa. Other posts he reportedly holds include chairman of one of Umezawa Kenji's political organizations and vice chairman of Akarui Yokohama Tsukuri Kai (Society to Build a Bright Yokohama), an organization which comprises mostly LDP prefectural and city assembly men from Yokohama. Fujiki's name was once floated as the conservative candidate for mayoral election of Yokohama in 1990, but was withdrawn after critics claimed that Fujiki was tied to the Mob.

The shadowy links between the LDP and the *yakuza* became prominent in the Sagawa scandal of 1992, when it was alleged that Takeshita relied on the mob to silence some Right-wingers who were embarrassing him with a smear campaign prior to his election as party president. While the alleged ties between the LDP and the *yakuza* in Yokohama have attracted little attention, the case of Fujiki suggests that such ties are not uncommon at the level of local politics. While some LDP assembly members benefited from their shady ties by raising money and manpower from the mob to support their *kōenkai*, the negative publicity which ensued after the outbreak of a scandal involving the mob invariably alienated some of the unorganized urban voters which the party has tried to woo.

The *kōenkai* approach: problems and prospects

By the 1995 Local Elections, 18.7 percent of all voters in the 12 largest cities were *kōenkai* members. Barely 28 years before, only 4.2 percent of all voters were organized in the metropolises. This increase is indeed an organizational feat in an environment least conducive to *kōenkai*-building. Yet, its expansion to the cities has brought along a mixed baggage of benefits and problems. *Kōenkai* help to integrate some of the urban residents into the local community through a range of activities in which they can participate and thereby acquire a sense of belonging. In the big cities, where anonymity and impersonality are some of the unattractive aspects of urban living, *kōenkai* contribute to local community-building by nurturing a sense of friendship and mutual help among members. Notwithstanding the many criticisms levelled against *kōenkai*, the organization does provide tangible and psychological benefits to its members. A voter with a personal problem is unlikely to be turned away at the door of the *kōenkai*.

While the *kōenkai* approach helps to address one set of problems faced by a segment of voters, it creates a new set of problems which may eventually undermine the legitimacy of the political system. Satō Seizaburō and Matsuzaki Tetsuhisa mistakenly believe that *kōenkai* absorbs the popular will or the people's will *(min i)*.[74] Implicit in their study is the desirability of *kōenkai*, since the absorption of the people's will is good by most accounts of political philosophy. The error of Satō and Matsuzaki's analysis of *kōenkai* is the failure to distinguish between people's will and particular will. In actuality, *kōenkai* absorbs not the people's will but only the particular will. It caters specifically to the parochial needs of a mere fraction of the electorate which is organized into the private clubs of assembly members. Those outside the political machine, including non-organized, soft LDP supporters have no share in the benefits offered by *kōenkai*. Close to four-fifths of urban voters are not represented by *kōenkai*. How can *kōenkai* possibly absorb the popular will when it caters only to one-fifth of the urban voters?

It is more appropriate to suggest that the people's will is towards a better quality of life – better housing conditions, lower consumer prices, and more humane commuting time – than the narrow and self-serving activities of *kōenkai*. More accurately, the epitome of private interests or interest politics is *kōenkai*.[75] A normative critique castigates the *kōenkai* approach as essentially lacking the vision of a good polity and thereby losing sight of the higher purpose of politics. Politics is diminished to the point of the mere provision of goods and services, and *kōenkai* thus become the patrimonial possession of professional politicians. *Kōenkai* cannot absorb the popular will because of a lack of institutional channels to reflect the voices calling for policy changes which range from political reforms, direct participation by citizens in policy-making, to a better quality of life in Japan. The political machine is the only mass organization of the LDP. But ordinary members exercise no direct influence on public policy-making, for it is not the inherent nature of *kōenkai* to be concerned about the public good but private interests and the task to get a candidate elected to office.

The *kōenkai* approach reminds us of the adage: "all politics is local." This approach calls forth assembly members who are skilful in interpersonal relationships, sensitive to the needs and feelings of their supporters, and able to bring pork-barrel projects to their constituencies. However, Japan is increasingly propelled by its great economic engine to play a larger role in the international political economy. The question will arise whether Diet Members who are skilful at *kōenkai* maintenance and pandering to parochial interests at the local level also have the vision and the necessary skill to deal with the complexities and broad issues of international relations.

Another problem associated with *kōenkai* is the emergence of second-generation politicians at both the local and national levels simply because they have the advantage of inheriting political machines from their fathers.[76] Political machines constitute a barrier to newcomers not born into local political dynasties. The rise of second-generation politicians riding on the back of an inherited machine has resulted in a structural nepotism which may create problems for Japanese democracy. At present, more than one-third of Diet Members inherit their seats. Second-generation politicians are not unknown in democracies, but the extensiveness of this phenomenon in Japan is unrivalled by any other advanced industrial democracies.

The most serious problem of the *kōenkai* approach is its insatiable demand for money. It is pointed out that "the fundamental reason for the high cost of campaigning in Japan is that every LDP politician must build and maintain his own political machine."[77] The escalation of services to solicit voters' support often leads to the slippery road of political corruption, scandals, erosion of support at the polls and, if left unaddressed, a legitimacy crisis for the political system.

Will the Japanese political machine wither away like its American counterpart? Will it be hemmed in by the rise of New Politics in Japan? The decline of the U.S. urban machines by the 1970s has little to tell us about the fate of the Japanese urban machines.[78] Two crucial factors which contributed to an end of urban machines in the U.S. are absent in Japan. First, the rise of the U.S. machines is intertwined with the recruitment of ethnic immigrants – Irish, Italian, and Polish – and the provision of services to them in exchange for their votes. When the descendants of white immigrants joined the American social, cultural, and economic mainstream, climbed the middle-class ladder, and fled to the suburbs to escape the urban ghettos, the machines were less able to organize a bloc of ethnic votes. Since Japan's ethnicity is relatively homogeneous, ethnicity is not related to the building of political machines.

Second, the U.S. urban machines provided patronage and jobs in the city bureaucracy to its supporters. When civil service reforms and the U.S. Judiciary placed restrictions on this well-worn practice, "To the victor, belong the spoils," an important source of patronage which had sustained the machine dried up. In post-war Japan, bureaucratic posts are not in the largesse of politicians to be distributed to their *kōenkai* supporters. Although money politics, corruption, and venality are features of both the U.S. and Japanese political machines, there is little popular revulsion against the *kōenkai* compared to the recurring anti-machine movements popular in the U.S. The insulation of Japan's bureaucratic posts from the politician and his or her supporters has helped to preclude an American-style backlash against the political machine.

Factors which were expected to affect the viability of *kōenkai* are: election laws which curb the use of media technology, the single-ballot, multi-member electoral system, and the tendency by politicians to cling on to a well-worn organizational strategy even when objective conditions which sustain the *kōenkai* have changed.[79] In January 1994, single-member districts coupled with proportional representation in the Lower House were introduced by the Hosokawa government as an electoral device to check political corruption. Theoretically, if a multi-member electoral system contributes to the perpetuation of *kōenkai*, the introduction of a single-member electoral system should contribute to its demise. There is no certainty, however, that tinkering with the electoral system would necessarily lead to such an outcome. In a first-past-the-post system, it is not inevitable that the machine will wither away and replaced by strong local-party organization. Since politicians, like most human beings, are creatures of habit, they may cling to organizational strategies that have served them well in the past. They will probably rebuild their political machines, even if their *kōenkai* were initially fragmented by changes to the electoral boundaries. Changing a medium-sized, multi-member district into smaller single-member districts will result in the fragmentation of political machines because large numbers of *kōenkai* members will be stranded in newly created electoral districts. LDP politicians may retain their political machines even in a first-past-the-post system to deter other conservatives from running in their district and also to compete against the opposition parties. In the U.S., a first-past-the-post system and the availability of media technology have not seen the disappearance of personal candidate support organization. Likewise in Japan, the single-member constituency system, if introduced, will not automatically lead to the withering away of *kōenkai*. It is premature to predict their demise.

Despite claims by LDP renegades that they are committed to clean politics, big business poured in money to fund the *kōenkai* of the rebels even before the 1993 Lower House Election to insure goodwill just in case they got into power.[80] Thus, these renegades are not only relying on their *kōenkai* but also strengthening their support organizations to win power on the platform to clean up politics. Ironically, these former LDP chameleons ostensibly support political reforms but persistently rely on political machines, which which can be seen as a fundamental cause of money politics.

Conclusion

In the early 1970s, many scholars hailed the dawn of New Politics, a novel form of citizens' direct participation in politics, concern about environmental issues, and the advent of a new political culture in Japan. Contrary to some expectations, urban political machines which are associated with Old Politics flourished. Moreover the "premodern" attachment to one's "former village" and neighborhood association is still strong in urban Japan. The so-called "post-industrial society" does not represent a total transformation of society. Rather, the "post-industrial" sectors continue to embrace more profound and persistent "industrial" and "pre-industrial" values and behaviors. Political parties ranging from the LDP to NET rely on organizations and strong local support groups. An organizational backbone is as necessary in a "post-modern" as in a "modern" democratic polity. This is despite the Greens' expectation that the advent of a post-industrial society and New Politics would lessen the need for organizations and oligarchic structures.

With the emergence of new urban communities, conservative politicians have tapped into local networks and also recruited urbanites into their *kōenkai*. Regardless of the attraction of "post-modernism" or "modernism", many urban Japanese continue to place a high value on small-group, communal ties and personal loyalties. The *kōenkai* is indeed comfortably nested in a Japanese post-industrial society whose values and behavior continue to stress such reciprocal relationships. Moreover, the unabated demand for personal and collective benefits from candidates among a significant segment of the urban voters is likely to sustain the political machine despite the persistent call for "clean politics" in Japan. Confronted by the established parties' strong political machines that have succeeded in organizing a large segment of the urban votes, NET faces an uphill task to build strong organizations and to increase its electoral support.

3 The Liberal Democratic Party's quest for local policy-making party organization

Any Green party in Japan that seeks urban political support is confronted not only by strong political machines but also by Old Politics parties that embrace certain aspects of ecological issues. In the 1960s and 1970s, the established opposition parties increased their urban support partly by championing stricter environmental protection. The LDP responded to this electoral challenge by becoming more sensitive to environmental issues. Thus, it is not easy for NET to woo urban support and expand its electoral power on the basis of environmental protection, especially when all established parties are also supportive of environmental protection.

Although the *kōenkai* network is a formidable grassroots organization even in metropolitan Japan, it is not able to reach large numbers of urban voters who are outside its social web. Responding to policy concerns including ecology among the urbanites, the LDP Kanagawa Prefectural Chapter introduced the Kanagawa Forum 21 (KF 21), a policy-making party organization to attract the support of urban voters. Although KF 21 has six policy-making divisions, the party has paid special attention to the environmental division. However, the conservative experiment in constructing local policy-making organizations has had only limited success. The new party organizations are hierarchical and technocratic in character. While ordinary citizens are invited to attend policy forums, they mainly involve top prefectural party leaders and assembly members, specialists, scholars, bureaucrats, and business and other interest groups. Thus, ordinary citizens are essentially offered only passive roles without real avenues to participate in policy-formulation. The only mass-based organization for the LDP is still *kōenkai*. Moreover, many LDP local assembly members are lukewarm to the new policy-centric organization. If they and their rivals within the same electoral district embrace similar policy issues, there is little to separate one conservative candidate from another in the eyes of the voters; a conservative candidate is unlikely to win an advantage over his rivals if they are all competing on similar issues. Ultimately, conservative politicians feel more secure concentrating on their *kōenkai* rather than spending time on policy-making organizations that do not guarantee any electoral rewards. Despite the prefectural leadership's intention of winning greater urban support for the LDP based on policy appeals, individual LDP candidates are more concerned about their own political survival than a policy renovation to strengthen the party organization.

The significance of KF 21 lies not in what it has achieved but rather in what it was unable to do. The inability to develop strong local policy-making party organizations by the LDP in Kanagawa prefecture despite concerted efforts by the party prefectural leadership highlights the fact the LDP faces an uphill task to avoid a singular dependence on *kōenkai*. The LDP's failure to reduce its dependence on political machines means that the attendant problems of money and political corruption will continue to bedevil the LDP and Japanese politics. However, the LDP's limited success in introducing ecology-centric party organizations does not necessarily benefit NET. If other parties energetically pursue Green issues, NET will find it difficult to win support beyond the social networks of the *han* purely on an ecology platform.

This chapter will first examine the importance of the urban votes to LDP rule and the party's thinking on the imperative to win urban support. We shall then look at the attempt by the LDP Kanagawa Prefectural Chapter to build local policy-centric party organizations to win urban support and the problems involved when the LDP tried to construct such a project at the local level.

The imperative for urban support

The fate of the LDP lies in urban Japan. It cannot rely primarily on its traditional supporters, the farmers of rural Japan, to capture power. Contrary to persistent images of the LDP as a rural party dependent on farmers, the LDP has transformed itself into a party that derives substantial support from urban voters. According to one survey, about half of the LDP supporters are from the big cities, a quarter are from medium and small cities, and the remainder live in towns and villages.[1]

A number of factors will inevitably increase the electoral importance of the city in relation to the countryside. First, Japan has become overwhelmingly urban. According to an *Asahi shinbun* classification, only 22 out of 130 electoral districts are classified as rural.[2] Moreover, rapid advances in telecommunications, transportation, education and consumerism have resulted in the penetration of urban lifestyle and values into rural Japan. Rural depopulation and the drastic shrinkage of the agrarian sector from

45.2 percent of Japan's population in 1950 to 6.6 percent in 1990[3] mean that the LDP cannot neglect the urban voters. *The Economist* noted:

> Nowhere . . . is the greying of Japan happening faster than down on the farm. In 1960 half of Japan's farming population was still under 42 years old. By 1990 the median had soared to 60 – retirement age for the rest of Japan. Demographers reckon that, by 2000, as much as a third of Japan's farming population would have died of old age.[4]

The failure of the agricultural sector to attract a younger cohort of farmers in sufficient numbers to replace the present members and the steady decline of the farming population will gradually reduce the electoral clout of the farmers in the long run.

Second, the Supreme Court ruled that the disparity between an urban and rural vote beyond a ratio of 3:1 is unconstitutional.[5] Reacting to judicial pressure, the Diet adopted stop-gap measures to reduce the urban–rural disparity to below the prescribed 3:1 ratio. By 1992, the disparity had once again increased to 3:4:1.[6] In the same year, 10 seats were subtracted from rural constituencies and nine were added to urban constituencies. After the redistribution of seats, the imbalance stood at 2.77:1.[7] In January 1994, the Diet introduced a new electoral system for the Lower House as an electoral device to check political corruption. Out of 500 seats, 300 are single-member constituencies while the remainder are distributed by proportional representation. With the introduction of the new system, greater weight is given to urban constituencies. Thus, it is logical for the LDP to reduce its dependency on the farmers and reinforce its new urban base. Rather than the rural rice producers, the LDP must strengthen its appeal to urban consumers as they will increasingly exercise greater electoral clout.

Third, Japan was pressured by GATT and especially the U.S. to open its protected rice market. Even though the liberalization of Japan's rice market will not substantially reduce the U.S.–Japan trade imbalance, rice is a bilateral issue because it symbolizes Japanese markets closed to various U.S. goods and services. Japan's inexorable trade surplus with the U.S., the dawn of the post-Cold War era where the U.S. is less inclined to subordinate its own economic interest to the maintenance of military alliances, and the advent of a new Democratic Clinton administration less bent on free trade rhetoric make it increasingly difficult for Japan to avoid opening its rice markets. In November 1993, Japan partially opened its rice market to foreign competition.[8] Consequently, Japan's cosseted farmers may stage an electoral revolt against the parties that gave in to foreign pressure. Since a political backlash from the farmers is expected, the LDP has an added incentive to woo the urbanites.

Fourth, urban Japan is an arena for fierce electoral competition. The competition is intense given the large number of parties chasing after a diverse group of voters. In the 1960s and 1970s, parties of the Left (JCP), Center (Kōmeitō, DSP) and Right (New Liberal Club) enjoyed temporary booms in urban support. From the 1980s, NET launched electoral challenges and captured seats in prefectural and city elections in half of the largest cities. In 1992, a second conservative party, the JNP, staged its debut with a program designed to appeal to urbanites. This included political reforms, rice market liberalization, and lower consumer prices. In the following year, the Shinseitō (Renewal Party) and Sakigake (Harbinger Party) became the third and fourth conservative parties to make their appearances. In 1994, all established opposition parties except the JCP merged to form the Shinshintō (New Frontier Party) to challenge the three-party ruling coalition comprising the LDP, JSP and Sakigake. Given the intensely competitive party system in metropolitan Japan, the LDP must woo urban support beyond the reach of *kōenkai*.

The 1985 system

In January 1982, the LDP's official journal, the *Jiyū minshu* (Liberal Democrat) proclaimed a new era of conservatism and boldly predicted the replacement of the 1955 system[9] with the 1985 system.[10] The essential feature of the 1955 system is its two major pillars, the LDP as a perennial party in power and its rival, the JSP in permanent opposition. Polarized by issues of war and peace, the LDP supported the U.S.–Japan Alliance and, in the earlier phase, the revision of Article 9 (the war-renouncing clause of the Japanese Constitution), while the JSP advocated unarmed neutrality and the safeguarding of the Constitution. Although the combined votes of the two major parties declined gradually but inexorably, the JSP, in terms of voter support and seats, remained approximately half the size of the LDP. Within the overarching framework of LDP one-party dominance, the 1955 system evolved. Minor parties proliferated, issues of environmental protection and welfarism became increasingly important while the issues of war and peace concomitantly declined and many urban voters became dealigned from the established parties.

When the *Jiyū minshu* proposed the replacement of the 1955 system with the 1985 system, it envisaged the bolstering of LDP one-party dominant rule. The defining characteristic of the 1985 system is not merely the perpetuation of LDP rule but the further strengthening of one-party dominance by co-opting new social bases of urban support. The *Jiyū minshu* gleefully pointed out that the belief that the LDP is weak in the cities is a myth. It highlighted a number of trends in the domestic politics of the early

1980s that it believed not only favored conservatism but also set it apart from the era of 1960s and 1970s.

First, progressive prefectural and city governments were on the wane. In the 1970s, many big cities were controlled by non-conservative governors and mayors; by the early 1980s, the conservatives had recaptured most of the local governments in the metropolitan areas. Second, the LDP 1980 double election victory ended the situation of near parity between the number of conservative and combined opposition seats in the Lower House. Opposition attempts to build a coalition government to displace the LDP were dashed by the conservative's strong electoral performance.[11] Third, the *Jiyū minshu* perceived that by the 1980s, mass movements had become less conspicuous and strident compared to those of the previous two decades. The conservative establishment in the 1960s and 1970s was rocked by unprecedented mass protest movements that included anti-U.S.–Japan Security Treaty demonstrations, resident and citizens' movements revolving around environmental protests, and *Beheiren*, the anti-Vietnam war movement. Protest movements in the early 1980s did not seem to register the same degree of intensity, scale, or challenge to the LDP. The party flattered itself by claiming that residents' movements had fizzled out because its policy-making process had absorbed the demands of the movements. (We must note that the supposed decline of social movements is merely an opinion of the *Jiyū Minshu*. According to other indices, the 1980s have seen an upsurge of social movements.) In 1982, in the wake of its 1980 double election victory, the LDP was too blind to see newly emerging movements which are oriented toward problem-solving rather than vociferous, physical confrontation and protests.

The *Jiyū minshu* then highlighted the appropriate strategy to establish a new conservative dominance, the 1985 system. In its self-evaluation, the LDP candidly acknowledged that, in the eyes of urban consumers, it was a party that represented producer interests such as agriculture and business while the JSP represented labor. The LDP mouth-piece believed that urban consumer interests were not represented by any political parties. It prescribed that the LDP must represent urban consumers in order to remain politically viable. A two-pronged strategy was recommended. First, the LDP must win the support of the urban housewives, students, youth, white-collar salary men, and it must also poach from the ranks of organized labor, the support bases of the JSP and DSP. Second, party organizations must be built to provide channels for urban voices in place of the personality-centric, *kōenkai* approach. Interestingly, the LDP made the argument that if it could not move beyond the *kōenkai* approach and construct alternative structures to organize the urban masses, the 1985 system would not come to fruition. The *Jiyū minshu*'s fascinating argument is not a mere regurgitation of the view that *kōenkai* hinders the growth of party organization. Rather, it made the intellectual linkages between the limitations of *kōenkai*, the lack of urban consumer interest representation, and the need to construct alternative LDP organizations to reflect those interests to ensure long-term conservative rule. Although the *Jiyū minshu* dissected the LDP's problems and opportunities, it stopped short of offering any concrete policies that would appeal to the urban consumers or explaining how the party could shift beyond the *kōenkai* approach at the grassroots. The issue of political corruption that often enshrouds the LDP, much to the chagrin of many urban voters, was totally ignored by the party journal.

Ironically, just a year after the advocacy of a 1985 system, the LDP did poorly in the 1983 Lower House Election. Barely maintaining an absolute majority, it had to form a coalition government with its conservative splinter, the New Liberal Club.[12] The guilty verdict in ex-Premier Tanaka Kakuei's corruption case, delivered prior to the 1983 Election, created a voters' backlash against LDP money politics.[13] The LDP's poor showing in 1983 highlighted the fragility of LDP political support in the cities and its vulnerability to negative publicity about its money politics. LDP money politics is intertwined with the high cost of running political machines. The LDP is caught in a contradiction: to expand political support in the cities, the party relies on the time-tested but resource-guzzling political machines. However, building expensive grassroots organizations often embroils the LDP in money scandals that alienate many urban voters from the party. Thus, the *Jiyū minshu*'s prescription that the party must move beyond *kōenkai* to garner support in the cities hits the problem on the head. Its glaring weakness is the absence of concrete ideas on exactly how the LDP can achieve that goal. The LDP's call for a new 1985 system was quietly abandoned after the disappointing 1983 Lower House results. But the electoral pendulum swung again, and the 1985 system was resurrected as the 1986 system by then Prime Minister Nakasone Yasuhiro in the aftermath of the LDP's stunning victory in 1986.

Visions and illusions: Nakasone and the 1986 system

The LDP won a historic victory in the 1986 Combined Upper and Lower House Elections when it captured 300 out of 512 seats, the largest ever since the party's formation in 1955.[14] At that moment, the LDP appeared invincible. Nakasone's clarion call for a new 1986 system seemed credible and within reach.[15] His address at the party's 1986 Karuizawa Lecture was hailed as a "landmark speech"[16] and was given considerable coverage by the media and the opposition parties. Nakasone repeated the same theme again at the LDP Number Eleven Research Seminar in 1987.[17]

The content of Nakasone's Karuizawa Speech was a repetition of the main points raised by the *Jiyū minshu* back in 1982. The essential point raised by Nakasone was: the LDP must win the support of housewives, youths, students, and salary men from urban Japan in order to maintain long-term conservative dominance. The weakness of Nakasone's proposal was identical to the *Jiyū minshu*'s call for a 1985 system: Nakasone failed to offer any concrete policies or organizational strategy for the LDP to adopt in order to build up its urban support. Barely six months after the LDP's jubilant victory, Nakasone ruefully noted that support for the LDP was like "shifting sand."[18] The party suffered a setback in the 1987 Local Elections when it was punished by voters who opposed the proposed introduction of a consumption tax. Ironically, both the 1985 and 1986 systems and visions of a new era of conservative dominance were proposed after the double election victories of 1980 and 1986. Both systems were shattered when some of the LDP's soft urban supporters abandoned the party.

The political commentator Matsuzaki Tetsuhisa argued that the LDP's weakness stemmed from the fact that many of its new-found urban supporters were not organized and lacked channels through which to articulate their interests.[19] Matsuzaki claimed that the 1986 system was not obsolete despite the loss of the 1987 Local Elections and implied it was possible for the party to win back its erstwhile supporters. However, the historic defeat of the LDP in the 1989 when it lost the Upper House Election for the first time since the Party's foundation underscored the fact that the 1986 system was still-born.[20] The roller-coaster-like electoral performance of the LDP from its electoral triumph in 1986 to its débâcle in 1989 shows poignantly that talk of long-term LDP resurgence was premature. Barely seven years after the LDP's smashing victory in 1986, it was toppled from power.[21] Although the party recaptured power in June 1994, its hold remained tenuous; it had to forge an unstable, three-party-ruling coalition.

In the wake of the LDP's vulnerability to persistent money and machine politics, political scandals and fierce electoral competition, the LDP's enterprise in Kanagawa prefecture to build policy-oriented local party organizations is an important experiment that holds out the hope of paving the way for other LDP Prefectural Chapters to follow suit and reconstitute the party as an organization that does not neglect policy-making at the local level.

Policy-making and local party organizations: the LDP Kanagawa Prefectural Chapter and KF 21

In terms of organization-building and institutionalization, the LDP has moved beyond *kōenkai* and faction and possesses complex policy-making divisions at the national level which parallel the various ministries. Diet Members join specific divisions such as construction or agriculture, acquire policy expertise, information, social networks to relevant ministries and interest groups, and obtain pork-barrel projects for their constituencies.[22] Sensitive to voter concern for ecological issues, LDP Diet Members also formed new policy groups (*shinkankyō zoku*) to examine environmental problems.[23] On the other hand, at the local level, the LDP had no complex and specialized policy-making organizations despite the urging of the *Jiyū Minshu* in 1982 to build organizations beyond *kōenkai* to absorb urban interests.

The LDP Kanagawa Prefecture Chapter is unique in constructing policy-centric organization at the prefectural level to win urban support.[24] In 1990, the LDP Kanagawa Chapter launched a policy-making party organization, the Kanagawa Forum (KF) 21.[25] Within Kanagawa prefecture, other established parties have yet to construct complex policy-making organizations. The office manager of KF 21 noted that the JSP was incapable of organizing specialized think-tanks at the local level since it was too dependent on labor unions and was unable to move beyond labor-related issues.[26]

KF 21 comprises six divisions: environment, education, industry, local government, city planning, and welfare (Figure 3.1). There are 78 committee members who are primarily scholars, specialists, and professionals. The policy-making process of Forum 21 is as follows: after the views of each division's committee members and LDP assembly members are synthesized, draft proposals are sent to the manager of KF 21 who will then forward them to the Prefectural Chapter's Executive Council (kenren seimu chōsakai) and General Secretary for examination and approval. The final proposal is then submitted to the Chairman for formal ratification. The position papers approved by the Prefectural Chapter will then serve as policy guides for LDP assembly members. Strictly speaking, LDP Prefectural Chapters have a policy-making mechanism, the Executive Council, but the Executive Council is not a specialized policy-making organization and is usually dominated by a few Senior Diet Members and local assembly members who often lack the expertise or time to be concerned with long-term planning, wide ranging issues, and policies affecting their prefectures.

KF 21 seeks to educate LDP local assembly members on issues beyond parochial road and sewer repair work.[27] LDP local politicians are invited to

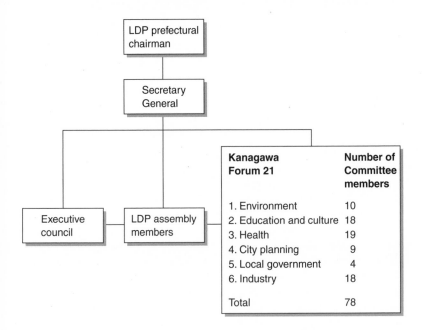

Figure 3.1 Structure of policy-making organizations in the LDP, Kanagawa Chapter.

be involved in lectures, discussions, and symposiums led by policy specialists. A popular division is the environment division, which attracts around half of the LDP prefectural assembly members to its meetings. After gleaning information and new knowledge from the study sessions, they discuss local, national, and global environmental issues before an assembly of their supporters. In their reports on assembly activities to their constituents, they tried to impress them by studying environmental issues. A conscientious participant in the environment division was prefectural assembly member Kojima Yukiyasu.[28] In his legislative report to his supporters, Kojima would demonstrate his keen interest in such environmental issues as the potential impact of industrial pollutants and acid rain from China on Japan's ecology. Increasingly, LDP local politicians in Kanagawa are joining the ecological bandwagon to polish their images as candidates and to appeal to their electorate.

Another advantage of the KF 21 is the opportunity to co-opt scholars, specialists, and interest groups who have previously been non-LDP supporters. Umezawa Kenji, the Prefectural Secretary General, pointed out that policy issues like environment, welfare, and education are non-ideological and thus, the party has been able to attract even scholars who lean toward the JSP. The LDP in Kanagawa opted for a broad inclusionary strategy to co-opt non-LDP partisans; it avoided dealing with divisive, exclusionary, ideological issues such as constitution revision.

Objective conditions, especially the special characteristics of Kanagawa prefecture, prompted the Prefectural Chapter to launch KF 21. According to the 1990 national census, Kanagawa is the second largest prefecture in terms of population.[29] The prefecture is heavily industrialized and urbanized, with large number of new residents, white- and blue-collar workers and very few farmers. These socio-economic conditions are not propitious for the LDP. Even in the LDP's 1986 landslide victory, the party captured only 15.3 percent of the votes for the Upper House local constituency of Kanagawa; its national average was 45.1 percent.[30] Kanagawa is probably one of the most competitive electoral battlegrounds in Japan. Although the formation of KF 21 can be interpreted as an organizational response to a competitive environment, subjective factors, especially personalities and leadership, do matter. KF 21 is the brain-child of Umezawa Kenji.[31] It is perhaps surprising that the initiator is not a LDP Diet Member but a senior prefectural assembly member. As a result of his leadership and affable personality, he won the support of LDP national and prefectural assembly members to set up KF 21, was granted a budget to establish a secretariat and a special Forum office within the Kanagawa Prefectural Chapter and, most importantly, attracted the active co-operation and participation of the prefectural assembly members.

A case study: the environment division

The environment division comprises seven environmental specialists and scholars, the office manager of KF 21, and two secretarial assistants. Approximately half of the meetings are among committee members and the other half are lectures and discussion sessions for local assembly members. Twice a year, the environment committee members meet with members from other divisions, participate in a general meeting and present their policy proposals to the Party Chapter.

Heading the environment division is Professor Saruda Katsumi of Kanagawa University, a veteran on environment policy, who describes himself as a person with socialist leanings (*"shakaitō teki"*) in terms of party identification.[32] To explain the seeming contradiction of having a person with JSP leanings heading an LDP think-tank, Saruda said that environmental issues transcend political ideology and that he wanted to stimulate LDP politicians to be more concerned about the environment. Saruda worked for 20 years in the Yokohama city bureaucracy's environment division and during the last 11 years of his stint in the bureaucracy, he was the environment division chief. He had also worked with JSP mayor, Asukata Ichio, who won prominence for his innovative environmental policies to curb industrial pollution in Yokohama. Saruda was a member of various environmental committees organized by the prefecture and national governments. Since Saruda had a large social network of scholars, bureaucrats, and specialists within the environmental community, he was eminently qualified to lead the environment division of KF 21. The co-option of such a prominent environmental specialist who had served under a socialist local government was a coup for the LDP and demonstrates its pragmatic nature.

The environment division was the first to kick off a series of big symposiums in 1991.[33] The Prefectural Chapter claimed that because the environment was the most important issue among the themes pursued by the six divisions, it was appropriate that a symposium on the environment was the first to be held.[34] Whether it was merely a public relations exercise or not remains to be seen. Prior to the symposium, it was announced in the press, and citizens interested in environmental issues and wishing to attend the symposium were encouraged to send their applications to KF 21.[35] The LDP boasted that this was no ordinary symposium because it was linked to the LDP and thus any proposals raised could be implemented. The symposium's theme was titled "Viewing Global Environmental Problems from Kanagawa."

The environment division was able to assemble panelists from varied backgrounds. The LDP top man on the environment, Kosugi Takashi (Chairman of LDP Environment Division and Chairman of the Diet's Environment Division), a representative from the Kanagawa Association to Prevent Industrial Waste (a group of 650 out of around 5,000 companies in Kanagawa), the environment division chief of Kanagawa prefectural government and a woman representing housewives' groups were active panellists at the symposium. Kosugi argued that after the end of the Cold War the next threat to mankind was environmental destruction. He also made an appeal to housewives: "Please do not let assembly members who are keen on environment issues lose their elections."[37] Policy issues and voter appeal are obviously intertwined.

Many of the pet themes of NET concerning the recycling of household rubbish, milk packs, beer bottles, disposal of cooking oil, and the use of natural soap were aired at the symposium. The LDP provided a forum to representatives from various housewives' organizations to articulate their views at that symposium. Thus, NET did not have the monopoly on these issues. NET is obviously not the only vehicle for urban housewives to articulate their interests. It is confronted by the Old Politics parties ranging from the LDP to the JCP that co-opt ecological issues which appeal to the urban housewives. It is not easy for NET to expand its political support beyond the social web of the SC purely on ecological issues, especially when other established parties woo urban support not only on the basis of political machines but also policy appeals that include ecology.

The environment division had submitted reports that were incorporated in detailed proposal booklets to the Prefectural Chapter.[38] These booklets included declaratory principles that warned against the dangers of air and water pollution, the loss of tropical rain forests, global warming, the destruction of the ozone layer, acid rain, and industrial emissions. They also pointed out that global environmental problems and Kanagawa prefecture's ecological problems are indivisible. Some of the more interesting, detailed proposals included:

1   The preservation of Sagami Bay, a wide expanse of Kanagawa's coastline. The LDP refers to it as "Shōwa no Umi" (Sea of the Shōwa Emperor).[39] The Shōwa Emperor, better known as Emperor Hirohito to foreigners, for decades conducted marine biological research along Sagami Bay in the post-war era. The division argued that there are around 1,300 species of life forms in the Bay, of which some are facing extinction. On grounds of sentimentality for the Emperor's work and the intrinsic value of preserving the natural environment, the proposals argued that the Bay must be preserved.

2   Strict regulations and laws on industrial waste: it advocated the stepping up of survey and inspection teams, the separation of rubbish (including batteries and vinyl), recycling efforts, and action against the illegal dumping of rubbish.

3   Aid to the International Tropical Timber Organization (ITTO), a United Nations organization located in Yokohama which monitors the tropical rainforests of the world.

4   Warning against the overdevelopment of tourism, golf courses, land rovers, four-wheel drives, and new camp sites which threaten the ecology of Kanagawa.[40]

Limitations to policy-centric, local party organizations

KF 21 was conceived to attract the participation of both LDP prefectural and city assembly members. In actuality, it attracted only prefectural assembly members.[41] The inability of the Prefectural Chapter to win support from LDP city assembly members from Yokohama and Kawasaki reflects the tension between the Prefectural Chapter and the two City Chapters. Both City Chapters are fiercely independent of the Prefectural Chapter and are reluctant to support a project that sprang from prefectural leadership.

Yokohama and Kawasaki are autonomous, "specially designated" cities with delegated powers normally associated with the prefecture. (Prefectural assembly members have only residual powers of supervising the police and education when they deal with specially designated cities.) Thus, city assembly members often view themselves as more important than prefectural assembly members. Since the two City Chapters handle their own affairs without subscribing to prefectural leadership, LDP city representatives are by habit reluctant to be involved in a project devised by the Prefectural Chapter.

LDP city assembly members have also expressed scepticism about the possibility that major policies can be decided and implemented at the local level. One city assembly member repeated the cliché that local government in Japan has only one-third autonomy (*sanwari jichi*) because the local government collects one-third of the tax receipts. He implied that KF 21 is just a talk show and a waste of time, since local government has very limited powers to shape important policies.[42]

A Yokohama LDP city assembly member intimated that some of the younger politicians from the Yokohama LDP City Chapter were keen to establish specialized policy-making divisions like KF 21 at the local level, but senior LDP Yokohama city assembly members were not interested in the idea of developing such local party organization.[43] According to a senior LDP Yokohama city assembly member[44] there was no need to replicate an organization similar to KF 21 at the city level because the LDP City Chapter already had an executive council (*seimu chōsakai*) that could decide on policies.

Although the LDP Prefectural Chapter boasted that it could execute the policy proposals of Forum 21, the structure of prefectural government does not guarantee policy outcomes favored by the party. Unlike the national level, the local level has a presidential system where the executive, governor or mayor, is elected directly by citizens. In the case of Kanagawa, even though the LDP formed the largest legislative party in the prefectural assembly, it had to compromise with the progressive-leaning Governor Nagasu Kazuji. Although Nagasu received endorsement from the LDP in his governorship race, he did not depend on the conservatives but on his personal popularity to win his election. Moreover, Nagasu must also consider the views of the socialists because he also received their endorsement. Thus, a delicate check and balance between the progressive-leaning executive and a conservative legislature majority resulted in a policy-making process in which many actors were involved: the governor, local bureaucracy, political parties, and interest groups. The LDP cannot act unilaterally and push its preferred policies.

In the July 1993 Lower House Election, the LDP fell from power. Even though the LDP is the largest party in the Kanagawa prefectural assembly, it had to "cohabit" not only with a non-LDP governor but also with a non-

LDP central government. Fortunately for KF 21, the LDP recaptured power in the following year. If the LDP had failed to recapture the national government, the Kanagawa Forum 21 would have been unable to take advantage of connections to the political center to further its goals.

A potential problem faced by KF 21 is the inherent tension between the environment division and two other economic-centric divisions (city planning and development).[45] The environment division is enthusiastic about preserving Kanagawa's natural environment from further ravages of over-development while the latter two divisions are recommending big development projects, especially a proposed third international airport within the Tokyo metropolitan area to be located in Kanagawa. Since large parts of Kanagawa are already densely populated, the only possible sites involve land reclamation that will destroy part of Kanagawa's coastline or the levelling of forested areas. The question remains: "how will the LDP harmonize the demands for environmental protection and economic development within KF 21?"

"New Politics" issues embrace not only ecology but also direct participation in policy-formulation by ordinary citizens. Although KF 21 is policy-oriented, it has few avenues for the direct participation in policy-formulation by ordinary citizens. KF 21's elitist and technocratic approach which caters only to elected politicians, hand-picked specialists, and academics is its basic weakness. Even ordinary LDP party members have no access to the six policy divisions. Although KF 21 sporadically organizes big symposiums where citizens are invited to articulate their views, there are no regular channels for ordinary citizens to be actively involved in LDP policy-formulation at the prefectural level.[46] The only conservative organization where ordinary citizens can participate on a regular basis is *kōenkai*. However, an organization that revolves around fun and games, the promotion of the career of a particular politician, and the parochial interests of the constituency is unlikely to attract those urban citizens who desire active involvement in policy-formulation and policy outcomes. In theory, such citizens would be the natural allies of New Politics parties that adopt an egalitarian approach. In reality, NET is not automatically a beneficiary of the LDP's limitations in attracting grassroots participation in its policy-making divisions. Although NET strives to attract the support and participation of ecology-minded citizens, its organizations are also hierarchical and essentially limited to the SC's social networks.

Conclusion

All urban political parties and some social movements have given attention to ecology. This is, in part, a response to growing awareness about environmental problems among the urbanites. Even the LDP in Kanagawa introduced policy-making party organizations at the prefectural level to deal specifically with ecology, but it has had only limited success. The possibility remains that other established and emerging political parties may strive harder than the LDP to respond to rising concerns for environmental protection. If these parties introduce policies and organizations that address these concerns, they will undercut the potential political support for ecology-minded parties like NET. If that comes to pass, the success of Green parties in Japan may be pre-empted by established parties that succeed in stealing their thunder.

4　The Japanese Communist Party: organization and resilience

With the effective exit of the Italian Communist Party (PCI) from communism, the Japanese Communist Party (JCP) became the largest non-ruling communist party in the advanced industrial democracies in terms of party and front organizational membership, party newspaper readership, and electoral support (Table 4.1).[1] Unlike the PCI, which had transformed itself into a social democratic party, the JCP has retained its Marxist ideology and the organizational principle of democratic centralism. Notwithstanding the collapse of communist regimes in Eastern Europe and the USSR, and an overall crisis of communism, the JCP succeeded in minimizing its electoral decline and even staged a modest electoral recovery in the 1995 Upper House Election.[2]

In that election, the JCP captured 9.5 percent of the votes cast in the party proportional list in contrast to 7.9 percent three years earlier. In the April 1995 Local Elections, the JCP obtained 6.6 percent of the votes in the prefectural assemblies and 12.0 percent of the votes cast in the special-designated cities. Four years earlier, it won only 6.3 percent of the prefectural votes and 11.8 percent from the special-designated cities. Even more impressive was the JCP's electoral performance in October 1996, when it won a historic high of 7.26 million votes or 13.08 percent of the votes cast in the proportional representation component of the Lower House Elections. The JCP did well despite its initial fear that the new electoral system which allocates 300 out of 500 seats to the first-past-the-post component of the Lower House would penalize smaller political parties like itself.[3] Moreover, the JCP achieved its best electoral results in the Lower House on its own strength; it did not rely on a united front with other political parties to boost its electoral support.[4] In the 1997 Tokyo Metropolitan Assembly Election, the party won 21.3 percent of the votes cast and doubled its number of seats in the 127-seat assembly to 26.[5] In that election, the JCP became the second-largest party in the national capital. This was the party's best result in the Tokyo Metropolitan

Table 4.1 JCP and elections to the House of Representatives, 1946–1996

Year	Seats won	Votes (million)^a	Percent
1946	5	2.13	3.8
1947	4	1.0	3.7
1949	35	2.98	9.7
1952	0	0.89	2.6
1953	1	0.65	1.9
1955	2	0.73	2.0
1958	1	1.01	2.6
1960	3	1.15	2.9
1963	5	1.64	4.0
1967	5	2.19	4.8
1969	14	3.19	6.8
1972^b	40	5.70	10.9
1976	19	6.03	10.7
1979	41	5.76	10.7
1980	29	5.94	10.1
1983	27	5.38	9.4
1986	27	5.38	9.0
1990	16	5.22	7.9
1993	15	4.83	7.7
1996^c	26	7.26	13.1

Sources: Peter A. Berton, "Japanese Eurocommunists: Running in Place," *Problems of Communism*, Vol. 35, No. 4, July–August 1986, p. 3, *Asahi nenkan*, various years and *Asahi shinbun*, October 20, 1996.

Notes:
a Figures are rounded to the nearest 10,000.
b Beginning with the 1972 Election, all figures for seats, votes and seats include communist candidates who ran as independents.
c In the 1996 Lower House Election, which adopted a new electoral system, the JCP won 24 out of 200 seats in the party proportional list while capturing another 2 out of 300 in the first-past-the-post component. The number of votes obtained and the percentage of votes captured are taken from party proportional list only.

Assembly Election since 1973 when it won 24 seats. Thus, the JCP is steadily gaining electoral support in the 1990s.

This chapter addresses a series of questions. Why has the JCP been able to hold its ground in the 1990s despite retaining its Marxist ideology in the world's second-largest capitalist economy? Why was the party able to ride out the crisis faced by most communist movements that resulted from the collapse of Marxist regimes in Eastern Europe and the USSR? What was the JCP's organizational response to the crisis of communism? What are its problems and prospects?

There are many reasons for the JCP's continued resilience in Japan's domestic politics. First, the negative Japanese media hype about the

Tiananmen Square Incident in 1989 and the end of the Cold War had virtually blown over by 1995. Second, the JCP has remained consistent in its policies, including an implacable opposition to the conservative parties, big business and the U.S.–Japan Alliance. When its traditional rival on the Left, the Japan Socialist Party (JSP) abandoned many of its policies to forge ruling coalitions with various conservative parties, the JCP became the only established party of the Left. Third, the JCP continues to adapt its policies and organizations to the Japanese social, political and cultural milieu. Especially important to the JCP is *kōenkai* (personal candidate support organization), a mass-based electoral political machine that supplements its party organizations. This electoral machine is usually based on group support for a political personality in exchange for patronage (individual and community) rather than party policies. Because other political parties in Japan rely on *kōenkai* for political mobilization and votes rather than party organizations at the grassroots level, the JCP too has developed *kōenkai* to compete against other parties in elections. Its *kōenkai* membership is larger than the party membership and, not surprisingly, the JCP cannot win its elections by relying on the party organization alone. Thus, the JCP adopts an organizational approach that is pervasive among Japanese parties but is uncommon in the Euro-communist parties. However, there are limits to the JCP's organizational adaptability. Its party leadership is unwilling to give up democratic centralism as its organizational principle. Thus, the JCP's reluctance and inability to further adapt its organizations to a new democratic Japanese political culture will limit a significant increase in its voter support.

The significance of examining the JCP

This study analyses how the JCP operates in a non-Western advanced industrial democracy. Although the party adheres to the parliamentary road of political action like its Euro-communist counterparts, it operates in a different institutional, social, and cultural milieu. Moreover, the JCP's viability is crucial to the health of Japanese democracy. Paradoxically, a communist party with an authoritarian and anti-system image helps to sustain Japan's democratic system because it is the only established party in parliament that has not been co-opted by the conservative parties. It performs a watchdog role against the ruling parties without fear or favor. More importantly, the JCP often offers the only opposition candidate in prefectural governorship, city mayoral, and other local elections. Despite the ostensible differences between the non-communist parties at the national level, they would often support a joint candidate for governor or mayor so that all parties are assured of being part of the ruling coalition (*ainori*). If the JCP did not offer a candidate, there would be a walkover and Japanese voters would be offered a *fait accompli* without an electoral avenue of protest. Promoting women candidates in elections to win women's votes is another characteristic of the JCP. More women are elected under the communist label than other political parties in Japan. The JCP also provided organizational training to many activists who subsequently left (or in some cases were purged from) the party to pursue activities in social movements. One example is the case of some activists and advisors of the Seikatsu Club who first cut their teeth as JCP members.[6] After obtaining organizational experience from the JCP, they were able to strike out on their own.

The significance of this case study also goes beyond the immediate question about the JCP's fate and deals with the very nature of change and continuity in Japanese politics. In the post-Cold War era, "change" (*henka*) became a catch word in Japanese politics and society. Political change includes the collapse of the LDP's one-party dominance, the adoption of a new electoral system in the Lower House, the emergence of new political parties and ruling coalitions, and increasing voter dealignment from the established parties. Amidst substantive changes to the party system and voting behavior, there is also profound continuity in political organizations and mobilization techniques based on patronage, social networks, and group solidarity. The JCP is the most unlikely case to adopt the *kōenkai* approach because it is the only Japanese party that has strong party organization at the grassroots level and an ideological foundation. Yet its continued adoption of *kōenkai* shows the pervasiveness of this electoral approach in Japan.

Coping with a hostile international and domestic environment

Although the JCP still retains residual influence on some students, academics, intellectuals, and professionals, especially doctors and lawyers, the allure of its ideology is on the wane due to the "embourgoisement" of Japanese society and the collapse of various Marxist regimes in recent years. The 1989 Tiananmen Square massacre and the subsequent collapse of the East European communist regimes sullied the JCP's image. Even though the party tried to disassociate itself from these regimes, many Japanese voters did not make the distinction. In one survey conducted just after the collapse of East European Marxist regimes, 42 percent of Japanese voters claimed that events in Eastern Europe would affect their vote.[7] The party leadership moved fast to limit the damage by explaining to its rank and file that party principles and policies were "correct" and that the collapse of communist regimes would not affect its reason for existence. The leadership also mobilized its organizations to launch a publicity blitz including the wide-scale distribution of pamphlets to the masses in an attempt to persuade them that the JCP was not related to the Marxist dominoes. The JCP eventually rode out the storm of negative publicity. Judging from the 1995 Upper House Election, the media no longer dwell on the Tiananmen Sqaure incident and the crisis of communism.

Besides the image problem, the JCP is confronted by the proliferation of new parties and the dealignment of voters from the established parties. Exasperated with political corruption and a lack of political reforms, many voters initially supported the new conservative parties including the Japan New Party (JNP), the Shinseitō (New Birth Party) and the Sakigake (Harbinger Party) instead of the JCP, traditionally a party of the protest votes. An important reason for the popular support for these parties was the fact that the mainstream mass media gave them extensive coverage and defined the central political issue as a contest to perpetuate or end the LDP's 38 years of one-party dominance. Many voters who desired to end the LDP's rule would rather support the new conservative parties that appeared a "safer" and more probable alternative to the LDP than to "waste" their votes on the JCP.

By the early 1990s, only around half of the adult population in Japan supported a political party. Disillusioned with the established parties, some of the non-party-affiliated voters cast their ballots for the "new" conservative parties. However, by the mid-1990s, the novelty appeal of these conservative parties had worn off for some voters. Moreover, these "new" parties did not demonstrate any substantive difference from the LDP when they became coalition parties in power. Similarly, the socialists expediently surrendered their traditional ideals, especially unarmed neutrality, when they joined the ruling coalition. The JCP indirectly benefited from some voters' disillusionment with the new conservative parties and the socialists. According to certain polls conducted after the 1995 Upper House Election and the 1996 Lower House Election, the JCP succeeded in drawing some support from voters who were non-party partisans and previous supporters of other parties especially the socialists.[8]

The JCP enjoyed remarkable continuity in its top leadership and ideology. Miyamoto Kenji, its 88-year-old paramount leader, led the party for 39 years until his retirement in 1997.[9] Strong discipline and consistency in its ideology meant that party rank and file, party sympathizers, and voters were not confused and demoralized by party factionalism and sweeping doctrinal changes. The JCP is the only established party that opposes the U.S.–Japan alliance, the Emperor system, "monopoly capitalism," and the consumption tax. Since it is now the only party to uphold the values of the traditional Left, it stood to gain when the JSP vacated its position at the left of Japan's ideological spectrum.

Organizational adaptability

The JCP has adapted well to the Japanese institutional, social, and cultural environment.[10] It has adopted policies and organizations to suit the changing domestic and international environment. Founded in 1922 as a branch of Comintern, the international organization of workers' parties controlled by the USSR, the JCP was an underground party until the American occupation of Japan permitted parties the freedom to organize and compete in elections openly. Since the 1960s, the JCP has maintained its independence from the communist regimes of the USSR and China. The party has abandoned the path of violent revolution and is committed to a "peaceful, democratic revolution" within the framework of capitalism and parliamentary democracy.[11] This switch was made even before the term "Eurocommunism" became fashionable in the 1970s to describe the West European communist parties that repudiated violent revolution and subservience to the USSR. The JCP also promised to honor political pluralism and safeguard the freedom of the individual.

During the 1960s and 1970s, the JCP made rapid gains in tandem with the rise of new issues such as ecology, welfare, gender equality, and citizens' direct participation in politics. The conjunction between the rise of these issues and the JCP was no coincidence. The party adapted to a new environment in which the electorate clamored for such issues to be placed on the political agenda and ably sought political support by actively promoting these issues. In a united front with the JSP and citizens' movements, the JCP supported progressive local governments that promoted dialogue between city hall and citizens, anti-pollution measures, and social welfare. Besides adaptability in policy-making toward new issues, the JCP has built and supported mass organizations that take root in the Japanese milieu to mobilize political support. These include party organizations, front organizations, medical co-ops, consumer co-ops, and *kōenkai*.

Poor voter turnout benefits political candidates with strong organizational support in Japan. Even if the weather is bad, JCP supporters are reputed to go to the polling stations while many "soft" supporters of various parties or non-party affiliates would stay at home. Because of disillusionment with money politics and a lack of choice between the established parties, voter turnout had registered record lows at local and national elections in the 1990s. In the midst of declining voter turnout, a party that possesses strong organizations and mobilizes its supporters to vote would suffer less than parties that rely on fickle non-party affiliates who may abstain from voting. While the JCP is noted for strong front organizations and is the only Japanese party that has viable grassroots party organizations, its linkages with co-ops and its dependence on *kōenkai* are less well known.

JCP, social movements and the consumer co-operatives

Close association with social movements is an extension of the JCP's ideology as a vanguard party leading the masses, a necessity for winning electoral support and resorting to extra-parliamentary forces to pressure the conservatives. In the post-war era, the JCP has been active in the labor movement, anti-war and nuclear disarmament campaigns, mass rallies against U.S. military bases in Japan, housewives' groupings, student activism, and consumer movements. Unlike its Italian and French counterparts, the JCP has only limited support from labor.[12] The lion's share of union support traditionally went to the JSP and DSP (Democratic Socialist Party). A lack of strong organizational support from the unions has encouraged the JCP to seek other organizational support, including *kōenkai*. Immediately after the war, the party initially made rapid inroads into the labor movement, but the advent of the Cold War in Asia, the "Red Purges" by the American Occupation authorities, and a futile attempt to conduct armed struggle in place of a promising parliamentary road resulted in the subsequent reduction of support within the labor unions for the JCP.[13]

The typical structure of Japanese labor unions is house union rather than enterprise union. Workers from big companies extend their loyalties to the company rather than to an overarching enterprise union whose members come from different companies. Company unions do not provide a fertile ground for communist agitation and support. Company paternalism and welfare coupled with the rising affluence of Japanese society have resulted in the "embourgoisement" of the workers. It is difficult for the JCP, the self-proclaimed champion of the working class, to seek support solely from a vanishing proletariat when around 90 percent of the Japanese perceive themselves to be middle-class.

Most consumer co-ops in Japan have a Leftist tinge. This is, in part, due to the longstanding association of the communists with the consumer movement. In post-war Japan, the Japanese Consumers' Co-operative Union (JCCU), the umbrella body of the co-op movement, is reputed to have a sizeable number of communist sympathizers in the midst of its leadership. The actual numbers are difficult to verify because party affiliation of the JCCU leadership is not disclosed. Just a stone's throw away from the JCP headquarters in Yoyogi, Tokyo is the location of the JCCU. Some anti-communist activists in the co-op movement have intimated that the close proximity between the JCCU and JCP is more than geographical.

Although some JCCU leaders may be communist sympathizers, the overwhelming majority of co-op members are not.[14] Even if the majority of members do not vote for the JCP, the party still finds it useful when sympathizers are found in strategic positions within the JCCU. Co-op members were mobilized to participate in anti-consumption tax campaigns, and anti-cruise missile and nuclear disarmament campaigns. Pro-JCP co-op offered help in the election campaigns of communist candidates.[15] Some office holders of various co-ops were drafted as JCP candidates. Top JCP leaders, including Fuwa Tetsuzō, Chairman of the Presidium of the Central Committee, personally campaigned for the candidates of allied co-op. However, many co-op members swung their support behind the JCP candidate on the basis of the interpersonal ties within the consumer movement rather than a support for communism *per se*.

Take, for example, the ties between the JCP and the Co-op Kanagawa. In Kanagawa prefecture (located in the greater Tokyo metropolitan area), the Co-op Kanagawa with a membership of around 800,000 households has historical ties with the JCP.[16] Its founder was a communist.[17] The Co-op Kanagawa continues to purchase advertising space and make annual public greetings in the JCP's national newspaper, *Akahata* (Red Flag) and the JCP's newsletter in the prefecture, the *Shin Kanagawa* (New Kanagawa), on New Year and May Day. When asked about the periodic greetings of the Co-op Kanagawa to the JCP, its top leader replied: it does so because the JCP is a long-time associate (*tsukiai*).[18]

Among the list of front organizations in Kanagawa prefecture mentioned by the JCP is the Co-op Kanagawa.[19] In the *Shin Kanagawa*, details and activities of the Co-op Kanagawa often appear. While the overwhelming majority of the Co-op Kanagawa members are non-communist supporters, a substantial number of the co-op's professional staff are party members, JCP *kōenkai* participants, and communist sympathizers. Co-op Kanagawa's workers' union is affiliated with communist-led unions. Professional staff and co-op members supporting JCP candidates would form a *kōenkai*. During the Local Elections, some of the co-op's professional staff would introduce JCP candidates to invited co-op members at their stores after closing time.[20] Candidates also conducted stump speeches outside the co-op stores appealing to the urban housewives. In pamphlets distributed at roadsides and train stations, endorsements of JCP candidates by former Co-op Kanagawa store managers were also printed. After the elections, the party also conducted its signature campaigns in front of the co-op stores where there was a constant flow of housewives.

Despite the historical ties between the JCP and the Co-op Kanagawa, the influence of the JCP on the latter is on the wane. Although the Co-op Kanagawa was first established by JCP members, it had grown beyond its communist origins partially due to mergers with a number of non-communist co-ops in Kanagawa prefecture in the 1970s for economic reasons especially to benefit from economies of scale in its operation.

Thus, the communist coloring of the Co-op Kanagawa has been diluted. Moreover, the co-op had cultivated ties with LDP and JSP politicians to protect its own interests. For example, the Co-op Kanagawa tried to build a "pipe" to LDP Diet Member Koizumi Junichiro (Kanagawa District Two) who was a Minister of Health and Welfare (MHW). Since the MHW supervises the co-op movement, the Co-op Kanagawa found it prudent to cultivate ties with Koizumi, who was reputed to have retained influence on the MHW. The Co-op Kanagawa's attempts to cultivate ties with LDP members were not unique among the co-ops. The JCCU also played the lobbying game by purchasing party tickets and hence contributing to the coffers of LDP Diet Members belonging to the Party's policy-making group (*zoku*) that supervises the MHW.[21] Despite its association with the communists, the JCCU sought allies within the LDP to protect itself from the encroachments of MITI (Ministry of Trade and Industry) and the party's business *zoku*. Since the support from friendly co-ops is less than solid, the JCP must build its own support organizations, especially *kōenkai*.

Better known than the relationship between the JCP and the consumer movement are the ties between the party and the medical co-ops. In the 1970s, when the JCP was making rapid gains, the LDP ran a series of articles on the medical co-ops claiming that the JCP was a wolf in sheep's clothing: "inside the white dress reveals a frightful armor, the Medical Revolutionary Corp."[22] The LDP warned that the communists were wielding medical co-ops as political weapons by inducing grateful patients to join party and *kōenkai* activities, subscribe to the *Akahata* and vote for them. The conservatives claimed that the JCP utilized the name lists of patients' phone numbers and addresses for election campaigns and that communist candidates were recruited from various medical co-ops. Although the LDP's statistics are already outdated, they indicate the scope of pro-JCP medical co-ops. In the mid-1970s, these co-ops had around 11,000 doctors, nurses, surgeons and hospital workers. Facilities included 350 hospitals and clinics with more than 8,000 hospital beds for patients. They served an average of 50,000 patients a day and more than 15 million patients a year.[23] Long-term plans included dental clinics, centers for disabled people, and centers for the treatment of occupational diseases. Tangible services were offered not only to potential supporters but also to party and *kōenkai* members. Even the LDP grudgingly admit that it was indeed an impressive mass organization.

The JCP and challenges from the co-op movement: the SC and NET

The JCP ambivalently viewed NET as a potential united front ally and a rival in the sphere of social movements. Eager for allies to avoid political isolation, the party publicized the alignment between the JCP, NET, and JSP in the 1993 mayoral election of Hoya city, Tokyo,[24] and the joint action between JCP and NET assembly women in Komae city, Tokyo to protest against the dispatch of Japanese troops for peacekeeping operations in Cambodia.[25] The JCP, NET, and JSP were coalition partners in the local governments of Kawasaki and Zushi in Kanagawa prefecture and Machida city in Tokyo. The JSP at the national level abandoned their united front with the communists in 1980 and condemned the JCP to isolation without a realistic hope of capturing power. The communists then defined a united front as a strategy which was not centered on established parties but citizens' groups and other mass organizations.[26] Within the united front framework, SC and NET are potential allies. In true united front style, the JCP was willing to extend a co-operative hand while at the same time it had no qualms about criticizing its partners or stealing their agendas and political support.

The JCP criticized NET for being a small "bourgeois" party which had benefited from publicity by the "bourgeois" press.[27] It slammed the SC for participating in electoral politics rather than sticking to the traditional role of a co-op. The party's view that the SC should steer clear of politics is no different from that of the LDP. Ironically, the JCP had no hesitation in receiving support from friendly co-ops. Other criticisms of NET include the presence of "anti-party elements" who were purged from the JCP and subsequently become advisors to NET and its think-tank, the Social Movement Center. NET was also criticized for its "incoherence" toward the U.S.–Japan Security Treaty and the presence of American bases in Japan, and an uncritical attitude toward LDP politics and big business.[28]

Although NET is a fledgling organization, it has not escaped the notice of the top JCP leaders. Miyamoto Kenji, the octogenarian leader of the party, expressed his concern about the contest between the NET and the JCP candidates in his home district, Tama city, Tokyo.[29] Barely a month after the 1991 Local Elections, Fuwa Tetsuzō alerted the party to the new challenges posed by citizens' groups making advances in local assemblies. Fuwa noted:

> [A] great number of people have been sensitive about and interested in various problems relating to people's daily lives, such as environmental hazards, waste disposal, food pollution and so forth. This has drawn a wide range of new people toward political issues that have been regarded as "non-partisan" or "people who have not chosen a political party to support". Also, on the basis of such interests, a conspicuous trend is emerging: candidates linked with citizen movements or local residents [sic] movements are advancing into local assemblies.[30]

The JCP is sometimes more explicit about the challenge of the NET and SC. NET is viewed as a competitor for political support in the public housing estates (*danchi*), the traditional hunting ground for the party.[31] The JCP reported that the influence of NET has penetrated into some of the estates by appealing to non-party supporters and housewives who are concerned with such issues as rubbish disposal, environment, safe food, and recycling activities. JCP activists were urged to pay heed to such issues. Sensitive to the challenges of NET and other citizens' groups in politics, the JCP has launched a series of publications expounding the party's position and efforts in developing recycling measures and environmental protection policies.[32] Besides policies to attract support, another strategy is to build party organizations and *kōenkai*.

The JCP and *kōenkai*

The JCP emphasizes its Four Basic Points as axioms for party members to follow in a hostile domestic and international environment for Japanese communism. The Four Basic Points comprise the daily activities it considers most essential: offering consultation services to the masses, increasing *Akahata* readership, carrying out mass publicity, and last but not least, expanding party and *kōenkai* organizations.[33] The activities of the first three Basic Points are carried out by party and *kōenkai* organizations. Often, the party stresses its commitment "to raise JCP organizations to be like big trees, never swayed by whatever anti-communist storm may rage."[34] To avoid being blown away by anti-communist storms, the JCP strives to plant deep-rooted *kōenkai* to bolster its party organization.

The JCP claims that *kōenkai* are unique to Japan and attributes their presence to the "lack of maturity in Japanese society."[35] The party implies that Japanese society is not yet fully "modern." Ironically, a party that claims to be the most "modern" in Japan, has adopted *kōenkai*, a type of organization often associated with "tradition." According to the JCP, the prevalence of *kōenkai* is, in part, due to a Japanese political culture which focuses on personality and patronage instead of party and policies.[36] The JCP has adopted *kōenkai* because it cannot win elections by relying only on party organization. According to Fuwa, its *kōenkai* membership is 55.8 percent of *Akahata* readership.[37] If this statistic is indeed accurate, the JCP *kōenkai* membership is around one and a half million, or more than three times larger than the party membership. The JCP even quoted Friedrich Engels to provide a Marxist justification for *kōenkai*. According to the party's interpretation of Engels, the communist movement must seek mass support beyond the working class.[38] *Kōenkai* is an organizational means to attain such support. If the JCP had remained a small, conspiratorial party pursuing revolutionary armed struggle, *kōenkai* which are essentially vote-reaping organizations, would be unnecessary. Since the JCP pursues a peaceful, parliamentary path to socialism – ballots instead of bullets – the party required *kōenkai* in workplaces, residential areas, and within other mass organizations such as labor unions and co-ops.

The JCP urged its members to recruit their family, neighbors, and friends into the political machine.[39] It also suggested that if it were to succeed organizing just 60 percent of the family members of its *Akahata* readers, it would possess a *kōenkai* membership that is larger than its readership of three million.[40] The organization's range of activities for members include bazaars, New Year parties, flower arrangement classes, chess, bowling, hiking, legal sessions, travel, and barbecues.[41] Thus, the emphasis is on the provision of services and companionship – and not ideology.

In July 1959, at the Sixth Central Committee of the Seventh Party Congress, the JCP gave its stamp of approval to *kōenkai* organizations.[42] Undoubtedly, electoral competition between the parties compelled the JCP to adopt *kōenkai*. In the attempt to raise support beyond the party organization, the JCP had been bedeviled by a long-running problem: how can *kōenkai* be expanded without it degenerating into organizations more loyal to particular candidates running on a JCP label than to the party itself? Prior to 1980, most of the *kōenkai* of JCP candidates were named after the candidate and not after the party. In November 1980, Miyamoto in his speech on "new electoral policy and *kōenkai* activities" proposed a name switch from personal candidate to a party *kōenkai*. In both name and substance, each *kōenkai* must be a party *kōenkai* rather than a personal candidate *kōenkai*.

From the viewpoint of its leadership, there are a number of compelling reasons why personal *kōenkai* must be reined in. First, when mass support is extended to a specific candidate there is no assurance that it will also be given to other JCP candidates who are competing at other local and national levels. When a specific JCP candidate retired or was removed, the support from his personal *kōenkai* was non-transferable to another JCP candidate. Second, the Upper House Electoral system was changed in 1982 whereby a voter thereafter cast two ballots, one for the candidate at the local constituency and another for a party at the national constituency by the d'Hondt system of proportional representation instead of the first-past-the-post system for the national constituency. In practice, supporters of a JCP candidate at the local constituency did not always cast votes for the party at the national constituency.[43] If supporters could be persuaded to support the JCP instead of specific personalities, the party stood to boost its standing in the proportional party listing of the Upper House.

Third, if JCP candidates have strong, personal *kōenkai*, they can establish a degree of autonomy from the party leadership. Its leadership demands conformity from the lower echelons, in line with democratic centralism. JCP assembly members who maintained their personal *kōenkai* or concentrated only on winning re-election in their constituencies were chided for "sectorism" or "localism."[44] In the worst scenario from the leadership's point of view, JCP assembly members could even desert with their support base intact if they have strong personal *kōenkai*. In 1990, shortly after the collapse of the Soviet empire, a number of local JCP assembly members bolted from the party to avoid being tainted by the demise of communism in Russia.[45] Although the defectors were few, it sent shock waves through the party. It was intimated that the renegades were able to split because they had independent sources of support, their *kōenkai*.[46] Although the JCP has the image of being a disciplined monolithic party, its center has perennial problems trying to control its roughly 4,000 local assembly members and their *kōenkai*. In October 1981, at the JCP's Special National Conference, activists from different prefectures were assembled to give a detailed report on their efforts to convert personal *kōenkai* to party *kōenkai*.[47] Activists also reported opposition to the new *kōenkai* policy because some *kōenkai* members did not wish to join a communist *kōenkai*. Even a decade later, Shii Kazuo, youthful Head of the Secretariat, lambasted assembly members for "sectorism" and clinging to personal *kōenkai*, but to no avail.[48]

Despite the problems of controlling an assembly member's *kōenkai*, the JCP has continued to emphasize *kōenkai* building. It is easier to persuade a JCP sympathizer to become a *kōenkai* member than to be a party member. JCP members are expected to donate one percent of their salary to the party, meet once a week to study and discuss party directives, attend rallies, distribute pamphlets, sell *Akahata* subscriptions and keep a strict code of personal conduct. Since it is very demanding to be a party member, a JCP supporter may prefer to join the *kōenkai* which imposes less demands on time, money and commitment. Although JCP *kōenkai* are supposed to explain party policies to members, activities usually revolve around fun, games and travel. *Kōenkai* members are not pressured to join the party and financial contribution is not a condition for participation. *Kōenkai* members are also not subjected to strict discipline and the dictates of democratic centralism.

Beyond *kōenkai*: problems and prospects

While the mass electoral organizations of *kōenkai* provide the JCP and its candidates a level of political support, there is a limit to this approach. Japanese parties including the JCP had organized 26.9 percent of voters as *kōenkai* members by 1995.[49] However, they have difficulties organizing voters who are not tied to the social and patronage network of *kōenkai*. Conceivably, if the JCP wants to improve its electoral position, it has to go beyond the *kōenkai* approach and to further adapt to a more democratic milieu in Japan. However, innovations to party organization and policies are fraught with uncertainties; this move may even backfire and further undermine the position of the party.

The JCP's main problem is the undemocratic image of its party organization. Democratic centralism is the organizational principle of the JCP.[50] In theory, ordinary members can freely express their views at party meetings. These views are supposed to be respected, synthesized and conveyed to the next level of the party hierarchy for consideration. The same process continues at each subsequent level, all the way to the Party Congress. After distilling the views of party members, the Party Congress is then supposed to lay out the party's resolutions and policies, and all members are then obligated to faithfully abide by the party line which has been adopted. In practice, democratic centralism is an oxymoron. Since the Party Congress meets infrequently, around once every two to three years, power is delegated to the Central Committee. Similarly, decision-making is located in the Presidium and the Secretariat because the Central Committee meets infrequently during the year.

Party members can neither criticize their leadership in public nor publish opinions which differ from those expressed at the top. Any appointment to a particular level of the organizational hierarchy requires the approval from the level above it; the top can veto the appointments and decisions made at the lower levels of the hierarchy. To attain the goals laid out by the party line, the JCP insists that party unity is indispensable. The individual must submit to the party line regardless of personal opinion; the party comes before self. The JCP insists on retaining an organizational principle first developed by Lenin and the Bolsheviks to promote social revolution in autocratic Tsarist Russia mired in poverty and misery and apply it to a post-war, affluent, and democratic Japan.[51] The oddity of applying a Leninist organizational principle to an advanced industrial democracy is lost on the JCP leadership.[52] In practice, the JCP recognizes political pluralism outside but not within the party. The JCP's authoritarian image is probably its most serious problem. This is a major contributory factor to the JCP's inability to significantly expand its political support. Miyamoto claims that the JCP's relative lack of support is due to the climate of prejudice reinforced by state propaganda and repression against communism since pre-war Japan.[53] The blame is laid on "reactionaries" and the inhospitable environment faced by the JCP instead of a soul-searching into the very nature of the party organization.

In contrast to the JCP, the Italian Communist Party (PCI) transformed itself in 1989.[54] It jettisoned democratic centralism as its organizational principle, agreed to elect leaders by secret ballot, permitted members to freely criticize the leadership and canvass ideas in party publications. Aspiring to a future role in Italian politics, the PCI dropped its ideological baggage and remade itself in the wake of momentous changes in Eastern Europe. Barely five days after the fall of the Berlin Wall, the symbol of the Cold War, the PCI proposed to reconstitute itself to become a social democratic party. The PCI finally crossed the Rubicon in March 1990 when it was reborn as the Democratic Party of the Left (Partito Democratico della Sinistra: PDS). The PDS adopted a Green image by asserting in its party program that environmental problems are the key issues facing humankind and also accepted the framework of the market economy. It also guaranteed women members a 30 percent share of leadership positions with a 50 percent quota envisaged for the future. Thus, the PDS boldly and swiftly shifted from Old Politics, whose axis was along class fissures, to seize a cluster of New Politics issues which include ecology, gender equality, and participatory democracy.

Although the JCP has a reputation for adaptability, it is reluctant to follow in the footsteps of the PCI because its leadership believes that its Italian counterpart was unprincipled and wrong.[55] The Japanese communists adamantly refuse to change their name like the PCI because such an act is considered to be a repudiation of the JCP's history and achievements. Fuwa asserted that a party changes its name only if it is wrong or embarrassed by its past.[56] He believed that it has no reason to do so because it has pursued a correct policy line. Moreover the PCI's labor pains in giving birth to a new party may also have dissuaded the Japanese communists from attempting a similar strategy. Attempts to reconstitute the PCI resulted in a schism – the PDS as a social democratic party and a die-hard communist remnant, the Communist Refoundation (Rifondazione Comunista: RC). The PDS became increasingly fragmented after democratic centralism was abandoned. Although the PDS has embarked on new policies and democratic organizational principles, the level of voters' support is lower than for its predecessor, the PCI. Similarly, if the JCP were to take a bold leap in the dark after the departure of Miyamoto, there is no assurance that a party split could be avoided or further decline in voter's support be arrested. Moreover, the party could suffer from an identity crisis if it were to jettison its Marxist ideology. The JCP will be pinned on the horns of dilemma: clinging to democratic centralism may condemn it to a gradual but inexorable decline, but a gamble to jettison it may lead to a rupture in its solid organization and presents uncertain returns. Thus, fundamental reforms to the party's organizational structure and processes will open a Pandora's Box and the outcome will be unpredictable and uncontrollable by its leadership.

Even though the PDS-led "Olive Tree" Alliance won the Italian General Election in 1996, it appears that the JCP is not tempted to follow the social democratic path of the PDS.

The JCP's long-term structural problems include: the end of rapid urbanization, the reduction of environmental problems of which the party had so deftly taken advantage, a post-industrial society where blue-collar jobs are being whittled away, and the acceptance of democratic norms among the Japanese. The retention of democratic centralism as an organizational principle is increasingly out of step with a more democratic political culture in Japan. In post-industrial Japan where knowledge, information, and affluence have multiplied, highly educated citizens are less willing to be led by a group of counter-elite. In an affluent and knowledge-intensive Japan, it is difficult for the JCP to act as a vanguard party offering the only correct interpretation of universal truths when the party elite are not much better educated than the masses they purport to lead.

Mid-term problems include declining *Akahata* readership (the financial and propaganda lifeline of the JCP). However, as the only established party that opposes the U.S.–Japan alliance, the JCP may benefit if more voters reject the presence of U.S. bases in Japan and the alliance as a consequence of the Okinawa Incident. In 1995, the rape of a 12-year-old Japanese girl by three American servicemen in Okinawa ignited mass demonstrations, especially in the same prefecture, and reawakened the Japanese domestic debate as to whether or not U.S. bases in the country are desirable. Since the JCP is the only established party that opposes the alliance, a further rise in anti-American sentiments among the Japanese may be an advantage to the party. Nevertheless, if a bellicose and powerful China were to emerge in East Asia, many Japanese would be less willing to give up the alliance. If anti-American sentiments in Japan are tempered by a fear of China as a rising regional hegemon, the JCP obviously would not benefit from this outlook in public opinion. None the less, it may also reap some support from workers and salaried employees if Japan's lifetime employment system continues to unravel. Unemployment in Japan is still relatively low compared to the advanced industrial democracies in the West, but many employees fear that Japan's industrial structure may be "hollowed out" when factories continue to shift abroad as a consequence of the yen's appreciation. The party may also poach on the erstwhile supporters of the JSP, since the latter has abandoned its traditional policies of the Left. However, even if the marginalized Marxist Left wing of the JSP were to abandon the party, it would not automatically support the JCP because they traditionally belong to rival sects of Japanese Marxism. At the national level, the JCP has to face the challenge of "new" parties; at the local level, the JCP must compete against local parties in metropolitan Japan, especially the Network

Movement. Although NET is a fledgling organization, it poses a threat to the JCP because it competes for the votes of the urban housewives by offering only women candidates that advocate Green issues.

In 1997, Miyamoto retired and became the party's emeritus chairman. Fuwa took over the helm at the age of 67 but it is uncertain whether he will (or can) move away from Miyamoto's shadow of Marxist orthodoxy. When Fuwa was a communist youth, he flirted with the PCI's Gramscian ideology before he returned to the orthodox fold. In his middle age, it is unclear whether Fuwa is prepared to spearhead any doctrinal, policy, or organizational changes in the post-Miyamoto period that may have the unintended consequence of splitting the party. After formally taking over its leadership, Fuwa again dismissed the speculation that the JCP might become a social democratic party. It appears that the JCP leadership has already groomed Shii Kazuo (44 years old in 1998) to be the third-generation leader to eventually succeed Fuwa as the party chief. Thus far Shii has not shown any tendency to deviate from the Marxist orthodoxy of the Miyamoto leadership.

Conclusion

Despite the global crisis of communism, the JCP has avoided a rout at the polls. It has developed organizations that cater to different tendencies and interests among the Japanese voters. The JCP has programmatic party organizations and political machines based on social networks and services. The JCP seems a most unlikely case to adopt *kōenkai*. But, driven by the need to compete in elections, the Japanese communists have adopted *kōenkai* to bolster their party organization. Even though the JCP is the most radical party in post-war Japan, it conforms to indigenous norms and acquiesces in the *kōenkai* approach. Its concession to this approach is a pragmatic choice that recognizes the preferences of many Japanese voters to belong to a group based on personal ties and shared interests rather than Marxist ideology. However, this social network approach has its limitations. The JCP must reach out to non-*kōenkai* members in order to win greater mass support. Unless it adapts and produces organizational structures, processes, and principles more attuned to a democratic political culture of a post-industrial Japan, the JCP's ability to significantly improve its electoral performance is rather bleak.

This case study also suggests that despite various substantial changes in the Japanese party system, all political parties, including the JCP, will continue to rely on time-tested strategies of political mobilization, especially *kōenkai*. Moreover, a substantial segment of Japanese voters continues to cling to the political machine given their disposition toward patronage and group solidarity. Notwithstanding recent changes in Japan's electoral and party system, social and political norms associated with "groupishness" still persist. This *kōenkai* approach is unlikely to disappear in the near future despite the introduction of a first-past-the-post component in the Lower House Election. Since resource-guzzling political machines are a fundamental source of political corruption, their persistence means that despite calls for political reforms, money politics will remain endemic in Japanese politics. Moreover, the organizational resilience and the adaptability of the Old Politics parties, especially the JCP in metropolitan Japan, is an important factor that limits the growth of the Greens in that country.

5 Social movements and the Seikatsu Club

Permissive conditions, especially an open political system that allows new-comers to enter the political arena, rising post-material values among the urbanites, and rapid urbanization, have contributed to the Seikatsu Club's (SC's) expansion. These permissive conditions are necessary but not suffi-cient for its rise. Favorable conditions such as an open system, rapid urbanization, and changing mass values must be seized by mobilizers before they are translated into social action. Especially useful is the focus on the various resources of SC members, including affluence, high levels of educa-tion, and free time to participate in social movement activities. Owning such resources does not automatically lead women to become social activists. They have to be mobilized by leaders and organizations to join the co-op rather than other competing social activities. While more Japanese appear to express post-material attitudes in opinion polls, post-material political *behavior* is still relatively weak. Thus, mass sympathies for certain Green issues are not automatically translated into political activism or votes for a New Politics party. Competition and the presence of formidable rivals in a pluralist system, the end of rapid urbanization, and the difficult task of mobilizing even voters with post-material values to support NET partially explains why the Greens are not a major political force in Japan.

Japanese social movements

Social movements in Japan have gained prominence since the 1960s.[1] According to one survey, citizens who had experiences in social movements have increased from 8.4 percent in 1976 to 14.1 percent in 1991.[2] Other features of social movements today include the diversity of issues pursued and a style that emphasizes alternative proposals to solve problems rather than mere protests or demand for monetary compensation.[3] A content analysis of 2,850 social movements' newsletters (Table 5.1) reveals that these movements deal with problems beyond pacifism.[4]

Table 5.1 Social movements' newsletters and content

Social movements and themes	No. of titles
Environment – anti-pollution	80
Development	48
Anti nuclear energy	85
Conservation of nature	274
Consumer movement	152
Medical – food contamination	108
Welfare	323
Education	123
Anti-war, anti-nuclear, peace movement	75
Human rights and anti-discrimination	93
Women's issues	97
Society and economics	73
Culture and religion	374
Freedom of speech and expression	257
Residents' movements	425
Labor	22
Overseas information and international exchanges	146
Total	2,850

Source: Jūmin toshokan, *Minikomi sō mokuroku*, p. 24.

The scope of movements tends to be universalistic in orientation, dealing with issues like ecology and human rights. If these goals are attained, the beneficiaries are not just that particular band of activists but also the general public including the "free riders." In contrast, some of the earlier citizens' movements were parochial in nature. Protests were launched against the placement of factories or rubbish incinerators in their neighborhood, but some activists were not concerned if these complexes were sited in other people's neighborhoods. Unlike the social movements of the 1960s, which placed a greater emphasis on the issues of war and peace, later movements have increasingly focused on ecological issues.[5]

Nevertheless, the end of the Cold War has not led to the demise of peace movements. The 1995 Okinawa incident ignited a new wave of mass protests against the presence of U.S. military bases in the country.[6] Moreover, the Clinton–Hashimoto Joint Declaration in April 1996 paved the way for Tokyo to assist Washington in the event of regional conflict in "areas surrounding Japan" including the Korean peninsula, the Taiwan Straits, the South China Sea, the Straits of Malacca and the Persian Gulf.[7] This fundamental shift in the nature of the U.S.–Japan alliance, from a limited posture of defending the Japanese islands to an expanded role to provide logistic support to the U.S. in the event of a regional conflict, eventually may unleash greater mass protests against the alliance if it threatens to drag Japan into an American-led war with her neighbors, especially North Korea or China. Besides peace movements, anti-nuclear activism has also gathered momentum because of nuclear mishaps and cover-ups.[8] Further attempts by the central government to build more nuclear stations are likely to provoke greater disquiet among and resistance from ordinary citizens.[9]

The uniqueness of the SC as a social movement organization

While Japanese social movements are increasingly sharing common concerns about the environment, they are not alike in terms of size, scope, activities, and organization. Among the myriad of Japanese social movements, the SC and its political arm, NET, are probably the most prominent and well organized.[10] In contrast to many social movements that came and went, both parent and child organizations have staying power. Since 1965, the SC has sought to mobilize and politicize ordinary housewives in an endeavor to promote alternative values and change in Japanese politics and society. The co-op has some characteristics that make it an atypical Japanese social movement. First, its activities are not limited to one specific village, ward, city, or region. It has grown rapidly from its birthplace in Setagaya ward, Tokyo to the greater Tokyo metropolitan region (Tokyo, Kanagawa, Saitama, and Chiba) and the prefectures of Iwate, Ibaraki, Aichi, Tochigi, Miyagi, Hokkaidō, Yamanashi, Nagano, and Shizuoka. Thus, it has expanded to 13 of Japan's 47 prefectures.[11] Excepting the traditional labor unions and certain religious organizations, most social movements in Japan are local and fragmented.[12] They lack overarching national organizations that can marshal their resouces to make a larger and more sustained impact on society. An encyclopaedic survey of 2,850 Japanese social movements shows that 60 percent of the respondents produce only between 200 and 500 copies of their newsletters for their members and sympathizers.[13] Thus, the survey reveals that a majority of social movements, unlike the SC, are small in membership, localized, and fragmented.

Second, in contrast to most social movements, the SC has strong organizations. The literature on Japanese social movements often gives the impression that most social movements have weak or non-existent organizations because of an ideological disdain for hierarchy.[14] Few Japanese social movements can match its size and scope. In 1997, it had a membership of 246,696[15] and if we include their husbands and children, the beneficiaries of SC household products and food comprise a group at least a million strong. Although social movements may idealistically renounce hierarchy and organizations, they are often forced by necessity to retain them. Many social movements do not abandon organizations. It has been suggested that "social movement organizations" is an appropriate description of social movements that utilize organizations to achieve their goals.[16]

Third, the SC is also an economic enterprise. As a co-op, it owns factories, farms, storage facilities, depots, buildings, land, transportation fleets, and a formal membership list.[17] In 1997, it employed 989 professional staff to develop and distribute products to members.[18] Staff members are often deployed to social movement activities and even election campaigns on behalf of NET. Few social movements in Japan have resources comparable to the SC.

Fourth, few social movements can match its involvement in electoral politics. It is not uncommon for Japanese citizens' movements to launch a recall of an incumbent mayor or to endorse a sympathizer to hold public office.[19] Such movements often fizzled out when the problem was solved or when they were defeated. In the SC's case, its participation in electoral politics via NET is not limited to a specific outbreak of a local conflict, but embraces a sustained challenge that, since 1977, has spread to different prefectures. Its presence in politics is not reactive to a single issue, but is an initiative to empower its members from different regions to have an impact on a wide range of issues in local politics. By July 1997, the distribution of NET female assembly members by prefecture is: 49 in Tokyo, 38 in Kanagawa, 15 in Chiba, 8 in Fukuoka, 5 in Hokkaidō, 3 in Saitama, 2 in Nagano, and 1 in Iwate.[20] Out of the 12 largest cities, NET has secured footholds in half of them: Tokyo, Yokohama, Kawasaki, Chiba, Sapporo and Fukuoka (Tables 5.2 and 5.3).

The SC and NET aspire to play a larger role in Japanese politics. There is a running debate within the SC about the appropriate political strategy it should adopt. The founding father of Kanagawa SC proposed the formation of a Green–Red coalition to contain the ruling conservative party, the LDP.[21] (Red included Labor and the JSP while Green encompassed NET.)

Table 5.2 NET's electoral record in April 1991 Election

Special designated cities	Population (million)	Total no. of seats	No. of NET candidates	NET candidates elected	Total votes cast in all wards	NET's votes	% of votes
Yokohama	3.22	94	11	4	1,084,784	66,774	6.2
Kawasaki	1.17	64	7	3	419,880	22,899	5.5
Sapporo	1.67	71	3	3	785,210	21,493	2.7
Fukuoka	1.24	64	3	1	461,347	11,666	2.5
Chiba	0.83	56	2	2	296,880	9,724	3.3

Source: *Shakai undō*, No. 134, May 1991, pp. 2–5 and Mainichi shinbunsha, *1991 Tōitsu chihō senkyo* [The 1991 Local Election] (Tokyo: Mainichi shinbunsha, 1991).

Table 5.3 NET's electoral record in April 1995 Election

Special designated cities	Total no. of seats	No. of NET candidates	NET candidates elected	Total votes cast in all wards	NET's votes	% of votes
Yokohama	94	11	6	1,140,459	81,579	7.2
Kawasaki	64	4	4	392,689	23,858	6.1
Sapporo	68	6	3	782,468	38,858	5.0
Fukuoka	65	2	2	401,649	9,691	2.4
Chiba	56	5	4	325,011	20,530	6.3

Source: *Shakai undō*, No. 182, May 1995, pp. 16–21, *Senkyo kanri iinkai*, 1995 [local election management committees], various cities.

In contrast, the founding father of Chiba SC advocated the forging of a nation-wide Green coalition based upon the SC, the Green Co-op and allied co-ops of other regions where the SC lacks an organizational presence. He hoped that the Greens spearheaded by the SC, NET, Green Co-op and other allied co-ops, would hold a casting vote in Japanese politics.[22] In the event of a split within the conservative forces, the Greens were prepared to support those conservatives who are concerned about environmental protection. The ambition for a casting vote in Japanese politics is of course premature given the relative weakness of the Greens. Although the SC has ambitions to play a larger role in Japanese politics, it is still dwarfed by the established parties. Nevertheless, NET has the potential of gaining greater electoral success in local politics especially in the Tokyo metropolitan region, where a quarter of Japan's population lives.

Fifth, few social movements in Japan have gained publicity from abroad. In contrast, the SC has won international recognition for its activities. In December 1989, it won the morale-boosting Swedish Right Livelihood Award, an annual prize given to outstanding individuals or organizations that promote peace, human rights, and environmental protection.[23] At the award presentation, the participants were told:

> Our Honorary Award Recipient this year is an inspiring step in that direction [right livelihood]. Alternative economics in order to have an impact cannot just withdraw from society but must aim to create a new mainstream. We honor the Seikatsu Club Consumers' Co-operative as a project which has successfully taken up this challenge, proving that it is possible to grow into an organization of over five hundred thousand members [sic] without losing the original vision. Seikatsu Club practices ecologically sustainable production, exchange and consumption based on co-operation, self-management and abolition of waste.[24]

Indeed, most social movements in Japan lack the SC's distinct character-istics: a presence in 13 prefectures, strong organizations, a resource-rich economic enterprise, keen participation in electoral politics, and interna-tional recognition. A number of plausible perspectives explain the SC's emergence.[25] They are neither mutually exclusive nor sufficient by them-selves to provide a convincing explanation for its success. The paradigms are: pluralism, urbanization theory and value change in post-industrial societies.

Pluralism

In a democratic polity, interest groups have opportunities to organize, enter, and compete in the political arena.[26] New groups will periodically emerge to take advantage of an open institutional framework to promote their causes. While the lack of formal barriers does not necessarily guarantee the success of any group or ensure that all groups compete on equal terms, the presence of formal restrictions will preclude newcomers from partici-pating in politics. Formal institutional barriers against female voters and candidates were removed after Japan's capitulation to the U.S. in 1945. A liberal constitution was introduced and the way was paved for women to participate in politics. Thus, a necessary though not sufficient reason for NET's emergence is the absence of formal barriers against its entry.

Urbanization theories

Urbanization coupled with industrialization will increase political competi-tion between the government party and the opposition; the percentage of the votes cast for the leading party decreases in unit size, degree of urba-nization, and social differentiation in a democratic polity.[27] As the size of the urban unit grows, increased social density and fragmentation of interests not only lead to greater competition, but also enable an individual to find allies of common interests more easily. With increased heterogeneity of institutions and occupations, the cost of dissent also decreases. This hypoth-esis is often used to explain the rise of political opposition in urban Japan.[28] Another hypothesis postulates that rapid urbanization leads to the erosion of traditional networks and community structures.[29] Urbanites who are not tied to the socio-economic and cultural networks dominated by traditional elites are less susceptible to mobilized voting often made on behalf of conservative candidates. This presents opportunities for non-conservative candidates. Implicitly, both hypotheses assume that urbanites can organize and gain access to the electoral process. Thus, both perspectives share the basic premise of pluralism.

The SC is predominantly an urban phenomenon, and its activists are mostly new residents who are not enmeshed by webs of old, communal ties (Table 5.4). Most of its members come from Tokyo, Kanagawa, Chiba, Saitama, and Hokkaidō prefectures. With the exception of Tokyo, these prefectures are experiencing urbanization. Within Kanagawa prefecture, at least half of SC members live in the large cities of Yokohama and Kawasaki.[30] Yokohama, the prefectural capital of Kanagawa, has experienced the second-highest rate of urbanization among the 11 largest cities of Japan (Table 5.5). Within Yokohama's 16 wards, Midori ward has the highest rate of urbanization (Tables 5.6 and 5.7) and is the strongest bastion of the SC and NET in Kanagawa prefecture, not just in Yokohama. Thus there is a strong correlation between the SC's expansion and urbanization. Patterns of rapid urbanization in Yokohama's new residential suburbs have provided a larger supply of potential recruits for the Kanagawa SC to organize than in the core areas of Yokohama, where traditional business districts and old residents prevail. The SC also encounters recruitment problems in the industrial belt of Yokohama, where large numbers of blue-collar, unionized male workers stay in company dormitories within the same wards.

Rapid urbanization may lead to anonymity in the cities. One incentive for lonely, new residents to join the SC is the opportunity to make friends and also obtain the benefits of mutual help. In districts with a higher percentage of old residents, the presence of a wider network of kinship and neighborhood ties make it unnecessary to join the co-op merely for the sake of making friends. Urbanization as an objective factor in the SC's growth is duly acknowledged by its founding father, Iwane Kunio.[31] The co-op has flourished in the suburbs and dormitory towns of central Tokyo that experienced the rapid influx of new residents. Within the giant loop of the Yamanote railway line that demarcates Tokyo's core, no SC organizations exist. The combination of old residents and availability of shopping centers, supermarkets, and neighborhood stores in central Tokyo preclude the co-op's establishment.

While there is a high correlation between rapid urbanization and the SC's growth, organizational growth is not automatic. Organizers must seize

Table 5.4 Residential length of Kanagawa SC members

Less than 5 years	5–9 years	10–14 years	Over 15 years
39.1%	29.2%	16.9%	13.0%

Source: Seikatsu kurabu rengō shōhi iinkai, *Shōhi seikatsu kenkyūkai hōkokusho*, 1991, p. 13.

Note:
N = 723

Table 5.5 Population shift of Japan's ten largest cities

Cities	1970 Population	Rate of increase	1975 Population	Rate of increase	1980 Population	Rate of increase	1985 Population	Rate of increase	1988 Population	Rate of increase
Tokyo	8,840,942	-0.6	8,646,520	-2.2	8,351,893	-3.4	8,354,615	0.0	8,323,699	-0.4
Yokohama	**2,238,264**	**25.1**	**2,621,771**	**17.1**	**2,773,674**	**5.8**	**2,992,926**	**7.9**	**3,151,087**	**5.3**
Osaka	2,980,487	-5.6	2,778,987	-6.8	2,648,180	-4.7	2,636,249	-0.5	2,644,691	0.3
Nagoya	2,036,053	5.2	2,079,740	2.1	2,087,902	0.4	2,116,381	1.4	2,147,667	1.5
Sapporo	1,010,123	27.1	1,240,613	22.8	1,401,757	13.0	1,542,979	10.1	1,621,418	5.1
Kyoto	1,419,165	4.0	1,641,059	3.0	1,473,065	0.8	1,479,218	0.4	1,474,507	-0.3
Kobe	1,288,937	5.9	1,360,565	5.6	1,367,390	0.5	1,410,834	3.2	1,447,547	2.6
Fukuoka	853,270	13.8	1,002,201	17.5	1,088,588	8.6	1,160,440	6.6	1,203,729	3.7
Kawasaki	973,486	13.9	1,014,951	4.3	1,040,802	2.5	1,088,624	4.6	1,142,953	5.0
Kita-Kyushu	1,042,321	0.0	1,058,442	1.5	1,065,078	0.9	1,056,402	-0.8	1,039,482	-1.6

Source: Yokohama shiritsu daigaku keizai kenkyūsha, *Yokohama no keizai to shakai 1990* [Yokohama's Economy and Society, 1990] [Yokohama: Yokohama shiritsu daigaku, 1991).

Table 5.6 Ward population as a percentage of Yokohama's population

Wards	1970 Population	Percent	1975 Population	Percent	1980 Population	Percent	1985 Population	Percent	1988 Population	Percent
Total	2,238,264	100.0	2,621,771	100.0	2,773,674	100.0	2,992,926	100.0	3,151,087	100.0
Tsurumi	256,360	11.5	242,808	9.3	231,477	8.3	237,083	7.9	246,489	7.8
Kanagawa	207,362	9.3	213,645	8.1	201,794	7.3	201,062	6.7	203,234	6.4
Nishi	97,906	4.4	89,015	3.4	80,539	2.9	78,858	2.6	77,830	2.5
Naka	132,470	5.9	131,346	5.0	121,476	4.4	118,274	4.0	117,793	3.7
Minami	193,221	8.6	198,187	7.6	192,020	6.9	191,578	6.4	193,988	6.2
Kōnan	104,426	4.7	151,682	5.8	185,713	6.7	206,980	6.9	222,766	7.1
Hodogaya	166,766	7.5	177,092	6.8	179,860	6.5	184,013	6.1	191,805	6.1
Asahi	161,187	7.2	200,245	7.6	210,887	7.6	234,544	7.8	244,439	7.8
Isogo	116,018	5.2	156,165	6.0	156,586	5.6	162,484	5.4	166,516	5.3
Kanazawa	108,693	4.9	135,349	5.2	154,687	5.6	176,055	5.9	191,785	6.1
Kōhoku	221,511	9.9	255,275	9.7	265,506	9.6	280,670	9.4	292,577	9.3
Midori	**147,156**	**6.6**	**236,251**	**9.0**	**289,766**	**9.0**	**365,934**	**12.2**	**410,927**	**13.0**
Totsuka	248,696	11.1	339,420	12.9	402,239	14.5	444,116	14.8	231,844	7.4
Izumi	–	–	–	–	–	–	–	–	119,860	3.8
Sakae	–	–	–	–	–	–	–	–	122,274	3.9
Seya	76,492	3.4	95,291	3.6	101,124	3.6	111,275	3.7	116,960	3.7

Source: Yokohama shiritsu daigaku keizai kenkyūsha, *Yokohama no keizai to shakai 1990*.

Table 5.7 Yokohama's population increase and rate of increase

Wards	Population increase				Rate of increase (%)			
	1970–75	*1975–80*	*1980–85*	*1980–88*	*1970–75*	*1975–80*	*1980–85*	*1985–88*
Total	383,507	151,903	219,252	158,161	17.1	5.8	7.9	5.3
Tsurumi	−13,552	−11,331	5,606	9,406	−5.3	−4.7	2.4	4.0
Kanagawa	6,283	−11,851	−732	2,172	3.1	−5.5	−0.4	1.1
Nishi	−8,891	−8,476	−1,681	−1,028	−9.1	−9.5	−2.1	−1.3
Naka	−1,124	−9,870	−3,202	−481	−0.8	−7.5	−2.6	−0.4
Minami	4,966	6,167	−442	2,410	2.6	3.1	−0.2	1.3
Kōnan	47,256	34,025	21,267	15,786	45.2	22.4	11.5	7.6
Hodogaya	10,326	2,768	4,153	7,792	6.2	11.6	2.3	4.2
Asahi	39,058	10,639	23,657	9,895	24.2	5.3	11.2	4.2
Isogo	40,147	434	5,898	4,032	34.6	0.3	3.8	2.5
Kanazawa	26,656	19,331	21,368	15,730	24.5	14.3	13.8	8.9
Kōhoku	33,764	10,231	15,164	11,907	15.2	4.0	5.7	4.2
Midori	**89,095**	**53,515**	**76,168**	**44,993**	**60.5**	**22.7**	**26.3**	**12.3**
Totsuka	90,724	62,822	41,877	29,862	36.5	18.5	10.4	6.7
Seya	18,799	5,833	10,151	5,685	24.6	6.1	10.0	5.1

Source: Yokohama shiritsu daigaku keizai kenkyūsha, *Yokohama no keizai to shakai 1990.*

favorable residential patterns and recruit new residents before it can expand. Urbanization *per se* does not guarantee its emergence. For example, the SC is absent in the Kansai region of Osaka, the third-largest city of Japan, along with the major urban centers of Kyoto and Kobe. There is also the atypical case of Nagano SC that has managed to flourish in a rural setting.

Value change in advanced industrial societies

While pluralism and urbanization theories suggest conditions that permit the SC's emergence, they do not tell us about the nature and character of these new groups or the direction in which they are heading. The paradigm of value change highlights the qualitative differences in values, material and post-material, between these groups and the general society, and is historically grounded in the affluent societies of the post-second World War era. Inglehart postulates that an affluent society gives birth to a new political culture based on post-material values. The rise of post-materialism in turn underpins the growth of new social movements and Green Parties. From this perspective, the SC is not just another group in the pluralist game or a typical organization thrown forth by urbanization, but a social movement that is underpinned by the transformation of mass values. Japan is one of the richest countries in the world. In terms of per capita income, Japan has even overtaken its post-war mentor, the U.S. (Table 5.8).

From the 1960s, Japan saw a rise in citizens' movements. Unlike the agrarian and labor protest movements of the past, the core concern was not material issues such as the lack of staple food, oppressive taxes, miserly wages, and economic layoffs, but environmental and peace issues.[32] The emergence of more assertive citizens' movements is due to the presence of such objective factors as environmental pollution, the initial indifference to environmental problems by the national government, and the rise of a new

Table 5.8 Cross–national comparison (per capita GDP in US$), 1995

Country	Per capita GDP (US$)
Japan	40,897
U.S.	27,799
U.K.	18,097
Germany	29,644
France	26,496
Italy	19,002
Canada	19,431

Source: Bank of Japan, *Comparative Economic and Financial Statistics: Japan and Other Major Countries* (Tokyo: Bank of Japan, 1996), p. 1.

participatory political culture. This culture shift is the outcome of a new post-war education system based on democratic principles and the consequence of an affluent society where increasing number of citizens have more resources at their disposal. These include higher levels of education (Table 5.9), income, leisure, information and confidence.

Since 1953, the Institute of Statistical Mathematics (an organization affiliated to the Ministry of Education) has been conducting surveys at five-year intervals on value change among the Japanese. These statistics over the years reveal a gradual shift from material toward post-material values. The findings confirm that the Japanese have an abundance of material possessions (Table 5.10). Moreover, in 1993, 81 percent of the respondents claimed to be fairly satisfied with the quality of their lives.[33]

Table 5.9 The rise in Japanese mass education

Year	Primary and junior high school (%)	High school (%)	University (%)	Others (%)
1953	68	24	6	2
1958	68	37	7	1
1963	62	29	8	1
1968	56	34	10	0
1973	45	42	11	2
1978	42	40	16	2
1983	37	43	19	1
1988	32	45	22	1
1993	27	47	25	1

Source: Institute of Statistical Mathematics, *A Study of the Japanese National Character: The Ninth Nation Wide Survey*, Research Memorandum No. 572, 1995, p. 3.

Table 5.10 Creature comforts, materialism and the Japanese

Indicator	1983 (%)	1988 (%)	1993 (%)
Private car ownership	70	78	84
Refrigerator	99	99	99
Personal computer	7	21	29
Land ownership	69	69	72
Home ownership	72	72	77
Vacation home	2	2	2
Compact disk player	–	24	37
Telephone	97	98	99
Video recorder	–	70	80

Source: Institute of Statistical Mathematics, *A Study of the Japanese National Character*, p. 5.

A litmus test of materialism is the individual's obsession with money.[34] Once poverty is no longer a gripping issue, the concern for money will tend to diminish as a core issue for some Japanese. Two sets of statistics support the above statement. By 1993, 40 percent of the respondents claimed to lead a life of based around their own interests and not one dominated by the desire for money and fame, while only 21 percent shared the same perception back in 1953.[35] Respondents were also asked about the most important thing in their lives. On child-rearing and socialization by parents, the respondents were asked whether they agreed with the view that children should be taught that money is the most important thing. Back in 1953, 65 percent supported the statement while only 35 percent shared the same sentiment in 1993 (Table 5.11). Despite the bursting of Japan's asset-inflated "bubble economy" in the early 1990s and rising anxiety among many Japanese about the state of the economy, the mass outlook today is markedly less materialistic compared to just a generation ago.

The rise of the SC and NET can be viewed in the context of an affluent society that places greater emphasis on quality of life issues including ecology. In surveys conducted by the Prime Minister's Office, the Japanese, especially those staying in the metropolitan areas, are well informed on environmental problems such as the destruction of the ozone layer and global warming (Table 5.12). Besides a knowledge of ecology problems which includes even the stratosphere, the Japanese have increasingly expressed concern about the general environment (Table 5.13).[36] Heightened ecological consciousness at the mass level creates permissive conditions for social movements to flourish.

Table 5.11 Money and child socialization

Question: Do you agree to the view that children should be taught that money is the most important thing?

Year	Agree (%)	Disagree (%)	Can't say (%)	Others (%)	Don't know (%)
1953	65	24	9	0	2
1963	60	23	15	1	1
1968	57	28	12	1	2
1973	44	38	17	1	1
1978	45	40	13	1	2
1983	43	42	13	1	1
1988	35	47	16	1	1
1993	35	45	18	1	1

Source: Institute of Statistical Mathematics, *A Study of the Japanese National Character*, p. 43.

Table 5.12 Urbanites and global warming problems

	Know well (%)	Quite well (%)	Don't know (%)
Total	41.2	45.9	12.9
Big cities	50.4	41.2	8.4
Villages	35.8	48.2	16.0

Source: Sōrifu kōhō shitsu, *Seron chōsa*, November 1992, p. 12.

Note:
N = 2,284

Table 5.13 Mass attitudes toward nature

	1986 (%)	1991 (%)
Very concerned	20.9%	28.2%
Concerned	57.5	56.2
Total	78.4	84.5

Source: Sōrifu kōhō shitsu, *Seron chōsa*, December 1991, p. 3.

Affluent electorate, the SC and NET members

Most regional SCs are located in the most affluent and urbanized prefectures. This correlation is also strong at the local level within these prefectures. For example, the Kanagawa SC and NET are strongest in the richest sector of Yokohama,[37] the northern part of Midori ward. When we examine the voters' concern in Midori ward we discover that the ward's affluent electorate shows great concern for post-material issues, especially ecology (Table 5.14). The typical Kanagawa SC or NET member is better educated (Table 5.15), more affluent (Table 5.16) and has a greater satisfaction with life (Table 5.17) than the average Japanese from the same prefecture. Thus, her involvement in social movements is not a result of relative deprivation or resentment against society. In a survey of Tokyo NET, not a single NET member believed that Japan should concentrate on greater economic growth, but it should instead protect the environment (Table 5.18).

The SC's backbone is its housewife activist. She is affluent and has the leisure time to be involved in activities outside the home. At least half of the members' husbands belong to the managerial class of large Japanese enterprises.[38] Since it is the norm for large Japanese companies to provide lifetime employment to Japanese male employees, SC members who are married to elite salary men are assured of long-term material security. Long

Table 5.14 Midori ward electorate's outlook

Ranking	Issues	Very concerned (%)
1	Environmental protection	66.8
2	Welfare	58.4
3	Stable Japanese economy	47.1
4	U.S.–Japan trade friction	43.9
5	Problem of the aged	43.0
6	Revision of the consumption tax	41.8
7	Bullying in school	41.5
8	Japan's participation in UN's peacekeeping operations	36.6
9	Market liberation of foreign rice	31.1
10	Political reforms	30.5
11	Security market scandals	25.7
12	LDP Presidential Elections	25.2
13	U.S.–Soviet co-operation	23.6
14	Establishment of peace in Cambodia	10.9
15	Yugoslavia's civil war	8.3
16	Party alignments in Japan	8.2

Source: Tanaka Aiji, *Shiji seitō o motanai yūkensha ni kansuru jisshōteki kenkyū* [Research on Voters who are Non-Party Supporters], (Yokohama: Toyo eiwa jogakuin daigaku nyubun gakubu, 1992), pp. 43–48.

Note:
N = 364 Multiple answers

Table 5.15 Education: comparison of Yokohama residents, North Midori electorate and Midori NET members

	Primary and junior high (%)	High school (%)	College and above (%)
Yokohama (N = 2,188)	19.3	45.2	35.2
North Midori (N = 2,695)	5.8	29.5	59.8
Midori NET (N = 104)	2.9	25.9	70.2

working hours at the office and time spent with colleagues after work to cement social relations mean that the husbands of many SC activists do not spend much time at home during the weekdays. Thus, their wives are free to pursue activities, including social movements, that appeal to them. Affluence also permits members, like most households in Japan, to afford time-saving devices such as washing machines, vacuum cleaners, refrigerators, and microwave ovens.[39] By lightening the load and drudgery of housework, members give themselves more time and energy to engage in activities outside the home.

Table 5.16 Annual household income (¥ million)

	0–0.59 (%)	0.6–0.99 (%)	1.0 and above (%)	No reply (%)
North Midori ward resident	29.3	28.5	29.7	12.5
Midori NET (Husband's income only)	5.8	59.6	28.8	5.8
Kanagawa SC member	28.7	55.0	17.9	–
Kanagawa resident	48.3	33.5	13.0	–

Sources: Seikatsu kurabu rengō shōhi iinkai, *Shōhi seikatsu kenkyūkai hōkokusho* [Research Committee's Report on Consumption and Livelihood], 1991 Booklet, p. 56 and Yokohama shi sōmukyoku gyōsei ku chōsa shitsu, *Kōhoku ku midori no chiiki seikatsu to gyōsei ni kansuru kumin ishiki chōsa*, pp. 21–22.

Table 5.17 Life satisfaction index (comparison between Kanagawa residents and Kanagawa SC members)

	Satisfied (%)	Quite satisfied (%)	Quite dissatisfied (%)	Dissatisfied (%)	No reply (%)
Kanagawa SC (N = 710)	20.1	67.9	10.2	3.0	–
Kanagawa Residents (N = 1,523)	4.2	42.5	20.8	2.9	29.6

Sources: Seikatsu kurabu rengō shōhi iinkai, *Shōhi seikatsu kenkyūkai hōkokusho*, 1991, p. 56 and Kanagawa ken kenminbu kenminka, *Kurashi nitsuite no kenmin ishiki chōsa* [Survey on the Outlook of Prefecture's Residents on Livelihood], 1990, p. 31.

Table 5.18 Outlook of Tokyo NET members (issues which Japan should grapple with)

Issue Priority	Percent
Protect the natural environment	37.3
Increase citizens' participation in politics	21.1
Increase citizens' welfare	18.5
Protect citizens' rights	12.6
Deepen international friendship	2.6
Maintain law and order	0.5
Develop Japan's economy	0.0

Source: Nasu Hisashi, Yamasaki Tetsuya and Watanabe Noboru, *Survey on Tokyo NET Members*, unpublished manuscript, 1991.

Affluent societies have seen the trend toward nuclear family and declining birthrates. However, in the unusual case of Nagano SC, many members belong to a three-tier extended family structure.[40] Thus far, it is the only large SC found in a rural setting. Many of the patriarchs and matriarchs of Nagano SC members' families are members of agricultural co-operatives that support conservative candidates. It is intimated that some members faced strong opposition from parents-in-law when they expressed their desire to become politically involved in social movements or NET campaign activities. However, most members from other regions do not face this dilemma.

Marrying at an older age (partly due to longer years at school and a period of work upon graduation), the higher cost of feeding, schooling, and housing more than two children and a sheer lack of living space for a large family in metropolitan Japan are disincentives to maintaining a large family. This changing demographic pattern means that the average SC member has fewer children to look after. Once her children are in school and her husband is at work, she is free to pursue co-op activities. Most members are in their thirties and forties and have studied in a post-war liberal educational system. They are not exposed to the discredited values of authoritarianism, militarism, and emperor worship of pre-war Japan. Indeed, the liberation of Japanese women from traditional household chores through technological innovations, higher levels of education, affluence, and the rising status of women pave the way for women to take a more active role in politics.[41]

It is perhaps ironic that the affluence of SC members is indirectly made possible by the LDP's stewardship of Japan's political economy. By being very supportive of producer interests, the party helped to catapult Japan to the forefront of economic powers. Paradoxically, the conservatives' emphasis on economic growth has created an affluent society that has become more demanding on quality of life issues and critical of the LDP's support for producer interests. The cornerstone of the LDP's foreign policy is the U.S.–Japan Security Treaty. Reliance on the U.S. security umbrella permits Japan to concentrate on economic growth rather than to channel scarce resources into non-productive military spending. Japan also benefited from the relatively open markets of her security partner. These are two crucial factors that have contributed to Japan's rise as an economic superpower and affluent industrial society. Even though the SC and NET are against military alliances, they are indirect beneficiaries of LDP's foreign policy that facilitated economic growth. Their emergence is, in part, an unintended consequence of the LDP's single-mindedness on economic growth and commitment to the U.S.–Japan alliance. The creation of an affluent society has facilitated the entry of SC members into social and political activism.

The three perspectives – pluralism, urbanization, and value change among the Japanese – highlight the permissive conditions for the SC's ascent but do not sufficiently explain the rise of social movements and New Politics parties. Favorable conditions are not automatically translated into political and electoral support; they are necessary but not sufficient conditions for social movements and Green parties to emerge. Leaders, mobilizers, organizations, and strategies must take advantage of favorable conditions before a social movement advances. SC members have the resources to participate in politics. A majority of them are affluent and well-educated housewives who have the time to participate in the activities of the co-op. That the SC was able to tap this social group for support was due to its successful mobilizing efforts.

6 Origins of the Seikatsu Club

To understand the SC's emergence, and its strengths and weaknesses, we must examine its origins. Its foundation was not pre-ordained by the transformation in the structures and values of Japanese society; it was established by an act of will by a charismatic leader who had the vision and drive to mobilize apolitical housewives into social activism. Peculiar characteristics that include a narrow support base of urban housewives, a male-dominated organization, and the type of issues the movement pursues, can be traced back to its founding moment.

The club is the brainchild of Iwane Kunio.[1] Although other leaders would play critical roles in establishing sister organizations in different regions, Iwane, more than any other leaders, has infused it with the spirit of social activism. While most co-ops in Japan abstained from electoral activities, the SC was unique in sponsoring women candidates in local elections.[2] The Founding Father of Hokkaidō SC, Kobayashi Shigenobu, when assessing the role of Iwane, remarked: "If there was no Iwane-san, there would have been no Seikatsu Club."[3] Likewise, if there was no SC, there would have been no NET. Its origins suggest that the vision and charisma of a leader are often critical to the launching of a social movement. Some observers believed that women had founded the club but this view is erroneous.[4] This inaccuracy was perpetuated by the co-op's brochures, which claimed that it was founded by a housewife who was invariably never identified. The SC downplays its male origins in order to project the image that it is a women-conceived and led organization.

Iwane participated in the massive demonstrations which erupted against the 1960 revision of the U.S.–Japan Security Treaty. The forces of the Left feared that an entangling alliance with the U.S. would drag Japan into a war with her communist neighbors while the conservatives believed that the Security Treaty would shield Japan from external aggression. Although the scale of the demonstrations was the largest post-war Japan has ever seen, the Left was unable to block the LDP from ramming the revised Security

Treaty Bill through the Diet. The 1960 demonstrations were a turning-point in Iwane's life.[5] Profoundly disappointed with the Left's failure to check the LDP, Iwane abandoned his career in photography and dedicated himself to revitalizing the JSP by becoming a party activist in Setagaya ward, Tokyo. Soon he became acutely aware of the JSP's organizational weakness at the local level. On the surface, Setagaya ward appeared to be a socialist stronghold, since two out of three Lower House seats were captured by the party then. At that time, Setagaya ward had a population of 800,000, but there were only two full-time JSP activists when Iwane arrived. Setagaya ward was devoid of socialist grassroots activities until election time when the unions were mobilized to help in the party's campaign.[6]

In 1962, Iwane became the chairman of the JSP's youth wing in Setagaya ward, Tokyo. In the local elections held in the following year, Iwane received an endorsement from the JSP Right wing "structural reform" faction which was the mortal enemy of the Marxist-Leninist factions.[7] He ran in Setagaya's ward assembly elections but was defeated. The failure convinced Iwane that a radically different approach must be adopted to win grassroots support. He realized that the lack of grassroots support was the JSP's fundamental weakness. This resulted from the party's indifference to the concerns and problems of daily life. The JSP's negligence of the grass-roots stems from three sources: a Marxist-Leninist ideology that focuses on the class struggle at the workplace at the expense of the residential place; the social composition of its most active supporters, who are invariably male unionists preoccupied with workplace issues; and an unimaginative leader-ship unable to transcend the narrow interests of its union supporters.

The key to obtaining grassroots political support was the direct involve-ment in the mundane issues of daily living. Since the housewives were virtually the only group of voters who were present at the residential neighborhood during the day, their support was indispensable to the endea-vor of forging support at the grassroots.[8] Iwane believed that many new residents in urbanizing Setagaya ward were unattached to the established political parties. It was therefore necessary to organize these "floating" voters in order to strengthen the JSP.[9] The problem was to pick a mobilizing issue that would attract the participation of apolitical housewives.

Milk as a mobilizing issue

Iwane, aided by his wife, started a daily milk delivery service in 1965 as a strategy to establish daily contact with local residents.[10] There were pre-cedents where local movements involving housewives had successfully dis-tributed cheap and safe milk in Japan.[11] Although milk as a mobilizing issue was not an untested approach, Iwane's approach was novel because he intended to use an innocuous issue as a political vehicle to strengthen the JSP against the conservatives.[12]

The club started with a staff of only four and around 200 housewives in Setagaya ward. To translate his vision into reality, Iwane personally delivered milk at four o'clock in the morning by bicycle whether it rained or shone during the co-op's early years.[13] Tenacious door-to-door canvassing in the new residential estates was adopted to recruit members. Reflecting upon its humble origins, Iwane would later remark that not even in his dreams did he anticipate that the SC would eventually become such a large organization (Table 6.1).[14]

The SC's prototype election campaign

Even though the club was still a fledgling organization in 1967, it supported Iwane's wife, Shizuko, when she ran for a seat in Setagaya ward assembly under the JSP's label. Iwane was her campaign manager. Mrs. Iwane, riding on the back of the organization, won an unprecedented number of votes; in

Table 6.1 SC and NET membership

Prefecture	Year established	SC (1997)	NET (1995)
Tokyo SC	1968	56,741	1,019
Kanagawa SC group			
SC	1971	47,739	–
Welfare Club	1989	8,792	2,700
Community Club	1991	17,304	–
Saitama SC	1975	25,220	179
Chiba SC	1976	30,978	997
Nagano SC	1977	14,040	32
Hokkaidō SC	1983	13,215	803
Ibaraki SC	1983	4,168	–
Yamanashi SC	1985	3,926	152
Iwate SC	1987	2,320	52
Shizuoka SC	1987	3,910	–
Aichi SC	1988	6,872	–
Tochigi SC	1990	2,634	–
Sendai co-op[a]	1997	8,837	–
Total		246,696	5,934[b]

Sources: Social Movement Center and *Seikatsu kurabu 1997*, p. 4.

Notes:
a The Sendai co-op (Sendai kyōdō kōnyū kai) was established in 1979 but joined the SC group in June 1997.
b If we include the 348 members from Fukuoka NET, the total membership is 6282. In the case of Fukuoka NET, its sponsor is the Fukuoka Green Co-op, North Block.

1967 it was the highest ever in Tokyo's ward electoral history.[15] The SC made use of its monthly newsletters to publicize and endorse Mrs. Iwane's candidacy,[16] and its professional staff and members formed the backbone of her campaign.[17] These tactics were later emulated by NET. The triumph of 1967 was in complete contrast to Iwane's electoral attempt four years earlier. The crucial difference between the two campaigns was the presence of an SC organization in 1967 which effectively mobilized the support of housewives.

The SC as a co-op

In 1968, the SC was legally reconstituted as a co-op. By becoming a co-op, it obtained the right to raise capital from its members and the opportunity to place the organization on a sound economic footing. With a strong economic base, it could independently engage in social movements. Moreover, the switch from individual home delivery to the group (*han*) delivery system was a time- and labor-saving device. The *han* of the SC consists of a group of housewives who regularly assemble to jointly order food and other items in bulk (*kyōdō kōnyū*).[18] The advanced orders are processed by the co-op and then passed on to its producers. Prior to production, the SC and its producers agree on a fixed price that is adequate for the producer's livelihood. In exchange for a promised fixed price and the assurance that the co-op will purchase items even if they are imperfect in appearance, the producers promise to avoid using health-damaging pesticides by adopting organic farming. When the organization receives the products, it delivers them to the *han* at a prearranged place and time where members distribute the items among themselves. By by-passing Japan's labyrinthine distribution process and avoiding the cost of fancy packaging and news media advertisement, the SC can pass on considerable savings to its members.

Until 1982, the SC relied exclusively on the *han* instead of a store system.[19] Since it did not run a chain of stores, risky land purchases, construction bills, store personnel costs, and overheads were not incurred. Unlike many bigger co-ops, whose members were merely passive shoppers, the *han* system demanded active participation from its ordinary members. Its structure and function encouraged social interaction, co-operation, and collective decision-making by members. *Han* meetings often result in the forging of friendships. From the SC's viewpoint, it is easier to mobilize *han* members than atomized individuals for social movement. If one or two members can be persuaded to support a cause, they might be able to win support from the rest of the members based on the social cohesion of the group. Thus, the *han* is the SC's building-block and launching pad for social action.

By reconstituting the SC into a co-op, it came under the jurisdiction of the Ministry of Health and Welfare (MHW). This was a potential problem because co-ops are not supposed to be involved in electoral politics. Chapter 1, Article 2, Para. 2 of the Consumer's Livelihood Co-operative Society Law (Co-op Law) reads: "Consumer's Livelihood Co-operative Society and Union of Consumer's Livelihood Co-operative Society shall not be utilized for any particular political parties."[20] The SC eventually tried to get around the law by creating a separate organization, NET, which does not fall under the jurisdiction of the Co-op Law.

The Co-op Law also prevented the co-ops from expanding beyond prefectural boundaries.[21] The MHW prohibited the co-ops from expanding beyond a single prefecture and clashing head on with the commercial supermarket chains. This legal requirement had a certain impact on SC and NET: by limiting the original SC to Tokyo, future sister organizations in other prefectures were required by law to retain legal and operational autonomy. Each regional SC had its own set of leaders, policies, and variation in organizational structures. Even though an SC Federation was established in Tokyo in 1978, the regional clubs were autonomous in their operations. Concomitantly, the SC's decentralized nature had resulted in the decentralization of NET. Each regional NET, like its parent organization, operated independently from the NET organizations in other prefectures. Although the regional clubs were kept distinct by law, informal ties and common values between their top leaders gave the group a common identity and coherence: alternative values, direct participation, a concern for the residential area, environmentalism, and social activism.

SC and the context of political activism

In March 1977, Iwane made the clarion call in the SC's newsletter for amateurs from the co-op to launch a citizen-centered New Politics and directly to compete for electoral seats in the local assemblies.[22] Iwane argued that social problems cannot be solved within the narrow framework of the co-ops and that there is a necessity to be involved in politics to promote desirable political change. He envisaged the pursuit of livelihood and ecological issues as mobilizing concerns and a new form of direct political participation by ordinary citizens.

The national context of Iwane's call for political activism was the pervasive corruption that discredited the political establishment. By 1977, there was profound disappointment with the established parties and strong impulses for changes in Japanese politics emanating not only from the public but also politicians within the LDP and the JSP. Iwane too was caught up in the maelstrom of political change: attempts to sweep away the corruption of established party politics. Japanese politics was rocked by the Lockheed scandal and party schisms within the LDP in 1976 and within the JSP in the following year. (LDP politicians including former Prime Minister Tanaka Kakuei were implicated for accepting bribes from the Lockheed aircraft corporation.) The political climate against the LDP's money politics led to the formation of a second conservative party, the New Liberal Club (NLC), that stood for clean politics.[23] On the socialist side, Eda Saburō, a charismatic, reform-minded leader of the Right faction broke away from the JSP after fighting a series of protracted battles with the Left factions. Iwane was sympathetic to Eda's call for "structural reform" in place of revolutionary class struggle as the ideological basis to rebuild the JSP.[24]

Structural reform was Palmiro Togliatti's[25] proposal that quantitative reforms made over time will cumulatively lead to a qualitative change in the structure of capitalist society and the advent of a socialist society.[26] Structural reform theory staged its Japanese debut around 1957 and gained adherents within both the communist and socialist parties. A number of communists who embraced structural reform were purged or quit the party of their own accord after fierce resistance from the JCP mainstream.[27] They include Andō Jinbei,[28] presently a top SC advisor, and Kotsuka Hisao,[29] former chairman of the Kanagawa SC. In 1961, the JCP put an end to the structural reform debate within its ranks. This resulted in a schism and seven central committee members defected. Some of the ex-communists who supported structural reform linked up with like-minded socialists and continued to propagate their revisionist ideology within the JSP. This group of structural reformers eventually found a champion in Eda. His call for an evolutionary approach to socialism was not only heretical to the Left but was also viewed as an ideological weapon to knock the Left in the internecine struggle for power between the factions.

In March 1977, Iwane received a telephone call from Eda asking him to leave the JSP and help Eda build a new party, Social Citizens League (Shakai Shimin Rengō), to reform Japanese politics.[30] After spending 17 futile years trying to revitalize the JSP, Iwane finally left in frustration and cast his lot with Eda. Eda then offered Iwane an Upper House candidacy for the new party but Iwane subsequently decided to let his wife run in his place in the coming elections. The SC's delivery center in Setagaya ward was converted into the campaign headquarters in anticipation of the Upper House Election.[31] For reasons that remain unclear, Iwane's candidacy was opposed by some of the activists from Eda's camp. When Eda died unexpectedly in the same year, Iwane decided not to join the new party. The ostensible reason was that his sense of obligation (*giri*) to Eda had ended with his death.

Perhaps Japanese politics might have taken a different course if Eda had lived longer. If Eda, often hailed as the first charismatic Japanese political leader of the television age, had survived, the Social Citizens League (SCL)[32] might have attracted a larger and broader based group of activists like Iwane. It might have made some impact at the polls and engaged in coalition building with the center parties, the DSP and Kōmeitō. Perhaps the SC and future NET organizations might have aligned with Eda, giving the SCL the grassroots base it has always lacked. If such a scenario had materialized, the trajectory of NET could possibly have been different from that of today.

The emergence of NET can also be seen as the failure of an established party, the JSP, to appeal to activists like Iwane and the urban housewives. Even though the LDP was mired in scandals, the JSP was unable to offer itself as a credible alternative, but was torn by internecine factional strife. The contextual factors of massive political corruption within the LDP, the paralysis of the JSP and the irrelevance of the established parties to the interests of urban consumers spurred Iwane to launch the NET movement.

Electoral breakthrough

In July 1977, the SC sponsored its first woman candidate, unaffiliated to any established party, to stand in Nerima ward for Tokyo's prefectural assembly, but the attempt was unsuccessful.[33] It was only two years later that the co-op's candidate finally won a seat in Nerima ward assembly election.[34] Other regional NETs, after observing Tokyo SC's successful experiment, eventually followed suit and fielded their own slate of candidates in local elections.

There was initially much resistance to Iwane's proposal that the co-op should support candidates for elections.[35] Members were afraid that the SC might break the Co-op Law and that it would be diverted from its task of food distribution. Some members even believed that involvement in electoral politics was a waste of time and resources.[36] Iwane's ability to cajole the organization's leaders and members to embark on electoral politics despite their misgivings is testimony to his charisma and powers of persuasion.

We will next examine how the SC and NET have expanded beyond Tokyo to neighboring Kanagawa prefecture. The inception and expansion of Kanagawa SC was similar to Tokyo SC in that the critical role of a founding father whose mission was to mobilize urban housewives for social movements.[37]

Kanagawa SC's founding father: Yokota Katsumi

Yokota participated in the 1960 anti-U.S.–Japan Security Treaty demonstrations and was deeply disappointed by the Left's failure to check the LDP.[38] He joined the JSP and through its youth wing, became acquainted with Iwane in 1963. Yokota was then active in the labor union of Tōkyū Railway Company. He was not interested in a labor movement centered around wage raises but was motivated by the desire to promote the power of labor. Yokota was also appalled that local residents along the Tōkyū rail tracks were dependent on the rail company not only for transportation but also for supermarkets, housing projects, and recreational facilities. Yokota first formed a *han* at his workplace that was linked to Tokyo SC, but subsequently shifted the area of organization from the workplace to the place of residence. The formation of a co-op was Yokota's strategy to help local residents and Tōkyū workers avoid the huge railway company's local monopoly of goods and services. Since a number of Yokota's *han* members from Tōkyū live in Midori ward, a newly urbanizng area in Yokohama city, he began his activities there. The Kanagawa SC's social composition changed rapidly as housewives quickly outstripped the original Tōkyū union members.

Kanagawa SC: crisis, opportunism and growth

The Kanagawa SC's growth was the result of luck and pluck in overcoming challenges. In 1971, Yokota established Midori Co-op, the predecessor of the Kanagawa SC in Tama Plaza, a new residential area in the northern part of Midori ward, Yokohama.[39] Tama Plaza was a newly developing housing estate that was not saturated by supermarkets, rival co-ops, or the presence of a traditional shopping district (*shōtengai*). It was served by a new railway line, opened in 1966, linking Northern Midori ward to Tokyo. Tama Plaza was and still is a dormitory town of Tokyo. Although Tama Plaza was a propitious environment for the Midori Co-op, success was not assured. The Midori Co-op was basically on its own since Tokyo SC had labor shortages and was unable to extend much help. Through tenacious door-to-door canvassing in Tama Plaza the Midori Co-op rapidly expanded.

The 1973 Oil Shock

The consumer panic triggered by the Oil Shock of 1973 presented both a crisis and an opportunity for the Midori Co-op. Consumer nervousness about Japan's dependence on foreign oil and other natural resources led to massive hoarding of basic necessities leading to severe shortages of items such as sugar, salt, detergent, and toilet paper. The co-ops, inclusive of Midori Co-op, were hit by inadequate supplies caused by abnormal consumer demands. Despite chronic shortages, co-ops shared what they had fairly among members; instead of one person hoarding many rolls of toilet paper, co-ops distributed a few rolls to each member to tide them over the crisis. Even though the co-ops suffered from shortages, the communitarian approach of members won for Japan's co-op movement a fine reputation for coping well in a difficult situation.

In the aftermath of the 1973 Oil Shock, the membership of the Midori Co-op soared, just like that of many other co-ops. The impetus to join a co-op was the desire to secure predictable supplies after the scare of 1973. Midori Co-op's leadership was also prescient enough to build two large oil tanks before the Oil Shock. Despite misgivings from many members about the high cost of this investment, Yokota was able to persuade enough members to go ahead with the plan.[40] Fortuitously, the oil tanks were completed before the oil exporting Arab countries placed an embargo on Japan for being "soft" on Israel. Through Yokota's foresight, Midori Co-op was able to supply kerosene oil to keep its members warm during the winter of 1973. Yokota's gamble was vindicated, the co-op's reputation was enhanced, and membership continued to soar. Paradoxically, the SC was almost destroyed by its own success.

Organizational crisis: the labor–management showdown of 1975

The SC's rapid expansion stretched both management and labor. A labor shortage in the midst of rapid growth contributed to discontent among its full-time staff. The labor–management conflict that culminated in violence at Kanagawa SC's General Assembly on May 28, 1975, almost destroyed the organization.[41] Yokota considered this débâcle to be the greatest crisis ever faced by the co-op.[42] Had the crisis not been contained, Midori Co-op might have collapsed, resulting in NET's absense in Kanagawa politics.

In theory, labor (Midori Co-op's full-time workers), management, and *han* members were partners, but in reality the relationship was conflict-ridden. Workers were often overworked and underpaid, and had to deliver heavy loads of co-op groceries to the *han*. There was also the question of how much influence the workers could exercise when, according to the co-op principle, ordinary *han* members were supposed to be in control of the organization. However, Yokota, being the founding father of Midori Co-op, wielded great clout in the organization. Thus, one aspect of the conflict was about the distribution of power and the future control of the organization.

One quarter of the workers were involved in the labor unrest and strikes were carried out at two of the six Midori Co-op delivery centers. According to one member's account, dissident workers with red headbands distributed handbills that condemned management, picketed with microphones, and demanded that management be "struck down."[43] Things came to a head at the 1975 General Assembly when the dissidents assaulted a guest from Tokyo SC who was then hospitalized with broken bones. Management retaliated and seven of the dissidents were dismissed.

Many of the genteel housewives of Midori Co-op were deeply shocked and disturbed by the outbreak of violence. The major incentive to join the co-op was the assurance of obtaining a reliable supply of safe and inexpensive food. When the strikes disrupted delivery services, members deserted the organization in flocks. In that year alone, 4,300 members quit out of a total membership of 9,000.[44] For the very first time, Midori Co-op's rapid growth grounded to a halt; the organization was plunged into a membership and financial crisis.

The near collapse of the Kanagawa SC shows that despite favorable objective factors for the growth of social movements – influx of new residents, presence of ecological problems, a more democratic political culture – success was by no means assured. The ability of leaders to rally the members and navigate the social movement enterprise through crises and opportunities is crucial to the organization's survival and growth. A concentration on structural factors such as the rise of a white-collar, middle class and value change may mislead us by giving the impression that the emergence and growth of social movements in post-industrial societies are inevitable; success often hinges on leadership and sometimes on pure fortune.

In 1977, two years after the labor–management débâcle, the Midori Co-op changed its name to Kanagawa Seikatsu Club. The ostensible reason was to avoid confusing members and potential recruits by the SC labels on products jointly produced by the group handled by Midori Co-op. Thus, the new name would be consistent with the product labels it was handling. Perhaps a new name had the added advantage of giving the organization a facelift after the negative publicity about the strife within the Midori Co-op.

The "Iwane problem" of 1981 and its impact on Kanagawa SC

In 1981, the club was faced with a crisis that embroiled its founding father, Iwane. When he accepted personal loans from SC's suppliers to build his home, some members felt that the loans represented a clash of interests: how could the club ensure that suppliers' food are of the best quality when the chairman might be beholden to the producers?

One branch of the Kanagawa SC in Midori ward decided to pursue the issue.[45] When news of Iwane's financial dealings came out in the open, many members in Midori ward quit the organization. The disclosure of the Iwane incident also caused a stir among the members in Kawasaki city.[46] The whole débâcle ended only after Iwane resigned from his post. The incident was reported at length by the *Mainichi Shinbun*, one of Japan's top newspapers, leading to much consternation among members.[47] The whole incident might have been a blessing in disguise for the SC group. When Iwane resigned, the loss of the group's founder did not lead to major organizational instability. After 16 years of institutionalization, the club was able to weather the departure of its founding father without serious disruption. Although Iwane left under a cloud, he bequeathed a legacy of social activism to the group. The SC's social activism, the NET movement, and a think-tank organization, the Social Movement Center,[48] were firmly set in place despite leadership changes. Even in the 1990s, Iwane was often invited to the NET regional lecture circuits to explain the meaning of SC and the NET movement.[49]

Soap as a mobilizing issue

The Kanagawa SC was in no position to participate in local politics immediately after the near collapse of its organization in 1975. After repairing and strengthening its organization, the co-op was poised to move beyond the realm of food distribution in 1980. Its soap movement was the vehicle to move apolitical housewives into local politics.[50] Why was soap picked as a mobilizing issue? First, the natural soap movement was not an esoteric movement in Japan. A successful precedent was established in 1979 when Shiga's Prefectural Assembly, in response to citizens' concerns about the pollution of Lake Biwa, prohibited the use of synthetic soap (*gōsei senzai*).[51] The local government's initiative had already gained publicity in the mass media by the time the co-op carefully picked its cause. Second, soap was not an abstract issue but a household item that housewives used daily. Housewives could be persuaded that the pollution of rivers, lakes, and seas by synthetic soap will inevitably contaminate the food chain and was potentially harmful to their families' health. An unpopular environmental issue such as the hazards of cigarette smoke was not selected by the SC.[52] The organization shrewdly picked synthetic soap as an issue which appealed to the housewives. Soap as a mobilizing issue satisfied three criteria: the successful precedent of soap as an environmental issue, the fact that it was also a concrete issue, and that water pollution was an objective problem which could gain widespread public support.

In 1980, the Kanagawa SC initiated a signature campaign against the use of synthetic soap.[53] About 220,000 signatures were collected and petitions were sent to various local assemblies in Kanagawa. Despite the large number of signatures collected, local governments in Kanagawa rejected a ban on synthetic soap. The unfavorable outcome was seized by the co-op as evidence of the local assemblies' lack of responsiveness to ordinary citizens' requests. The only means to implement their proposals, it argued, was the direct participation by ordinary housewives in the electoral process so that their views could be reflected in the local assemblies.

In the 1983 local elections, Terada Etsuko became the first candidate supported by the Kanagawa SC.[54] In that year, it supported only one candidate as a prelude to running more candidates in the 1987 Local Elections. Terada was the co-op's representative in Kawasaki city's special commission on the use of synthetic soap. She never dreamt of standing for elections until Yokota approached her to run as an independent candidate.[55] After vacillating for a month, she was finally persuaded by Yokota to become a candidate. The whole episode demonstrated the critical role of a founding father in spearheading the NET movement in Kanagawa prefecture. After Terada won her seat in Miyamae ward, Kawasaki city, together with two SC male workers she established NET as a political organization that was distinct from the co-op. Between 1983 and 1987, four more candidates supported by Kanagawa SC were elected to local assemblies. By the 1987 Local Election 13 NET candidates were elected to local assemblies in Kanagawa. From that year, NET became a feature of Kanagawa's local political scene.

Conclusion

By tracing the SC's origins and development, we can see that permissive conditions for social movements in Japan, an open political system, rapid urbanization, and value change did not automatically lead to social movement activities. Members were assiduously recruited and organizations were painstakingly built over the years before the co-op was strong enough to participate in electoral politics. Mobilizers and mobilizing issues that included safe milk and natural soap were necessary to the growth of the SC and its activities. Crucial to the inception and consolidation of social movement enterprises was the role of strong leadership. Iwane was indispensable to the emergence of the SC and NET. National events especially the anti-U.S.–Japan Security Treaty demonstrations in 1960 acted as catalysts to Iwane's involvement in social movements and the formation of the SC in 1965. Massive political corruption in 1976 and other contextual factors including Eda's split from the JSP in 1977 prompted Iwane to launch an amateur-based political participation rooted in Green values. Even though the 1970s saw the rise of citizens' movements and a new participatory culture in Japan, the formation of the SC and NET was by no means assured. It was inspired by the vision and the will of a single man.

The transformation of apolitical housewives into social movement activists is the result of Iwane's grand design. Most members were initially drawn to the co-op's seemingly innocuous provision of services and friendship rather than a concern for participation in social movements. Many ordinary housewives became enthusiastic participants in social movement activities after sustained exposure to the SC's propaganda, values, and activities, and only after being locked into the *han*'s social networks.

The weaknesses of the SC were already sown in its founding moment. The founding fathers left an indelible mark on the co-op. However, the dependence of the organization on a small band of male leaders is a potential source of weakness. It is not possible for the organization to make a full-hearted appeal to gender equality, especially when it has been directed by males for around three decades. Club members in local elections seek voters' empathy by harping on their status of "ordinary housewives" playing the traditional role of a caring mother rather than women in search of gender equality.

The SC was too dependent on a singular base of urban housewives. Moreover, these housewives were more preoccupied about issues relating to their families' health than with a broader concern to forge a new social and political order. Thus, policies advocated by the SC had a limited appeal to other social groups. Participation in the *han* was also an outcome of a desire for belonging, friendship, and mutual support in an urbanizing milieu. The club could mobilize even apolitical *han* members on the basis of group solidarity, but it had problems mobilizing other groups outside the social webs of the *han*. Japanese norms of belonging to a group, personal loyalties, and reciprocal obligations are a double-edged sword for the co-op. On the one hand, it was able to mobilize even club members who are not interested in politics; on the other, Green policies had limited appeal to groups outside its social networks.

7 Seikatsu Club: ideology and organization

Why did the SC emerge and make a sustained challenge in local politics? Why is a women-populated organization led by men? What are the limitations of the Greens in Japan? The answers to these questions partially lie in the organization's leadership, structure, and ideology. To make an impact on society, its male leaders shaped the ideology and organizations of the group. Oligarchic tendencies within the co-op and NET resulted from the founding fathers' dominant role in designing their organizations and ideology.

To fulfil the grand design to attain, in Gramscian terminology, a "local hegemony," its leaders have succeeded in building an impressive range of organizations, activities, and services at the grassroots level. These include the *han*, a chain of supermarkets, workers' collectives, and even daycare centers. By meeting the daily needs of some urban residents, the co-op wins their loyalties and participation in social movements. Enmeshing local residents in the social networks of its parent organization, NET can count on the support of co-op members in elections. However, NET's appeal is limited by the difficulty in attracting urban residents who are not beneficiaries of the co-op's goods and services.

Many top SC leaders still cling on to Gramscian ideology, a variant of Marxism, even though it is passé, not only in Western Europe but also in Japan. An inability to detach themselves from an intellectual and political fad from the late 1950s and 1960s means that they will face greater difficulties obtaining political support beyond the social networks of the *han*. In theory, post-materialists are the natural constituents of the New Politics party. However, many post-materialists in Japan today are unlikely to find Gramscian ideology attractive. The values and beliefs of its top leaders are traceable to eclectic sources: Gramsci's concept of hegemony, the tradition of the co-op movement, and ideas indigenous to the SC. After discussing its ideology, we will examine its influence on the organizational structure of the Kanagawa SC.

The SC's interpretation of "hegemony"

The term "hegemony" often appears in the written and spoken words of its top leaders.[1] When Iwane was a JSP youth leader, he held and led study sessions on Marx, Lenin, and Gramsci. Among these Marxist giants, Iwane acknowledges Gramsci to be his greatest source of inspiration.[2] To most of the founding fathers, Gramsci's concept of hegemony is a key in explaining "conservative dominance" and, conversely, the Left's weakness in Japan. Moreover, it prescribes a solution to contain the dominance of conservatism. Yokota's framework of analysis often echoes Gramscian ideology. In a flattering introduction to Yokota's book, a friend acknowledges Yokota as falling within the Gramscian tradition: "He [Yokota] is not a scholar, but should be regarded in the same light as the Italian intellectual author and social activist Antonio Gramsci."[3]

The organization's clearest exposition of Gramsci's concept of hegemony transplanted to Japan's social and cultural terrain was given by Kotsuka Hisao, the successor to Yokota's chairmanship in 1992.[4] Kotsuka argued that the weakness of the JSP stems from its concentration on politics while neglecting other important spheres such as culture, education, and intellectual ideas; the conservatives' strength is derived from conservative values which pervade Japanese society. In contrast, the JSP was unable to create a "hegemonic alternative" or system of alternative values which could have taken root in civil society. Kotsuka advocated that the co-op movement should create a set of alternative values, lifestyles, and organizations to resist "conservative hegemonism."

The Kanagawa SC's efforts in organization-building, including the formation of NET, Workers' Collective, and Community Club, are ongoing processes in constructing an "alternative hegemony" at the place of residence.[5] By offering a wide range of goods, services, and social activities to local residents, the co-op hoped gradually to transform the outlook and values of its members and citizens in the neighborhood where its organizations exist. By casting its net of innocuous organizations the SC sought to rope in political support based on the social ties and a sense of community engendered by its values and institutions. In accordance with the Gramscian grand design, the organization since 1965 had been developing an alternative to the conventional route of capitalism's production, distribution, consumption, and disposal.[6] It invested in milk factories and food production resulting in the co-op becoming its own producer, distributor, and consumer of certain items. In the perceptions of its leaders, their provision of alternative products, services, lifestyle, values, and social circles is a grand strategy to create a "counter-hegemony" to the conservatives at the grassroots.

The co-op ideal

The SC group traces its ancestry to the English co-op first established by workers in 1844 in the town of Rochdale, near Manchester.[7] The Rochdale workers pooled their resources to make bulk purchases of consumer goods in order to obtain a better deal and to avoid being exploited by rapacious merchants. The Rochdale Co-op's set of principles has been codified in Japan's Co-op Law. These principles include open membership, democratic control of the co-op by ordinary members, and the organization's role to educate and promote the economic and cultural well-being of its members.

According to one account, Japan's first co-op was established in Kobe city in 1921.[8] The co-op movement soon spread throughout pre-war Japan but was subjected to government repression during the war years because of its Leftist orientation. Some of the co-op activists were communist sympathizers who believed that improving the livelihood of the workers was an extension of the class struggle against capitalism. Left-leaning co-op organizers were incarcerated during the war years.[9] However, Japan's defeat by the U.S. in 1945 ushered in a far more democratic and favorable milieu in which the co-op movement could flourish.

The SC group takes a serious view of its mission to educate and improve the lifestyle of its members, a principle enshrined in the Co-op Law. It refuses to produce what is merely profitable. Instead, the organization produces only what it considers good for its members' health and well-being.[10] It advocates a transformation of members' lifestyles and does not restrict its activities to the collective purchasing and distribution of food. After launching the natural soap movement, at least 90 percent of its members were converted from the use of synthetic soap to natural soap.[11] Initially, many members joined the SC simply to obtain food items rather than intending to participate in social movements.[12] Nevertheless, many members were subsequently socialized by the organization and were drawn gradually into its social networks and social movement activities (Table 7.1). Inglehart's theory of value change assumes that the transformation of political culture in advanced industrial democracies leads to greater democratic participation, social movements, and Green parties. The case study

Table 7.1 SC's impact on members' political interest and participation

	Before joining SC	After joining SC	Change
Interest in politics	42.7%	63.9%	+21.2%
Participation in local movements	31.0%	40.2%	+9.2%

Source: Seikatsu Kurabu Rengō Shōhi Iinkai, *Shōhi seikatsu kenkyūkai hōkokusho*, p. 17.

shows that the causal chain also moves in the opposite direction: participation in social movements may lead to a transformation of values.

In its newsletters, members are kept informed about environmental issues and NET activities. The group has taken the co-op ideal of lifestyle transformation one step further. Instead of limiting its educational role to just members, the SC tries to promote desirable values and habits among the general public too. One attempt to change the outlook of local residents is to promote NET in local politics and politicize pet themes like safe soap and the recycling of rubbish. Mass consciousness is raised by, among other things, disseminating information about SC and NET activities in the mass media, involvement in election campaigns, legislative activities of its assembly women, and daily organizational activities at the local level.

The group is also influenced by intellectual trends in the international co-op movement. The International Co-operative Alliance (ICA), a forum for the co-ops from different countries, initiated a study at the 1980 ICA Congress in Moscow to analyze the movement's future role. Dr A. F. Laidlaw's paper "Co-operatives in the Year 2000" is quoted at great length in Yokota's book.[13] The paper argues that co-ops should create a different socio-economic order rather than be assimilated by industrial society. First, workers' collectives should be promoted as the basic structure of a new kind of industrial democracy where workers are owners as well as employees. Second, the co-op should strive to build village communities in the cities centered around workers' collectives:

> The general objective should be to help create an identifiable community served by many types of co-operative organizations: housing, savings and credit, medical services, food and everyday household needs, day-care, baby-sitting services and nursery schools. . . . In addition to the various departments of a well-developed consumers' society such as restaurants and funeral services, there could be a variety of workers' co-operatives, for example, repair service for household appliances, bakery, barber shop and hairdressing parlor, shoe repair, dry-cleaning and auto repair. Thus many co-operators in the area would be engaged as producers or workers as well as consumers.[14]

The idea of a co-op acting as an agent of socio-economic transformation dovetails with Gramsci's concept of hegemony. The common ideological thread is the creation of an alternative to the established order. The Kanagawa SC is setting the pace within the group in promoting the growth of workers' collectives. If it were to introduce funeral services in the future, the co-op would become an organization that provides cradle to grave services for its members.[15]

While top leaders may speak about the concept of hegemony, many ordinary SC members are unfamiliar with the term. The typical member obtains most of her information from the mainstream newspapers.[16] Since Gramscian terminology does not usually appear in Japanese newspapers, the average member is probably unfamiliar with the idea of hegemony. In its written form, the term "hegemony" is transcribed into *katakana*, a script used for foreign words imported into Japan. Some of the ordinary members who are aware of the term dislike the word because it sounds alien and intimidating.[17] One thoughtful member who reflected on the concept said that any form of "hegemony" is not good, implying that even an alternative "hegemony" in its extreme carries the potential for totalitarianism – the exchange of one form of domination for another.[18] Rather than "hegemony," the term "alternative" goes down much better among members.

The NET assembly woman: citizen's messenger and agent

According to Yokota, depot (SC's chain of supermarkets), workers collectives and NET assembly women form a triangular strategy to attain an alternative "hegemony" in the neighborhood.[19] Thus, NET's involvement in politics is merely one component in a grand strategy to secure local support. To distinguish the NET assembly women from the politicians of the establishment parties, the group adopts a special terminology, *dairinin*, to refer to the NET assembly women. The term *dairinin* has different nuances: a representative, an agent, or a messenger.[20] The concept of a *dairinin* was first formulated by Iwane in March 1977 when he urged members to run for political office.[21] The *dairinin* is supposed to represent citizens who are concerned about various issues of daily living rather than the interests of production.[22]

In theory, the agent's status is no higher than an ordinary co-op or NET member. To maintain a sense of egalitarianism between the agent and the citizen, NET assembly women decline to be called *sensei* (teacher), an honorific term in Japan reserved for politicians and professionals such as lawyers and doctors. With the exception of the JCP and NET, all politicians from the established parties are addressed as *sensei*. Moreover, NET assembly women do not pin the assembly member's special badges on their lapels to set themselves apart from the citizens. In reality, most NET assembly women are not ordinary members. They were typically local leaders in various SC grassroots activities before they were drafted into electoral politics.

SC organization and power

Organization-building, the expansion of membership, and winning seats in local assemblies fall within the framework of constructing a local "hegemony." When NET made its gains in the 1987 Local Elections, it was the outcome of the SC's organization-building over a span of 22 years.[23] From its humble origins in 1965 with only 200 members in Tokyo's Setagaya ward, the co-op has rapidly expanded to 13 prefectures with a membership of 246,696 households by 1997 (Table 7.2). In terms of membership size (Table 7.3) and sales turnover (Table 7.4), the SC has made it to the top 10 out of 669 co-ops in Japan. Although a few co-ops are larger, their memberships are not predominantly based on the tightly knitted *han* structure, as in the case of the SC, but on members making individual purchases from co-op stores. The average figure for *han* participation among Japan's co-ops was 45.5 percent in 1990.[24] In contrast, 91.9 percent of SC members belong to a *han*.[25] What the co-op lacks in quantity, it makes up for in the quality of its members' participation in SC activities (Table 7.5). Among Japan's co-ops, the SC is second to none when it comes to political activism and involvement in social movements.

Table 7.2 Regional SC: size and business turnover (1997)

Region	Membership	Annual turnover (¥10,000)	Monthly purchases per family (¥)	No. of Staff
Tokyo	56,741	2,040,851	30,285	255
Kanagawa SC group	47,739	1,836,435	31,972	243
Welfare Club	8,792	194,030	19,915	25
Community Club	17,304	462,959	22,827	32
Chiba	30,978	916,337	25,148	130
Saitama	25,220	902,640	29,843	91
Nagano	14,040	387,140	23,392	47
Hokkaidō	13,215	341,025	21,751	48
Miyagi*	8,387	220,483	20,791	29
Aichi	6,872	171,579	21,867	26
Ibaraki	4,168	118,499	23,215	14
Yamanashi	3,926	95,346	20,605	12
Shizuoka	3,910	102,100	20,906	16
Tochigi	2,634	61,745	20,560	11
Iwate	2,320	48,388	17,522	10
Total: SC Group	246,696	7,899,557	26,895	989

Source: Seikatsu Kurabu, *Seikatsu kurabu gurūpu: 1997*, p. 4.

Note:

* Although it became part of the SC group in 1997, the Sendai Kyōdō Kōnyū Kai has retained its name rather than call itself the Miyagi SC.

Table 7.3 Japan's top ten co-ops (1990)

Ranking	Co-op	Membership size
1	Co-op Kobe	1,005,439
2	Co-op Kanagawa	811,823
3	Co-op Sapporo	673,113
4	Tokyo Citizen Co-op	401,108
5	Miyagi Co-op	312,111
6	Kyoto Co-op	304,921
7	Saitama Co-op	293,665
8	F Co-op	258,139
9	**SC**	**204,945**
10	Osaka Izumi Co-op	198,674

Sources: JCCU, *Co-Op Facts and Figures: 1990*, and Seikatsu Kurabu, *Seikatsu kurabu: 1991*, p. 2.

Table 7.4 Sales turnover (1991)

Ranking	Group	Turnover (¥ Million)
1	Co-op Kobe	327,880
2	Co-op Sapporo	149,413
3	Co-op Kanagawa	140,799
4	Tokyo Citizen Co-op	88,068
5	Saitama Co-op	71,995
6	Miyagi Co-op	68,664
7	Toyota Co-op	65,969
8	**SC**	**60,487**
9	Kyoto Co-op	59,085
10	F Co-op	58,232

Sources: JCCU, *Co-Op Facts and Figures: 1990*, and Seikatsu Kurabu, *Seikatsu kurabu: 1991*, p. 2.

Kanagawa SC's organizational structure

The organizational cornerstone is the *han* (Figure 7.1). The typical *han* comprises six to eight members who meet regularly to order and distribute food and household items. Through constant interaction, friendships are often forged in the *han*. Taking advantage of the *han*'s social bond, the co-op can use the *han* as a conveyer belt to disseminate information and to obtain feedback. About 125 *han* or 1,000 families form a branch. The branch was also the training and testing ground for many future NET assembly women where they gained experience and recognition before they were nominated to run for elections. The branches are grouped into nine regional blocks. Since a substantial number of members stay in Yokohama and Kawasaki, they are organized into four blocks in Yokohama and two in Kawasaki. The block has a unique social movement division (Figure 7.2). Its mission of not

Table 7.5 Participation in the SC's activities (percent)

Activity type	
"Soft" Activities	
Lectures and study sessions	44.7
SC Producers-consumers festival	35.8
Membership drives	33.2
Movies and dramas	17.2
Bazaar	17.1
Tour of producers' farms and factories	11.0
Social Movements	
Natural soap movement	16.3
Recycle movement	11.7
NET election campaign	9.0
Peace movement	5.9

Source: Seikatsu kurabu rengō shōhi iinkai, *Shōhi seikatsu kenkyūkai hōkokusho*, 1991, p. 46.

Note:
N = 2,209 (Multiple answers)

being limited to collective food purchases is institutionalized by the social movement division's establishment. Some of its activities include natural soap campaigns, recycling and anti-nuclear activities. The blocks are then linked to the Kanagawa SC headquarters in Kōhoku ward, Yokohama which in turn is connected to the SC Federation in Setagaya ward, Tokyo.

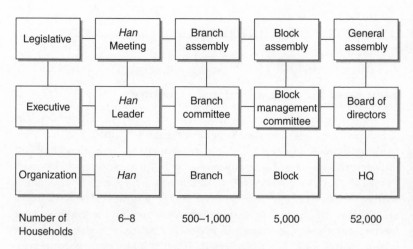

Figure 7.1 Kanagawa SC and organization structure.
Source: Seikatsu kurabu seikatsu kyōdō kumiai, *Orutanatibu: Seikatsu kurabu kanagawa 20 nen no ayumi*, 1991, p. 140 and Seikatsu Club Consumer's Co-operative, *Facts and Figures 1993*. A pamphlet in English.

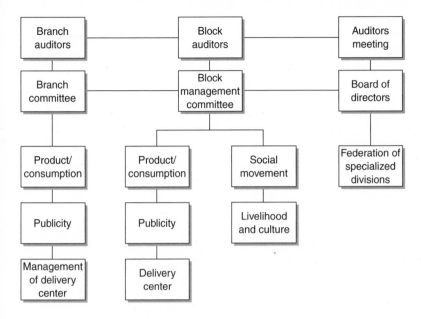

Figure 7.2 SC's specialized divisions.
Source: Seikatsu kurabu seikatsu kyōdō kumiai, *Orutanatibu: seikatsu kurabu kanagawa 20 nen no ayumi*, 1991, p. 143.

Kanagawa SC: Organization building toward a "local hegemony"

Within the group, Kanagawa SC is at the vanguard of organization building to meet the anticipated changes in Japanese society, especially declining numbers of housewives and the greying of Japan. According to the co-op, in order to create a "local hegemony," it is necessary to organize at least ten percent of the total households within the ward.[26] Thus far, Kanagawa SC has succeeded in recruiting only three percent of the prefecture's households in areas where it has an organizational presence.[27] Since it cannot rely on the *han* to break through the three percent barrier, it has to establish new organizations to capture other social groups especially women working outside the home, the elderly, and the physically disabled. If the co-op limits itself to the *han*, it will be restricted to only a social group comprising housewives in their thirties and forties.

It is not inevitable that an organization becomes a captive of its social base because an imaginative leadership can win over new social bases of support. Yokota envisages a group of organizations to spearhead the creation of a "local hegemony" – community clubs, workers' collectives, welfare clubs, an Earth Tree Club, an Ecology and Third World Club, livelihood halls, delivery centers and a male residents' club. Through the establishment of new organizations, the co-op plans to attract working women, senior citizens and even salary men to broaden its bases of social support beyond the urban housewives. Thus, social movements and New Politics parties are not always mere reflections of social bases; they may create new bases of social support.

Community club

Also known as the depot or store, a community club caters to those who are unable or unwilling to join the *han*. Since certain fresh groceries and perishable foodstuffs such as bread, fish, and vegetables cannot be obtained through the *han*, the depot may attract residents who wish to obtain such food. Busy women who work outside the home and cannot join the *han* may find it convenient to use the depot. When the idea of a chain of SC depot was first floated, many members opposed the scheme on the following grounds: the co-op lacks the managerial expertise to run a chain of stores; it is expensive to buy land and build depots in metropolitan Japan; personnel and overhead costs would be incurred; and the fear that depot members will lack the *han*'s social cohesion. There were worries that, unlike the *han*'s active participants, depot members will become passive customers no different from the shoppers of commercial supermarkets. The critics feared that depot members might not participate in social movements and thus negate the very reason the SC was established in the first place.[28] Nevertheless, by 1997 a string of 18 depots had been established in Kanagawa.

To prevent depot members from becoming passive customers, it is mandatory for ordinary members to serve at the depot at least three times a year.[29] Newsletters and invitations to SC activities are also sent to members. Applicants are limited to residents staying within a radius of 700 meters from the depot in order to create a thicker density and rapport among its members. Yokota saw the depot as the creation of an alternative urban community that will rival the *chōnaikai* or neighborhood associations often associated with conservative politicians.[30] The target is to organize 40 percent of the total households within the radius of 700 meters.[31] Some depots have reported an organizational rate of 30 percent within their vicinity.

Workers' collectives and the Welfare Club

These are enterprises which allow women workers to be their own bosses.[32] By helping women to manage their own enterprise, workers' collectives help to improve economic and social conditions, for women cannot be truly independent unless they attain economic power. They offer an impressive range of services such as wedding consultation, housing construction, travel, medical services, child care, and welfare for the elderly (Table 7.6).

After leaving his post as Kanagawa SC Director in 1992, Yokota became the Chairman of the Welfare Club. In the long run, the Welfare Club may enjoy strong growth given that the greying of Japan will become a serious social problem.[33] For the convenience of women with babies, the elderly, and the physically disabled who have difficulties leaving their houses, the Welfare Club offers individual home delivery services for co-op products. Delivery persons will enquire about the well-being of members, engage in conversation, and help to alleviate their loneliness. Other services include day care services for the elderly and taxi services for the disabled. The Welfare Club also intends to set up homes for the elderly in the near future.

Table 7.6 Kanagawa SC's workers' collectives

Workers' collective (Kanagawa)	No. of enterprises	No. of workers
Depot	3	295
Welfare services	3	200
Medical	4	23
Cleaning services	3	13
Restaurants	1	8
Bakery	1	18
Take away food service	1	14
Ice cream parlors	1	9
Handicraft shop	1	3
Recycle enterprises	4	23
Art studios and exhibition	7	30
Housework and cleaning services	15	964
Rehabilitation for the old	1	7
Cooking classes	1	8
Community college	1	53
Child care	1	5
Editing and publishing	3	17
Video shop	1	5
Soap factory	1	7
Third world handicraft center	1	7
Translation and interpretation services	1	33
Total	56	1,748

Source: Seikatsu Kurabu, *Seikatsu kurabu gurūpu: 1992*, pp. 17–18.

Livelihood halls, delivery centers and other SC organizations

Many of the workers' collectives and welfare services are located in the SC's "livelihood halls."[34] These halls function like community centers where members can gather for meetings and events, and during the local elections the halls were used for political rallies. Delivery centers are facilities where products are stored for distribution. Auditoriums and guest rooms are also available at the centers, making them convenient places for members to organize their activities.

The Earth Tree Club espouses human rights, peace, democracy, and environmental protection as its themes. It seeks to organize residents in Kanagawa who are concerned about global issues. The Earth Tree Club adopts a North–South paradigm in international relations and expresses solidarity with the South. It advocates the protection of Third World's rainforests and criticizes Japan for importing 90 percent of the world's tropical timber products while having less than two percent of the world's population. The club sponsors people-to-people aid to selected Third World countries mired in poverty, such as helping pre-school children struggling in the slums of the Philippines. The Earth Tree Club has a membership of 2,000.

The only non-female SC organization is the oddly named Jaoh Club, a phonetic inversion of the word *oyaji*, or parent in Japanese.[35] The members are mostly members' husbands and retirees. The aim is to encourage men to be more concerned with their places of residence rather than to be totally immersed in their workplace. Started in 1991, it has a membership of only 50 men. The small number of men directly affiliated with the SC reveals the difficulties faced by the organization in its attempts to broaden its social base.

Conclusion

Strong male leadership, grassroots organizations, a mobilizing ideology, a strategic outlook to develop alternative institutions, and the cultivation of social networks are some factors that contributed to the SC's growth. Although the co-op proclaims a doctrine of egalitarianism and direct participation in decision-making by ordinary citizens, its organization and ideology are essentially shaped by founding fathers. The case study shows that despite the idealism of direct democracy and suspicion of organization, with its attendant hierarchy, by social movement activists, organizations, oligarchies, and leadership are as necessary in a post-industrial society as in an industrial society. The nurturing of social networks in the *han* and other sister organizations as an approach to garner political support fits in well with the cultural milieu of Japan, but the SC and NET will find it difficult appealing to urban residents outside its social webs. Given the proclivity of Japanese society in stressing social bonds even in a post-industrial society, it is difficult for the Greens to win political support purely on policy appeals. Unlike the West European Greens, top SC leaders are still wedded to Gramscian ideology, a variant of Marxism. Their reluctance to scuttle such ideological baggage from the 1960s suggests that the Japanese Greens are more doctrinaire than their Western counterparts. Such attachment to outmoded ideology may inhibit them from winning greater support from voters beyond the social webs of the SC.

8   The Network Movement: a Japanese Green party?

No significant Green parties have arisen in post-industrial Japan despite changes to the structures and values of Japanese society. That there are no significant Green parties can be explained in two ways. First, there are no Green parties that have made a substantial electoral impact. In the case of Japan, none won seats at the national level; unlike the European Greens, the Network Movement (NET) won seats only at the local level. Second, the dearth of a Green party may be viewed as the absence of a party having the characteristics of a New Politics party. A party cannot be regarded as a genuine New Politics party even if it has won elections on a Green label but failed to display fully Green characteristics. If NET were a perfect New Politics party, we would expect it to exhibit the following features:

1   an egalitarian organization whose members imbibe a participatory culture;
2   a female-led organization;[1]
3   amateurish activists motivated by purposive rather than material incentives;
4   great stress on Green issues rather than a personality-centric organization which revolves around the distribution of patronage;
5   clean politics instead of money politics; and
6   adoption of a strategy of representing NET's constituency, policies, and values instead of vote maximization at the expense of its ideals.

NET qualifies as a *quasi*-New Politics party because it manifests only some of the characteristics that are associated with New Politics.[2] Thus, it is difficult for the party to secure the support of post-materialists who are outside the social networks of the SC and *kōenkai* of its candidates. To verify this assertion, we shall examine its organizational principles and practices to highlight the discrepancy between the ideals of direct participation and the reality of oligarchic control. Many NET candidates have adopted personality-centric *kōenkai* (candidate support organizations) as their vehicle of mobilization even though this is an approach usually associated with Old Politics in Japan. Ironically, a movement that espouses Green values has conformed to Japanese political norms even in post-industrial Japan. These norms by stress on social networks based on personal ties rather than a concentration on policy appeals. Moreover, oligarchic structures and practices seem unavoidable once a movement embarks on electoral competition, regardless of its post-modern origins and aspirations.

NET's organizational principles

NET is unique among the Japanese political parties. The party imposes term limits on its assembly women. Two terms are imposed in the case of Kanagawa NET while three terms are the norm for Chiba and Tokyo NET.[3] Incumbents are denied party endorsement if they run again after their terms are up. This rotation system was inspired by the German Green Party to promote a systematic flow of amateurs into legislative politics and to prevent the emergence of professional politicians within its ranks, which also ensures that the idiosyncrasies of an entrenched personality cannot dominate the organization.[4] Even though the rotation system has been modified or abandoned by the German Greens, NET thus far has maintained a fidelity to term limits.[5] Another feature patterned after the German Greens is the requirement that its assembly women must surrender their paychecks to the party in exchange for a stipend from NET.[6]

Its assembly women are not motivated by material incentives to participate in politics for they do not retain their salaries or form lucrative ties with established interest groups. They can abide by this unique scheme without incurring financial hardships because they are affluent housewives married to high-income (Table 8.1), well-educated, top-ranking salary men (Table 8.2). The Japanese industrial structure whereby husbands are typically breadwinners and spouses are housewives has the unintended consequence of facilitating the transplant of an ideal from the German Greens – the control of a representative's pay by the party – to Japan. Ironically, the gender inequality in Japan's industrial structure that shuts out women from lifetime employment after childbirth has created a leisured class of housewives who can stake a claim for greater gender representation in politics.

With the accumulated reserves from its assembly women, NET sponsors the re-election campaigns of its incumbents and supports new candidates in other districts to boost its influence in local assemblies. With a war chest, it

Table 8.1 Annual household income of NET assembly women before they were first elected

Income (million ¥)	No. of assembly women	Percent
Below 3	3	4.9
3–3.9	2	3.3
4–4.9	0	0
5–5.9	8	13.1
6–6.9	9	14.8
7–7.9	5	8.2
8–8.9	13	21.3
9–9.9	4	6.6
10–15	12	19.7
Above 15	2	3.3
Don't know	3	4.9
Total	61	100.0

Source: 1992 nation-wide questionnaire survey of NET assembly women by author (1992 NET Survey for short). The questionnaire was sent to all 79 NET assembly women and 66 responded. Subsequent tables on the NET assembly women and their views are derived from this survey unless otherwise stated.

Table 8.2 Occupation of NET assembly women's husbands

Occupation	No	Percent
Salaried		
Managers (above Section Chief level)	33	53.2
Professionals (doctors, lawyers, etc.)	10	16.1
Administrators	4	6.5
Salesmen and retailers	2	3.2
Self-employed		
Agriculture, shopkeepers	1	1.6
Professionals (doctors, lawyers, etc.)	2	3.2
Others	10	16.1
Total	62	100

also subsidizes regular activities in non-election years such as publications, seminars, and recycling shops to propagate its beliefs. There are two benefits to its candidates' reliance on party funds. First, candidates need not be obsessed with fundraising and can concentrate on policy studies and grassroots activities. Second, NET has a clean image since its candidates, assured of financial aid from the party, are not tempted to raise money through shady undertakings.

Party organizations

Regional NETs are loosely tied together through the informal links between SC's founding fathers, annual national symposiums for assembly women, and a liaison office, the Social Movement Center in Tokyo. The center monitors and publishes periodicals on regional NET activities.[7] NETs in the prefectures of Tokyo, Chiba, Saitama, Kanagawa, Nagano, Fukuoka, Iwate, Yamanashi, and Hokkaidō operate independently of each other because of a desire to avoid centralization of power.[8] Local autonomy also stems from the independent inceptions of their parent organization, the regional SCs. Since the clubs in various prefectures and the Green Co-op in Fukuoka are established by different sets of leaders, their offspring have also followed the independent courses of their parent organizations. There are variations in the organizational structures of regional NETs. Kanagawa NET is a union with a headquarters (HQ), five blocks, and 36 branches; Tokyo NET is a federation of loosely tied units; Chiba NET has independent local organizations tenuously linked through a liaison office.[9]

A New Politics party will practice decentralization of power. In the case of NET, there is no powerful, centralizing agency in Tokyo; decision-making lies with regional organizations in different prefectures. Besides an ideological commitment to dispersion of power, its decentralization is also an indirect consequence of the position of Japan's legal regime toward the co-op movement. The MHW and the Co-op Law forbid co-ops to expand beyond prefectural boundaries. Hence, regional clubs are autonomous, even though they have established a SC federation in Tokyo. Created by different club leaders, regional NETs reflect the decentralized nature of their parent organizations that are confined to each prefecture by Japan's legal system.

Is NET a policy-oriented, egalitarian organization? In Kanagawa prefecture, NET is divided into five regional blocks. Each block comprises local NET organizations at the ward level. The blocks are linked together by a headquarters located in Yokohama city (Figure 8.1). The HQ is staffed by a office manager, two full-time paid women assistants, and other volunteers. There is a multiplicity of activities every day when various sub-committees gather to do their planning at the HQ (Figure 8.2). The management committee of Kanagawa NET comprises a mix of assembly women and local leaders who do not hold public office. There is a high annual turnover of committee members to permit other local leaders opportunities to participate in the running of NET.[10]

All three levels (HQ, block, and ward) have policy-oriented divisions. NET members have ample opportunities to join sub-committees of their choice. Besides the regular sub-committees, local NETs at the wards organize seminars, movies, signature campaigns, questionnaire surveys, and

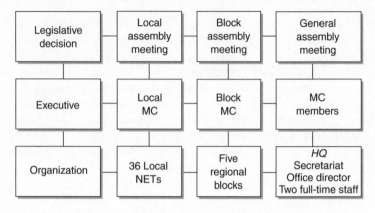

Figure 8.1 Kanagawa NET organization (branch, blocks and HQ).
Key: MC = management committee.
Source: Inaba Mitsuru, Office Manager, Kanagawa NET HQ.

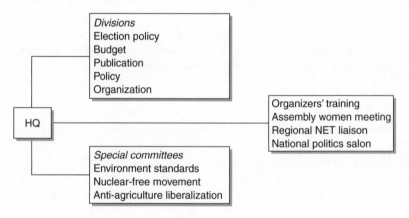

Figure 8.2 Kanagawa NET HQ.
Source: Inaba Mitsuru and *NET*, No. 85, August 1 1992, pp. 2–3.

mini forums (Figure 8.3). The last activity resembles New England town house meetings where citizens, friends, neighbors, and club members are invited to raise problems concerning the neighborhood. Mini forums promote political participation by ordinary citizens and are also avenues for the local NETs to propagate their messages and win political support, even in non-election years.

The style of NET meetings is highly informal; NET assembly women and ordinary members interact on the same social level. NET assembly women are not addressed as *sensei* (teacher), the customary term of respect reserved

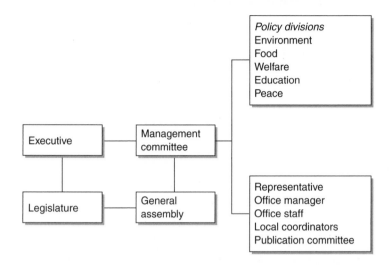

Figure 8.3 NET's grassroots organization in Midori ward, Yokohama City.
Source: Mukaeda Eiko, NET assembly woman, Midori ward, Yokohama.

for politicians and distinguished professionals. Hierarchical and honorific language is avoided between the assembly women and ordinary members.[11]

NET and *kōenkai*

Although NET has policy-centric organizations down to the ward level, many of its assembly women possess a second organization, *kōenkai* (Table 8.3). The *kōenkai* of its assembly women share certain similarities with those of the established politicians. Each *kōenkai* is a personality-centric organization which helps a politician get elected and in exchange provides services and promotes a sense of belonging among its members. Some assembly women have *kōenkai* as a formal organization with a membership list, annual meetings, newsletters, and regular activities. However, variations are found in the character of their *kōenkai*. At one extreme the *kōenkai* is a "fan club" of the assembly women.[12] One assembly woman intimated that the votes of her *kōenkai* will not be automatically transferred to her successor since the members are personally loyal to her and not to NET.[13] She also pointed out that her *kōenkai* is more active than the local party organization. At the other extreme are policy-centric *kōenkai* of some assembly women. When their term limits are due, their *kōenkai* members will then swing their support behind the next candidate. The typical NET *kōenkai* is a personalistic structure (Table 8.4) with a range of activities (Table 8.5). Unlike the

Table 8.3 NET assembly women and *kōenkai*

Prefecture	*Have* kōenkai	*No* kōenkai
Saitama	0	1
Nagano	1	0
Hokkaidō	4	0
Chiba	7	3
Tokyo	8	13
Fukuoka	0	3
Kanagawa	26	0
Total	46	20
Percent	69.7	30.3

Note:
N = 66

Table 8.4 Character of NET assembly women's *kōenkai*

Is your kōenkai *a personal candidate support organization?*	*No*	*Percent*
Yes	30	66.7
No	15	33.3

Note:
N = 45

Table 8.5 The activities of NET assembly women's *kōenkai*

Activities	*No. of assembly women*
Travel	1
Study groups	10
Sports meet	0
New Year Party	9
End of year party	4
Grape-gathering outing	2
Flower viewing	1
Distribution of representatives' pamphlets to ward households	27
Others	13

Note:
N = 46 (multiple answers)

established parties, NET assembly women's *kōenkai* solicit financial contributions from members and do not provide free services and patronage to participants.

The divergence in organizational structures and whether *kōenkai* is dor-

Table 8.6 Status of *kōenkai* after elections

Regional NET	Active	Inactive
Tokyo	1	7
Kanagawa	18	7
Chiba	2	5
Hokkaidō	2	2
Nagano	1	0
Fukuoka	0	0
Saitama	0	0
Total	25	21
Percent	54.3	45.7

Note:
N = 46

mant after the election (Table 8.6) is partly the result of the decentralized nature of NET leadership. In Kanagawa, the regional leadership actively encourages candidates to bolster their party with a second organization, the *kōenkai*.[14] In Tokyo and Fukuoka NETs, the top leaders have reservations about *kōenkai* because of the fear that personality-centric *kōenkai* may displace policy-centric party organizations.[15] The puzzle of regional variations in organizational structure is explained as follows: in the city elections of Kanagawa prefecture, a candidate running in Yokohama or Kawasaki needs around 7,000 votes to get elected. Because the margin to win election is higher in Kanagawa, candidates cannot rely merely on the SC and NET. They need a second organization, *kōenkai*, to win elections. In the ward elections of Tokyo, as few as 2,000 votes may be sufficient for a candidate to be elected. Since fewer votes are needed, the candidate can dispense with *kōenkai* because the SC and NET can mobilize enough votes.[16] However, such an argument is not entirely persuasive. In the smaller cities and villages of Kanagawa, NET assembly women have adopted a *kōenkai* approach even though they need as few as 1,000 votes to get elected.[17] Moreover, both Tokyo and Kanagawa are neighboring prefectures experiencing urbanization that disrupts the traditional community and inhibits the growth of *kōenkai* based on quasi-familial ties. The choice of a *kōenkai* approach is also influenced by leadership outlook; while Tokyo NET is lukewarm toward *kōenkai*, Kanagawa NET has aggressively promoted *kōenkai*.

Even though Kanagawa NET has adopted a pragmatic approach to winning more seats by utilizing *kōenkai*, it is ambivalent toward *kōenkai*. Occasionally, it warned that *kōenkai* of assembly women should not degenerate into personalistic organizations. Discussions were held to study how party organizations and *kōenkai* could complement each other.[18]

Nevertheless, the tension between the two organizations remains. Kanagawa NET adopts a dual organizational approach to win more votes in order to promote its Green agenda, but the reliance on a personality-centric organization has the danger of diluting policy issues in the party's campaigning style.

NET members' participation at the grassroots

Is NET a participatory organization? Its meetings and activities at the ward, city, or prefectural level are well publicized in newsletters and these are open to ordinary members. Although the party encourages the active participation of members, only a minority of members are involved in grassroots activities beyond the election campaign (Table 8.7). This reluctance to be actively involved in grassroots activities is because the top priority of many members is their family and other private pursuits rather than local politics. While many are willing to help during the short election campaign, few are willing to shoulder responsibilities on a regular basis during non-election years. Undoubtedly, most club and NET members subscribe to post-material values, but post-materialists do not necessarily have a higher propensity to directly participate in politics even if they believe that such actions are highly desirable. There is a gap between values and action that must be bridged by mobilization. That NET has difficulties trying to woo greater participation from its members should not come as a surprise. Even the German Green Party fails to attract greater participation among its members, especially women; posts in the German Green Party that are allocated to women on a quota system often go unfilled.[19]

Table 8.7 Rate of participation among NET members

Regional NET	A Total no. of members	B Participation in elections	B/A (%)	C Very active in daily NET activities	C/A (%)
Kanagawa	1991	1361	68.4	452	21.8
Fukuoka	170	90	52.9	35	20.6
Tokyo	984	682	69.3	263	26.7
Chiba	1140	435	38.2	73	6.4
Hokkaidō	191	191	100	35	18.3
Nagano	3	3	100	3	100
Saitama	110	100	90.9	15	13.6
Total	4589	2862	62.4	876	19.1

Note:
N = 66

The selection of candidates: how open?

We expect ordinary members to have a say in the nomination process if it is indeed a New Politics party. Moreover, any committed member should be eligible to run as a candidate. The criteria for a suitable candidate are: the nominee must be a woman, a track record of participation in club activities and other social movements, the ability to represent the viewpoints of the SC and NET, no opposition from the candidate's husband to her quest for public service, and someone who can devote her time wholeheartedly as the citizens' representative.[20] As a result of the screening process, most of the candidates have held top posts as the club's Board of Directors or as Chairwoman of the local SC branch (Table 8.8). They are usually in their late thirties and forties and therefore no longer need to nurse babies or tend to young children. Some of them have also had experience in social movements before they joined the co-op (Table 8.9). Thus, not any member can become a candidate; there is an obvious preference for a woman with a proven record before she is co-opted to run for elections.

How are candidates nominated? Names are informally solicited among active co-op and party members; there are no formal meetings where all members at the ward gather together to pick their candidate. Instead, recommendations are submitted to a small selection committee comprising NET and SC representatives. After interviewing a number of potential candidates, the committee selects a suitable candidate. In other cases, the nomination comes solely from the party's initiative while SC representatives in the screening process exercise a veto power. Despite the party's desire to promote a participatory form of politics, its candidate selection process does precisely the opposite. The selection committee comprises a small group of local leaders who often hand-pick one of their own numbers to run. The

Table 8.8 SC and Green Co-op posts held by NET assembly women

Posts	No.	Percent
Board of Directors	23	34.8
Auditor	7	10.6
Chairwoman of co-op branch	32	48.5
Committee member of co-op branch	33	50
Head of consumption section	13	19.7
Member of consumption section	8	12.1
Professional SC/Green co-op worker	3	4.5
Others	24	36.4
Not held any co-op posts	6	9.1

Note:
N = 66 (multiple answers)

Table 8.9 Experiences in social movements prior to being elected

Social movement activities	No.	Percent
1960 Anti-U.S.–Japan Security Treaty demonstrations	3	4.5
1970 Anti-U.S.–Japan Security Treaty demonstrations	7	10.6
Anti-Vietnam War demonstrations	11	16.7
Anti-nuclear movements	8	12.1
Student activism	12	18.9
Anti-pollution citizens' movements	9	13.6
Women's liberation	5	7.6
Other *non*-co-op related activities	35	53
No prior experiences	20	30.5

Note:
N = 66 (multiple answers)

selection of candidates by a small circle of leaders appears odd given NET's rhetoric in favor of direct democracy.

Power distribution between the sexes

NET's formal leadership comprises women. In reality, the founding fathers of the regional SCs wield disproportionate influence on the organization. The first assembly woman supported by the Kanagawa SC, Terada Etsuko, was hand-picked by Yokota to run as a candidate. After her election, Terada and two SC male workers set up an organization distinct from the co-op: the Kanagawa NET. She then became its representative. Terada made the following argument: during the early years there were suspicions over the preponderance of male influence on the party, but such misgivings have subsequently died down. She asserts: "NET is not a male's puppet. Initially, members have to learn from the SC males because of the women's unfamiliarity with electoral politics but as members increasingly gain in experience and confidence, women have taken control of the organization."[21] A top SC advisor, Andō Jinbei, remarked: "The power distribution between men and women in the SC is fifty–fifty. But power is shifting toward the women."[22] In reality, men exert disproportionate influence despite their small numbers. The paradox of a female co-op and political party led by males lies in the SC's origins. Since the co-op was established by males, the founding fathers retain substantial prestige among its members and they remain the designers of organization, ideology, and grand strategy.[23]

Male SC leaders and women office holders play different roles in NET. The men tend to propound on the historical and structural causes of social movements in Japan, preach abstract principles of direct participation, and plot the long-term strategic options for both the SC and party; women members tend to confine themselves to issues of motherhood[24] and concrete local problems, especially rubbish collection, soap contamination, and recycling activities.[25] Few women within both parent and child organizations have yet boldly to exercise their leadership on ideological, organizational, and strategic issues beyond the limitations of their immediate neighborhood. Male dominance is perpetuated by the SC's masculine staff structure; positions above section chief level are usually occupied by males as a result of the Japanese seniority system. When a co-op junior staff member is recruited, he usually begins at the bottom of the ladder as a delivery worker. Job responsibilities involve driving a truck and carrying heavy household items to the rendezvous for the *han*. Few women find the job of an SC worker attractive because it is physically taxing to lift heavy items.[26] After a worker gains experience as a delivery worker and learns the operation of the *han*, he will subsequently be promoted. It is difficult to promote a woman to the post of a division chief and let her leapfrog over her male seniors if she has not chalked up years of experience in the co-op's service. Even though the organization is committed to a social movement to redefine the status quo, it has not escape from Japanese social norms of promotion by experience and seniority.

The lack of women leaders among the SC's professional structure is also the outcome of Japan's industrial structure whereby the husband is a corporate warrior while the wife minds the home.[27] It is not easy for the co-op to attract women to work after marriage or child birth and attain the necessary years of experience and seniority. This is because of the social expectation that the wife will devote her time to the family rather than to her career. The SC is a multi-billion yen enterprise. Technical, managerial, planning, and accounting knowledge are needed to run the organization. Women who lack work experience due to the cultural imperative that mothers sacrifice their careers in Japan usually do not have sufficient technocratic skills to run the co-op. Despite the aspirations to create an egalitarian organization and civil society, the organization conforms to social norms in Japan to ensure its economic viability. If the co-op lacks sound management, its demise will concomitantly lead to NET's eclipse. Thus, the SC faces a dilemma: if it promotes women who lack managerial experience to the upper echelons for the sake of gender equality, it will lead to resentment among better-qualified or senior male workers and risk mismanagement of the economic enterprise; if it does not, the SC cannot claim to be an organization led by women.

Regional SCs each have a board of advisors that include former club leaders, academics, and social movement activists who advise both parent and child organizations on policies and electoral activities. In the case of the Kanagawa SC, with the sole exception of a retired woman activist, all board members are males.[28] Regional clubs' board of directors are overwhelmingly female; some of the posts of chairperson are occupied by women. It is intimated that these are mostly ceremonial and the role includes public relations with the press, public, and visitors. The person who usually leads the organization is the Special Director (*senmu riji*) (Table 8.10).

During election campaigns, professional SC workers (invariably males) are despatched to help local NETs by driving campaign vehicles and offering logistics support. In some cases the campaign strategist (*sanbō*) is a member of SC professional staff.[29] In the 1991 Local Elections, Yokota was present at various campaign offices to seek feedback and exhort campaign workers to strive for their best. Male SC leaders and advisors provided ideological and political training to candidates. Yokota and Yokoyama Keiji, a scholar on social movements in Japan, lectured NET candidates on a wide range of issues, including the functions of local assemblies and social movements, over a number of weeks prior to the local elections.[30] Periodically, Kanagawa assembly women would gather for discussions and pep talks by Yokota. Indeed, Yokota is the brain behind Kanagawa NET.

Until 1995, the office manager of the Kanagawa NET was Inaba Mitsuru, a male who worked at *Tōkyū* Railway Company (Yokota's former workplace), before he joined the SC.[31] Inaba was subsequently despatched from the SC to instil some expertise in the running of NET HQ. Besides keeping records, arranging meetings, and writing editorial articles for the party's newsletter, Inaba acted its press spokesman.[32] Why did a feminine organization lack a spokeswoman? The lame excuse given by NET is that, since Inaba was at the NET headquarters most of the time, it was convenient for him to talk to the press when they visit the HQ. Nevertheless, arrangements could be made to divert reporters to interview the representative of NET (an assembly woman) rather than the office manager. NET's dependence on a male spokesman signifies its lack of political maturity as a genuine women's organization.

Table 8.10 SC leadership and gender

Position	Male	Female
Chairperson	7	7
Special Director	9	1
Division Chief	18	4

Source: SC Group's Telephone Directory. (In addition, the 12 regional SCs, the Community Club and Welfare Club from Kanagawa are also included. Figures from the SC Federation HQ are excluded.)

When the party deals with outsiders such as labor unions and political parties, SC males act on its behalf. Top leaders from the SC and NET's office manager would negotiate with outsiders for political endorsement and organizational support.[33] Why were NET women at the periphery when NET had to interact with other organizations? The excuse offered was that NET housewives lack the experience of interacting with male unionists and socialists. Conversely, males from the established parties and unions may feel awkward negotiating with the NET women because they come from different social worlds. Top SC leaders can bridge the two worlds because of their past involvement in the JSP, trade unions, and social movements. If its assembly women lack the confidence, opportunities and the experience to deal with outsiders, it is difficult for the NET convincingly to portray itself as an autonomous, all-women party. Ordinary members are not consulted by the informal male leaders when they engage in high-level talks with outsiders. Those women who know – usually the formal female leadership – do not seem perturbed that male leaders are engaged in talks with outsiders without the knowledge or consent of ordinary members. There appears to be another division of labor of female activists and the informal male leadership. Activists appear to be happily engrossed in local politics and enjoy "autonomy" in their daily activities free from the interference of the informal male leadership. Similarly, the male leadership engages in grand politics and strategically steers NET in a preferred direction without the restraint of ordinary members.

This disregard for consultation has erupted in conflict between male SC leaders and a small minority of NET members.[34] Prior to the 1993 Prefectural Election in Tokyo, the NET organization in Suginami ward suffered a schism when an assembly woman and her supporters broke away over alleged manipulation of local NETs into an alliance with the JSP without prior consultation and consent from local party organizations. Critics of the unilateral action by SC male leaders to promote a Red–Green alliance were fearful that NET was being used to promote the JSP's fortunes. The top leader of Tokyo SC, Kōno Eiji, argued just the opposite. In order to promote NET's agenda, it is necessary to make use of the JSP since the party lacks adequate strength to go it alone in prefectural elections.[35] The means was an alignment with the JSP but the end was to further NET's position.

The débâcle of Tokyo NET over strategies and a lack of consultation highlighted a contradiction in regional NETs. In the quest to promote a Green agenda, informal male leaders circumvented the ordinary membership and contravened the expectation of consultation, egalitarianism, and the control of the organization by ordinary members. If the informal male leadership were to abstain and leave politics to women alone, the women might face difficulties getting elected due to a lack of electoral knowledge and a reluctance to enter arenas beyond the ward. Since the women are most concerned about neighborhood problems, they might be engrossed with parochial issues without making an impact at the prefectural or national level. There is a bifurcation of concerns between the informal male leaders and most female members. The women are most comfortable and concerned about the issues of motherhood and neighborhood while the men are trying to nudge them to play a larger role by forging alliances with other established parties to displace the LDP in the unfamiliar terrain of prefectural and national politics.

Its organizational principles (the rotation system and financial control of the assembly women's paychecks by the party) reflect the desire to be a participatory party. However, the rotation system is not applicable to the hidden, male leaders who are not formal party members; they are neither elected nor accountable to ordinary members. The gender relationship in SC and party is symbiotic; without the presence of the founding fathers, there would be neither SC nor NET. Without female participation, the male leaders will be unable to develop their political agenda. Yet the male–female partnership is an unequal one with the balance of power tilting toward the males.

Green issues

NET's pursuit of ecological issues has a style that is distinct from the Western European Green parties. While it pursues separation of rubbish, the banning of synthetic soap, is anti-nuclear power stations, advocates food free from radioactive contamination, and values ecological protection, this is done under the guise of traditional motherhood rather than feminism. The traditional role of a mother is used to justify and legitimize women's involvement in politics. By portraying themselves as concerned mothers out to protect the well-being of their families from environmental hazards, members can win sympathy from other housewives and encounter less resistance from those politicians and citizens who view politics as a male preserve. Although the role of women in Japanese politics has gained increasing acceptance, it is culturally more acceptable for women to campaign as concerned mothers rather than as radical feminists. Thus, NET has deftly used traditional norms of motherhood to promote a Green agenda.[36]

Few NET assembly women have prior experience in the feminist movement. Those with political experiences before their stint in the party were mostly involved in the anti-war movement, environmental, and citizens' movements. Limited attention is given to feminist issues in their grassroots activities after winning elections (Tables 8.11 and 8.12). The organization

Table 8.11 Issues enthusiastically pursued at grassroots level by local NETs

Issues	No.	Percent
Environment	62	93.9
Distribution of assembly women's reports to ward residents	60	90.9
Welfare	59	89.4
Study sessions	49	74.4
Questionnaire surveys	45	68.2
Children's education	41	62.1
Safe food	41	62.1
Pacifism	24	36.4
Anti-nuclear	22	33.4
Human rights	17	25.8
Recycle shops	17	25.8
Women's issues	**11**	**16.7**
Others	10	15.2

Note:
N = 66 (multiple answers)

Table 8.12 Active pursuit of women's issues by NET assembly women

Are they actively pursued?	No.	Percent
Yes	9	13.8
No	56	86.2

Note:
N = 65

sporadically speaks out on the discrimination against women. Regional NETs have criticized local bureaucrats for assigning only women employees to serve tea, and schools for placing male students first and female students last in the name list of the class.[37] Hokkaidō NET also took issue with the city of Sapporo for its financial subsidies to an annual festival and parade which glamorizes the traditional courtesans of that city.[38] It pointed out that traditions that exploit women should be rejected, even if the annual parades reap revenues for the city from tourists.

Attempting to attract more support from women voters in the 1995 Local Elections, Kanagawa NET issued a manifesto which included greater attention to gender issues. Eschewing gender confrontation, it advocated co-operation with like-minded males to end gender discrimination in Japan. Moreover, it called for the improvement to the working environment for women, including equality at the workplace, flexible labor hours, retraining programs for the female work-force, 24-hour childcare services, and paid leave for mothers to take care of their children.[39] Despite rhetoric about gender equality, especially during the elections, these issues are not a top priority for NET.

NET and clean politics

A clean image is an asset in the midst of rampant corruption among the major established parties. The party's ingenious way of fundraising without receiving a single yen from corporations and producers is probably the best claim to its status as a New Politics party.[40] NET can function on a shoestring budget because it taps the free labor provided by amateur housewives and the professional co-op staff during the election campaigns, and saves expenses by using SC delivery centers and depots as venues for its meetings and political rallies. Local NETs also rely on the compulsory savings from the salaries of incumbents, donations from individuals,[41] membership fees and, in certain cases, money from *kōenkai*. Other novel ways of fundraising include recycling shops, garage sales, and selling foodstuffs at bazaars.

A key reason why NET can avoid incurring huge political expenses is because it has a ready-made audience, the *han* of the SC. Politicians from the established parties have to sink enormous resources into building a patronage machine in order to woo an audience. SC members' support for the party is not based on patronage but shared values on ecology concerns and more importantly, the social networks within the *han*. Six months prior to the official election campaign, candidates attended numerous home meetings where they met SC and party members and their guests on a face-to-face basis. Armed with a membership list and addresses of SC members, NET candidates tried to visit the homes of all members in their respective districts to solicit support.

Strategic dilemma

Herbert Kitschelt theorizes that established parties will adopt a strategy of vote maximization with the objective of participating in government while Green parties will follow a strategy of representing their core constituency.[42] The assumption is that Green parties ascribe greater importance to their principles and policies than the imperative of winning votes at the expense of their ideological soul. The debate about the appropriate strategy for NET was held between the founding fathers: Iwane (Tokyo), Yokota (Kanagawa), and Ikeda (Chiba). Thus far, the issue of political strategy has not been discussed at NET's local meetings or regional and national conferences. Assembly women have mixed views about appropriate strategies but do not take the lead in canvassing strategic options and problems with the grassroots (Table 8.13). It appears that the assembly women and their supporters are preoccupied with ward activities and have conceded the debate about strategies to the founding fathers. Among the assembly women, 40.9 percent cast their votes for the JSP in the proportional list of the 1992 Upper House Election (Table 8.14); slightly more than half voted for the conservative JNP and other minor parties. There is therefore a lack of consensus within NET about the most appropriate strategy, even if some of the male leadership were to push for a Red–Green alignment.

Iwane was extremely critical of the JSP and he rejected an alliance between NET and JSP.[43] Instead, he advocated the strengthening of NET at the grassroots before it ventures into national politics. Anticipating the inexorable decline of labor unions and the rising numbers of elderly people in Japan, Iwane repudiated a Red (JSP and labor)–Green alignment, but proposed a Green–Grey (senior citizens) alliance. He pointed out that if the SC and party can serve the interests of the old in an aging society, NET will have a new role to play in social movements. Ikeda envisaged a Green

Table 8.13 Perceptions of NET assembly women toward political alignments

Strategic preference	No.	Percent
Solo at the local level	6	9.4
Align NET with other organizations at local level	8	12.5
Greens holding a casting vote at the national level	25	39.1
Red and Green alignment (JSP, NET and labor) to contain conservatives	10	15.6
Others	15	23.4

Note:
N = 64

Table 8.14 NET assembly women and voting patterns in 1992 Upper House Election (proportional list)

Party	Assembly women's votes	Percent
LDP	0	0
JSP	27	40.9
Kōmeitō	0	0
DSP	0	0
JCP	1	1.6
Shaminren	12	19.4
JNP	12	19.4
Others	10	16.1

Note:
N = 62

movement that holds a casting vote in Japanese politics.[44] The core of Ikeda's Green alliance comprised NET, SC, the North Block of Green Co-op of Fukuoka prefecture, and other co-ops. He argued that NET and its allies should strive to capture at least 10 percent of the votes. In the event of a split between the established parties or even within the conservative ranks, NET should even support a conservative party if there is a consensus on ecological issues. Yokota was a top advisor of the JSP and Jichirō (All Japan Prefectural and Municipal Workers' Union).[45] Not surprisingly, he advocated a Red–Green alliance between NET, JSP, and the labor unions to contain the conservatives. Some mid-level SC staff joked that it is more appropriate to call this strategy a Pink–Green alliance because socialism within the JSP has been watered down over the years.

While the founding fathers were debating the party's strategic options, NET in Hokkaidō, Tokyo, and Kanagawa forged *de facto* alignments with individual JSP candidates. Local NETs and JSP women Diet Members exchanged mutual endorsement and support. At NET's annual party conference, JSP Diet Members appeared, exchanged greetings and made speeches.[46] In the April 1993 Tokyo Prefectural Election all three NET candidates won their seats after receiving endorsement from the JSP.[47] The relationship between NET and the JSP was rather convoluted. On the one hand, NET supported JSP women candidates at the national level while, on the other hand, it competed with union-based, male JSP candidates at the local and national levels. To individual JSP male politicians, NET posed a threat. For example, in the 1993 July Lower House Election Zendentsu (All Japan Telecommunication Workers' Union) withdrew its endorsement of a JSP male incumbent Diet Member and gave it to the NET candidate who ran in Kanagawa District Two.[48] In the July National Election in the same year, NET ran three candidates in Kanagawa Districts One, Two and Three. Besides gaining the endorsement of Eda Satsuki of Shaminren,[49] the NET candidate of District Two also obtained the official endorsement of two labor unions, Zendentsu and Denkirōren (Japanese Federation of Electrical Machine Workers' Union).[50] To some NET members this was an unholy alliance. Zendentsu is a Right-leaning union that supports nuclear energy and the despatch of Japanese troops abroad for peacekeeping. These are policies that are diametrically opposite to NET's. In order to maximize its votes, the party accepted Zendentsu's endorsement despite sharp policy differences.

Aspiring to have an impact on national politics and to preclude a conservative domination of Japanese politics, various regional NETs have persisted in forging alliances with various national parties. In the 1995 Upper House Election, Kanagawa NET endorsed both the JSP and Sakigake candidates within the same constituency.[51] This policy was confusing and contradictory to many NET members because both national parties were competing against each other within the same Kanagawa constituency. In addition, Kanagawa NET supported both parties which were coalition partners with the conservative LDP in government. In the following year, certain regional NETs endorsed the Minshutō in the Lower House Election in the hope of bolstering a "liberal, third force" in Japanese politics.[52] In the quest to influence national politics through strategic alignments, NET risks compromising its ideals of amateur-based politics by associating with national parties that do not subscribe to such values. It may also suffer from a rupture in its party unity because many members prefer the organization to focus on local politics and not be entangled and tainted by its alignment with certain Old Politics parties.[53]

Conclusion

No Green party in the real world can measure up to an ideal-type New Politics party. NET is no exception. Rather than a black and white categorization of the organization as either a New Politics party or not, it is more helpful to assess the degree it attains certain qualities of a New Politics party. NET certainly has New Politics-like features: an all-women party, a rotation system, the surrendering of its incumbents' salaries to party control, and the pursuit of such Green issues as ecology, alternative economy, human rights, and pacifism. Its members are amateurs who are not motivated by material incentives to participate in politics. The party is also a practitioner of clean politics.

Yet there are countervailing features that challenge its credentials as a New Politics party. Like the German Green Party, it is vulnerable to oligarchic tendencies despite its original intent to curb autocratic leadership.[54] A professional male leadership, which is neither elected nor accountable to NET, dominates the organization. Ordinary members are not consulted on the party's strategic direction. Most members are unaware of the male leadership's interaction with outsiders (established parties and unions) to solicit additional support for NET candidates. There is genuine participation, autonomy, and an egalitarian spirit at the grassroots among ordinary members; the male leadership does not interfere in the day-to-day activities or the specific issues pursued at the grassroots. Yet any sensation of autonomy felt by members is an illusion because the males continue to shape its ideology and plot its future direction.

An ideal-type Green party would not sacrifice the representation of its constituency and Green beliefs for the sake of gaining more votes. Nevertheless, NET developed close and pragmatic ties with the JSP, Sakigake, Minshutō, and certain labor unions. The JSP's opportunism in joining local or national ruling coalitions with conservative elements despite the socialist principles of unarmed neutrality and anti-nuclear energy was conveniently ignored by NET. In its quest to win votes, the Kanagawa NET accepted endorsements from unions with markedly different policies. Despite the disquiet of some party members, the informal male leadership adopted this expedient approach at the expense of core principles.

Since NET operates in a different national context, it has evolved certain features absent in Western Europe. Because *kōenkai* is an entrenched aspect of Japanese politics, certain regional NETs have been influenced by its political environment to adopt an organizational approach which appeals to many Japanese voters. We expect a New Politics party to abandon a personality-centric organization, but the imperative to win votes has resulted in a party adapting to its environment despite its original intent to change certain aspects of that environment. The presence of an external sponsor, the SC, behind NET is another feature that sets it apart from the West European Greens. With the co-op's organizational backup, the party is able to win seats in local politics. However, it is excessively dependent on the SC. Although the party has the stated goal of wooing students, youths and women,[55] its core support is limited to housewives with children. West European Greens seem to have broader social support, especially among youths and the white-collar middle class, including males. Another of the party's distinctive features when compared to West European Greens is its exclusivly female membership. Housewife activism is made possible by Japan's industrial structure whereby men work in the office or factory while their spouses tend the home. The feminine composition of NET's formal leaders and members suggests that it is unique in Japanese politics, but any interpretation of NET as a New Politics party has to be tempered by the fact that it is led by an informal male leadership.

After examining the contradictory tendencies of NET, we may classify it as a quasi-New Politics party. A defining characteristic of a true New Politics party is one whose ordinary members actively and directly participate in the formulation of policies and keeping their leaders under a tight rein. Such an ideal situation has not been realized by the German Green Party, let alone by NET. The latter's credentials as a New Politics party will improve only if the women audaciously seize the ideological and strategic reins from the informal male leadership.

9 The Seikatsu Club and NET: problems and prospects

According to various surveys of mass attitudes, the Japanese have increasingly expressed a greater concern for post-material issues. Even if post-materialism among the Japanese continues to rise unabated, there is no certainty that it will be translated into political support for Green organizations. There are a number of problems that may dampen the SC and its offspring's growth and involvement in politics, even in a post-industrial milieu. The multitude of problems faced by the co-op includes the inexorable decline in the number of housewives, changing urban architecture which makes recruitment of members increasingly difficult, attempts by the Ministry of Health and Welfare (MHW) to clamp down on the involvement of co-ops in politics, and the elusive pursuit of alternative values in Japanese society. Unlike the German Greens, NET is too dependent on a diminishing social base of housewives, places too much emphasis on the narrow issues of "motherhood, soap, and rubbish," and operates in a very competitive and crowded party system. NET may encounter other potential problems: vulnerability to changing voter concerns, counter-actions by established parties, confinement to local politics by the nature of the electoral system, and the inability to project itself as an authentic female organization. These are key reasons why the "Greenest" party in Japan is likely to remain a marginal political force.

Structural changes in Japanese society

The most serious problem faced by the SC in the long run is a stagnant and aging membership. Tokyo SC suffered a membership decline for the first time in 1991. After years of steady growth, this erosion may be a precursor of potential decline in other regional SCs.[1] Two structural changes in Japanese society will limit the co-op's growth in the Tokyo metropolitan area: the slowdown of urbanization in the capital region and increasing numbers of women working outside the home. Since the co-op benefited from the rapid influx of new residents (the SC's potential recruits), a sustained slowdown in urbanization will have the opposite effect in shrinking the pool of recruits. Since Chiba and Saitama have high rates of population growth, we should expect greater organizational expansion in these new dormitory towns of Tokyo. However, Saitama and Chiba too are faced with a slowdown in their recruitment drives.[2] Even in these prefectures, favorable trends in urbanization are counteracted by social trends unfavorable to the SC, especially the relative decline in the numbers of housewives.

Iwane Kunio points out that the population decline of Tokyo's Setagaya and Nerima wards (the areas where the SC was first established), inhibits the organization's growth.[3] Tokyo's urbanization has been described as a "doughnut" phenomenon whereby the population in Tokyo's central wards is hollowed out while there is population increase in the suburbs. The "doughnut" effect may hamper the expansion of Tokyo NET since the parent organization thrives in an urbanizing milieu.[4] While Tokyo's population is expected to stagnate, it is anticipated that Kanagawa, Chiba and Saitama will register steady growth in the next two decades.[5] The influx of new residents to Tokyo's dormitory towns should be beneficial to the SC in the three prefectures. However, if increasing numbers of women among the new residents were to work outside the home, the co-op's pool of potential recruits will continue to shrink.

The relative decrease in the number of housewives may undermine the viability of the *han*, the SC's base of social action.[6] If the percentage of housewives continues to shrink inexorably,[7] housewife participation in the *han* will be weakened. Thus, the co-op must appeal to other social groups to avoid an erosion in membership. Anticipating changes in Japan's social structure, the Kanagawa SC is constructing welfare clubs to cater to the old, workers' collectives to provide avenues for women to be their own bosses, and depots for busy working women who cannot join the *han*. Although the depots were conceived to offer working women the convenience and the spontaneity of making immediate purchases as individuals rather than through the time-consuming ordering process of the *han*, few full-time working women can patronize the depots except on weekends. The astronomical cost of land in metropolitan Japan and high labor costs make it difficult for the Kanagawa SC to build more depots in Yokohama and Kawasaki. Between 1985 and 1991, the cost of land in metropolitan areas more than doubled.[8] Even if the co-op succeeded in building an extensive chain of depots, depot members may end up like the passive customers of the conventional, commercial stores. Although newsletters and invitations to various social movement activities are sent to depot members, the rate of participation in contrast to the *han* is poor among depot members. The depot system lacks the vitality and the tightly knitted structure of the *han*. The development of workers' collectives and welfare clubs is innovative, but it is uncertain whether this new approach will attract a large membership prepared to participate in social movement activities.

Iwane has shrewdly identified two major trends in the demographic structure of Japanese society which will have a serious impact on the club and NET.[9] They are the declining numbers of housewives and the rising numbers of senior citizens. The founding father has sounded the clarion call that the SC must address the needs of the aged and capture a new social base of support in order for the co-op to remain socially and politically relevant. Iwane noted that the *han* system of collective purchase in bulk for the family will become less effective as around one-third of residents in Tokyo are already living alone. Moreover, within a decade, one out of four Japanese would be over 65 years old. He envisaged the SC providing goods, services, and companionship to lonely senior citizens and mobilizing them for social action. If the SC can meet this challenge, both parent and child organizations will gain a new lease of life in the Japanese social and political arena.

Changes in urban architecture

New urban architectural designs also pose difficulties to its recruitment campaign. When the Kanagawa SC first started organizing in Tama Plaza, Midori ward, house-to-house canvassing was easy and effective because low-rise apartments had no security devices such as auto-locks which barred the way of the canvassers. The new housing estates in Midori ward are high-rise apartments equipped with auto-locks and intercoms. Strangers are screened by residents and admittance may not be granted to canvassers. In the absence of face-to-face contact, it is much more difficult to persuade a new resident to join the co-op.

This situation is similar to the difficulties faced by the legendary political machines of New York City which found that the time-honored method of door-to-door canvassing was rendered ineffectual by the installation of auto-locks in apartments due to the fear of crime in the city.[10] While metropolitan Japan is not plagued by endemic crime, the desire for privacy and the availability of hi-tech, auto-lock gadgets have made door-to-door canvassing obsolete in the newest residential areas of Midori ward. Ironically, Midori ward is the bastion of the Kanagawa SC and NET movement. The increase in the number of working women outside the home has also made door-to-door canvassing a less effective means of recruitment because the women in more than half of the households visited by the SC canvassers were not at home.[11]

Enforcement of the Co-op Law?

If NET makes significant political inroads in the big cities, the major parties may respond by leaning on the MHW to exercise stricter regulatory control of the SC group. The Ministry insists that co-ops must not support any specific parties or candidates according to its interpretation of the Co-op Law. It is conceivable that parties in power may exercise their clout by pressuring the MHW to curb the co-op's political activities. A triad of LDP small business policy-makers (*zoku giin*), small and medium-sized retail businesses and the Ministry of Trade and Industry (MITI) have already attempted to restrict the co-op movement.[12] In 1983 the LDP small business *zoku* (tribe or policy sub-committee) reviewed the Co-op Law because of the clash of interests between its clients, the small and medium-sized retail stores, and the co-ops. The criticisms levelled against the consumer movement included its Leftist orientation, lack of restriction on non-members who patronize co-op stores, and the continuous friction with small business caused by the establishment of new co-op stores. The critics also proposed a brake on these new stores and measures to increase the tax bracket of co-ops to the level of big stores.[13]

This concerted attack against the co-ops resulted in the formation of a countervailing triad: the LDP's health *zoku*, the MHW, and the co-ops. The LDP health *zoku* and some female LDP Diet Members warned that there were also LDP supporters among co-op members and that the party should not antagonize the urban housewives, especially when it was attempting to transform itself from a rural-based party to an urban-based party.[14] Since the MHW considered MITI's actions to be encroaching on its turf and the protection of its co-op clients to be a core issue, the MHW and its coalition doggedly resisted and were successful in warding off MITI and its allies' attempts to check the consumer movement. In 1986, the MHW reviewed the Co-op Law possibly to pre-empt further interference from MITI and the LDP small business *zoku* from undermining the MHW's autonomy.[15] The MHW's advisory committee suggested a number of guidelines including the imperative for the co-ops to maintain strict political neutrality.[16]

The LDP's annoyance with their political participation was apparent in a lengthy article in the party's newspaper, the *Jiyū Shinpō* (The Liberal) shortly after the April 1987 Local Elections, when NET made conspicuous progress. In this article, the LDP attacked the SC for allegedly breaking the Co-op Law, manipulating members to engage in politics while using "safe food" as a mobilizing issue, and for its "close ties" with the JSP. The conservatives sarcastically praised the SC as an effective and impressive political party (*rippana seitō*), since many of its endorsed candidates were elected.[17] The Kanagawa LDP Women's Division followed up the attack by circulating pamphlets to LDP supporters in the Tokyo Metropolitan region accusing the SC of being an extremist co-op (*kagekina seikyō*) and reiterated the criticisms made by the party's newspaper.[18] The MHW was probably aware of the LDP's irritation with the SC and NET when the Ministry tried to dissuade the consumer movement from participating in politics.[19] The Ministry probably tried to dissuade the consumer movement from participating in politics after the LDP became agitated about the advances made by co-op-supported women candidates in the 1987 Local Elections.[20]

In June 1987, MHW sent a "notification" (*tsūshin*) to various co-op prefectural headquarters with a set of guidelines explicitly warning them not to support political parties and candidates. The Ministry acknowledged that co-op members and staff could freely participate in politics in their individual capacities to improve the cultural and economic livelihood of members, but, as organizations, they should not be ensnared by politics. The MHW warned that if these organizations were drawn into politics, they could be torn asunder by the confusion among members holding different political views. Moreover, political entanglement might lead to misunderstanding and prejudices against the co-ops and would harm their development. The MHW also specifically mentioned that the co-ops' Board of Management and General Assembly should not endorse any political parties and nor should their newsletter endorse any party or candidate.

Just before the 1991 Local Elections, the MHW again cautioned the SC and its ally, the Green Co-op North Block of Fukuoka city, to steer away from politics. Warning letters from the Ministry were sent to co-op federations in various prefectures. The leader of the Green Co-op, North Block was also summoned by MHW's prefectural representative to receive a verbal warning on political entanglement.[21] The SC's strategy to refute the Ministry's demands was to claim that it was involved in social movement activities and not in party politics. (This position is untenable in the case of the Kanagawa SC because it supported Kanagawa NET, a self-proclaimed local party.) SC leaders also argue that the Co-op Law is open to different interpretations. They believe that the Co-op Law does not preclude the consumer movement from political participation and that the Constitution guarantees organizations and individuals the right to be involved in politics.

Although the MHW sends notifications to the co-ops' federation headquarters located at the prefectural level prior to each election, it is not legally binding on them.[22] Issue of notifications falls within the ambit of the bureaucracy's "administrative guidance" (*gyōsei shidō*), which depends on the co-ops' voluntary compliance. The Co-op Law does not provide for any appropriate punishment when a co-op disregards the MHW's notification or chooses to participate in politics.[23] Against the backdrop of the Co-op

Law, the SC's political activism is open to differing legal interpretations. Some of its members were uneasy and fearful that their organization may be breaking the law.[24] If the MHW were to take a hard line against the organization, some members and other potential recruits might be frightened away from it.

Pursuing an elusive "hegemony"?

The SC envisages the forging of an alternative lifestyle that caters to the daily needs of local residents, the inculcation of desirable values, and the bypassing of capitalism's wasteful production, distribution, consumption, and disposal processes. In certain areas of Kanagawa prefecture where the SC is located, it has successfully organized an average of 3 percent of the total households. Although Yokota Katsumi had the vision of constructing a multitude of mass organizations offering a wide range of services and activities to local residents, it was difficult for a local "hegemony" to be brought to fruition. A hermetic local community based on its values is impossible to maintain.[25] The access to alternative sources of information, interpretation and values, the involvement in non-SC activities (such as PTAs, neighborhood associations, charity organizations, and other social circles) by ordinary members will mean that, even if members are influenced by the co-op, it cannot expect to obtain a monopoly of values. Even if the SC succeeded in socializing some of its members, there would probably be a bifurcation of values within the members' families because their husbands, the lieutenants and captains of Japanese capitalism, are too busy at work to be involved in the co-op's activities.

Counter-actions by other political parties?

A more serious challenge to NET is the counter-actions of other parties, both old and "new." In the case of Germany, the SPD tried to poach on the Greens' support base by co-opting some of the Greens' environmental platform.[26] In contrast, the JSP was not as flexible as its socialist counterpart in Germany.[27] NET has little to fear from the JSP and its successor, the SDP. Rather than the former socialists, it is more likely that the conservatives may incorporate some of NET's platform given their impressive record of stealing the opposition's programs to win over new bases of support. If there is increasing voter support for its pet themes like natural soap and the recycling of rubbish, it is not inconceivable that the conservatives may embrace such policies as their own.[28] The conservatives introduced comprehensive welfare and anti-pollution policies once proposed by the opposition, and the formulation of "rubbish and soap" policies should not be problematic if there is an electoral incentive for them to do so. If other parties were to steal NET's rubbish and soap policies, NET might have difficulties finding new mobilizing themes which appeal to SC members, housewives, and the general voters. Its remaining policies, opposition to nuclear energy and support for demilitarization and direct democracy, may have less universal appeal than environmental protection, especially when the first two are also regarded as Old Politics issues in Japan. Unless there is a catastrophic nuclear accident in Japan, complacent voters may not heed Green appeals for safer alternatives to nuclear power plants.

Despite various nuclear mishaps in Japan, a powerful, nation-wide, anti-nuclear Green movement has yet to emerge. In so far as there is no immediate, wide-scale nuclear threat to their well-being, many voters are resigned to the fact that resource-poor Japan is reliant on nuclear energy for approximately one-third of its energy requirements and in the near future, other non-oil alternatives are likely to be more expensive and less techno-logically feasible. While pockets of local anti-nuclear movement have emerged in areas threatened by the development of nuclear stations, NET and other Green activists in Japan find it difficult to appeal to the Japanese since they do not perceive themselves to be directly vulnerable to nuclear accidents. Moreover, Green organizations have problems appealing to indi-viduals and groups outside of their social web because political mobilization in Japan relies heavily on tapping social networks rather than policy appeals.

Another threat to NET is the mushrooming of "new" parties. In rapid succession, the Nihonshintō, Shinseitō, and Sakigake were formed by ex-LDP renegades between 1992 and 1993. In 1994, the established non-communist opposition parties united to form the Shinshintō to challenge the three-party ruling coalition comprising the LDP, JSP, and Sakigake. In 1996, many members left the JSP and Sakigake to form a "liberal" alter-native, the Minshutō. These newly formed parties claimed to be purveyors of "New Politics" because they advocated political reforms, a consumer-oriented society, and greater autonomy to the prefectures. Such policies are already advocated by NET.

In the July 1993 Lower House Election, NET failed to win a single seat in Kanagawa prefecture because its electoral appeal of representing consumers and ordinary citizens in national politics was overshadowed by other issues. In that election, voters were preoccupied with the question of whether LDP rule should be retained or overthrown in the wake of its pervasive corrup-tion.[29] Many voters who wanted the LDP out of office opted for the "new parties" that opposed the LDP rather than wasting their votes on NET. New Politics parties are vulnerable to issue shifts in elections. A Green agenda may be overshadowed for voters when a national issue dominates the political discourse of the election. The issue of German reunification was the paramount concern of voters in the German 1991 National Election; political corruption and LDP's tenure as a ruling party were the core issues in the Japanese 1993 National Election. Ecology and direct citizen participation in politics were simply drowned out by the issue of the day.

The proliferation of "new" parties means that Japan's party system has become increasingly crowded. "New" parties with fresh reformist images undercut NET's attempts at the national level to appeal to urban voters alienated from the old, established parties. Indeed, it is difficult for NET to achieve a breakthrough in national politics given the intensity of competition among the many parties. In the case of the German Greens, they had an easier task in winning representation at the national level. West Germany had two large parties; the CDU and SPD with a smaller third party, the Free Democrats.[30] In certain regions, the German Greens were able to displace the Free Democrats and became the third party in local assemblies.

Another potential counter-action by other parties is the promotion of a larger slate of women's candidates at the local elections. At present, a conspicuous difference between NET and the established parties is its exclusive support for women candidates. However, if other parties were to open their doors wider to women candidates, NET would face greater competition for the support of women voters.

Electoral system: A barrier to small parties?

NET has obtained modest successes in three different local electoral systems: a small or medium-sized city forming one large electoral district, Tokyo's ward assembly elections, and the medium-sized, multi-member district adopted by the big cities for city assembly elections.[31] At the prefectural and national level the smaller number of seats in each electoral district and the need to win a much larger number of votes pose difficulties to NET's expansion beyond the ward and city levels. The introduction of a single-member district in the Lower House in 1994 makes it an uphill task for small parties like NET to compete against the big parties at the national level.[32]

There are proposals to extend single-member district system to the prefectural, city, and ward levels in tandem with the proposed electoral changes to the Lower House.[33] If a single-member district is introduced only at the national level, a discrepancy will arise when a Diet Member from a shrunken national district will represent a smaller number of voters than a local assembly member whose ward, city, or prefectural districts remains unchanged. If a single-member district system is extended to the local level, NET will probably be wiped out by an electoral device that discriminates against smaller parties.

The presidential system adopted by the city and prefectural levels presents opportunities for NET. By aligning themselves with progressive governors and mayors, they can obtain executive support to implement welfare and environmental policies. At the national level, the presidential system has not been adopted. While non-conservatives have succeeded as executives of local governments, the conservatives have monopolized the executive branch of the national government except for a hiatus between 1993 and 1994.[34] Even if a few NET candidates were to win elections at the national level against the odds, they will face tremendous obstacles in implementing their policies. In such a scenario, they may use the Diet as a forum to canvass their policies, seek support from public opinion, educate the masses on environmental issues, and obtain access to the national bureaucracy, but they are unlikely to make any headway to implement their programs unless they join a ruling coalition as a junior partner. Unable to win seats at the national level on their own, Kanagawa, Tokyo, and Hokkaidō NET, have aligned themselves with the Minshutō.[35] In the 1996 Lower House Election, the Minshutō performed disappointingly and failed to capture more than the 52 seats held by its incumbents. In the following year, the Minshutō again failed to make an impact in the Tokyo Metropolitan Election.[36] If the Minshutō were to fizzle out after failing to make an impact on Japanese politics, NET would lose a vehicle to play a larger role in national politics.

Beyond rubbish and soap at the Prefectural and National Elections?

Besides the challenge of fewer seats and the need to obtain a much larger number of votes to win at the prefectural and national levels, NET also faces the problem of espousing suitable prefectural, national, and global policies that appeal to voters. Municipal issues, such as the separation of rubbish and the use of natural soap, are less salient at the national level. Moreover, issues of international relations, national defense, the constitutional status of the Self Defense Force (SDF), the question of supporting or rejecting the U.S.–Japan Security Treaty, macro-economic policies, lower consumer prices, land policies, and affordable urban housing are some areas where NET has demonstrated no interest, mastery, or coherence. Terada Etsuko, the first candidate supported by the Kanagawa SC to win a city assembly seat in 1983, argued that one reason why she lost in her bid to obtain a prefectural seat in 1991 was the lack of knowledge of appropriate policies that could appeal to a larger group of voters at the prefectural level.[37] Policies and issues that have voters' appeal at the city assembly level may not necessarily have the same appeal at the prefectural and the national level.

Instead of appealing primarily to local problems, it is necessary to identify prefectural and national problems and offer viable solutions to voters beyond the ward level.

The lack of aptitude and a positive attitude toward issues beyond the ward and city boundaries is, in part, a result of the SC's social composition. Even though about half of the ordinary members have college education, they lack exposure and experience in the field of business and politics. Despite this handicap, NET members have made tentative steps to study issues beyond the ward and city levels. Seminars were held to examine the Japanese constitution, the implications of despatching troops abroad for the first time in post-war Japan ostensibly for UN peace-keeping in Cambodia,[38] and the impact of the Uruguay Round of GATT talks on trade negotiations and market liberalization on Japanese agriculture. The realization that fundamental problems cannot be resolved merely at the local level may force NET to look beyond the local level and study national and global issues.[39]

Even if NET can take advantage of the local presidential system by supporting a progressive mayor and becoming a part of the city's ruling coalition, there are limits to the local government's authority. A case in point is Zushi city in Kanagawa prefecture. NET backed mayor Tomino Kichiro whose main platform was to prevent the destruction of Ikego, an old-growth forest, to make way for the construction of U.S. military housing. In November 1992, NET successfully supported the Green mayoral candidate, Sanwa Mitsuyo, who became the second woman mayor in Japan's political history. The three NET assembly women in Zushi were members of the local coalition in power.[40] However, Zushi's local government was frustrated in its attempts to halt the construction project. It cannot veto or override the national government's decision since foreign and defense policies fall within the domain of the national government.

Female organization without feminism?

One of NET's assets is its unique sponsorship of only women candidates to redress the lopsided gender representation in Japanese politics. With the exception of the JCP, the other parties are relatively indifferent to the promotion of more women candidates within their party organizations and in the local and national elections. Since there is a lack of competition from most parties to advance the position of women candidates, NET is in a unique position to attract support from women who are dissatisfied with the male-dominated, political status quo. We expect the organization to promote the interests of women on the principle of gender equality and to seize an opportunity to win greater support from women voters. Paradoxically, its most glaring omission is its lack of attention to gender issues. Although the term "feminism" or the more popular expression "woman's viewpoint" is featured sporadically in its literature and pamphlets, the assembly women do not address issues such as the lack of equal employment opportunities for women, sexual harassment at the workplace, and the exploitation of local and foreign women by Japan's flourishing sex industry.

NET's legislative agenda with a "woman's viewpoint" includes requests for more child-care centers, stricter standards for school food and the use of natural soap in schools. The promotion of these issues stems more from the idea of "motherhood" to protect the family rather than the determination to seek gender equality. Instead of promoting gender equality, it may unwittingly reinforce gender inequality and the stereotype that things related to soap, food, child care, and rubbish are women's responsibilities.[41]

Why is NET apathetic to the promotion of gender equality? Its indifference does not arise from the ignorance that gender inequality is acute in Japan. A NET assembly woman explained that her organization's omission is due to a constellation of problems it has to deal with that mean feminism is simply not a priority issue. NET has to be pragmatic by dealing with issues it can solve rather than to bite off more than it can chew.[42] Another candidate remarked: "Gender inequality is something known in the head but not felt in the heart."[43] The lack of passion to pursue gender equality is, in part, due to the social composition of the SC and NET members, many of whom are housewives. As homemakers, they lack personal experiences of the problems which full-time working women have to face outside the home. To the genteel SC housewives, issues such as workplace inequality and the sexual exploitation of Third World women in Japan are mere intellectual issues that are far removed from their social universe.

In two separate surveys of the values and attitudes of NET members from different prefectures, the results consistently show an astonishingly low interest in gender equality. According to one survey, only 2.3 percent of members feel that the organization should wrestle with the problems of gender equality, and only 0.8 percent of members believe that gender equality should be its most important issue.[44] The issues of welfare, recycling of rubbish, safe food, and children's education rank much higher in members' consciousness. In another survey of members from Midori ward, Yokohama, only 7.7 percent are interested in promoting the re-employment of women.[45] Even though NET members are expected to be more politicized than the SC's rank and file, it is obvious that they have little interest in gender equality. Since its assembly women also come from the same socio-economic background as their supporters, it is not surprising that there is no strong commitment to an agenda for equality.

Perhaps the term "feminism" is largely shunned by NET to avoid projecting the image of radicalism and confrontation which may scare away many voters.[46] Past forays into the electoral process by self-proclaimed feminists include the Japan Women's Party that was led by a former leader of *Chupiren* (Women's Liberation League Against the Abortion Law and for the Pill), an organization that criticized Japan's abortion law and supported the use of birth-control pills.[47] *Chupiren* gained notoriety as the "pink-helmet" women who demonstrated at the offices of men who allegedly mistreated women. The reluctance of NET to be associated with "feminism" is perhaps a reflection of the nature of Japanese society that places little value on gender equality despite the constitutional guarantee that women must not be discriminated against. By avoiding the term "feminism," NET disassociates itself from past women's liberation movements deemed to be on the lunatic fringe by Japanese society. It could, however, avoid the term "feminism" and yet actively support the cause of gender equality. To date, it has shown little inclination to so. However, after the 1995 Upper House Election, Kanagawa NET advocated a quota system for greater women's participation in politics and society, but it has neither elaborated how this quota system should work nor demonstrated any tenacity in pursuit of this declaratory goal.[48]

The SC founding leaders and the key personnel in the organization are men. If both parent and child organizations were to champion gender equality, they might open themselves to attack for not practicing what they preach, since few women have taken over the top leadership and administrative posts from men. Rather than be accused of hypocrisy, both organizations have concentrated on the narrower issue of motherhood, that encompass the interests of only a particular set of women, rather than the pursuit of equality for women. Nevertheless, regional SCs are grooming more women to take over top leadership positions while NET is providing women with the opportunities to acquire greater political skills. In the long run, women probably will play a larger role in both organizations after the retirement of the founding fathers.

The major challenge for NET is whether it can transcend its well-to-do housewives' sensibilities and view of the role of women as mothers by becoming a movement that also takes a passionate interest in the problems of women working outside the home. The reason that the workplace is ignored can be traced to the SC's roots. When the organization was first formed, it attempted to avoid the JSP's over concentration on the workplace by organizing at the residential place. Ironically, by concentrating on the place of residence, the co-op has ended up ignoring the problems of the workplace. Its emphasis on the place of residence is a mirror image of the JSP's one-legged approach of concentrating on the workplace. NET needs to develop a two-legged approach that strikes a balance between the place of residence and the workplace. The party need not be a prisoner of its social composition; it can consciously take a greater interest in the problems of women working outside the home.

The formulation of policies concerning the workplace is also an approach for it to obtain political support beyond the urban housewives. While NET has embraced many worthy causes, it has also remained silent on the problems of the weak, the less fortunate and the pariahs in Japanese society that include the Ainu (Japan's original inhabitants),[49] ethnic Koreans who are born in Japan, the *burakumin* (Japan's caste system of social untouchables), the daily-rated workers, the homeless visible in metropolitan Japan, and the "guest" workers from abroad who do dirty and dangerous manual tasks shunned by young Japanese today.[50] This is the consequence of its concentration on the issues of motherhood and the place of residence.

Contributions

The main contribution of NET is its promotion of New Politics in Japan: the enhancement of women's participation in politics, offering a Green option to voters, the injection of New Politics issues in policy formulation, and the formation of Red–Green ruling coalitions in local governments. Notwithstanding NET's many problems and shortcomings, it has made a positive impact on Japanese politics. Its most conspicuous contribution is the promotion of women participation in politics. Although women form half of the electorate, the percentage of women holding political office at all levels remains very low despite the electoral gains made by women in recent years (Table 9.1). NET's involvement in local politics has encouraged many previously apolitical women to venture into politics. Despite the strong political allergy among SC members, there is a growing realization among them that politics is too important to be left to professional politicians only. The corollary is also true: politics is too important to be entrusted to males

Table 9.1 Percentage of local assembly women in Japan

Local elections	Total no. of Assembly Seats (A)	Total no. of assembly women (B)	Percent (B/A)
1987	68,462	1,420 (32)	2.1
1991	66,440	2,030 (72)	3.1

Source: *Yomiuri shinbun*, September 20, 1991.

Note:
Figures in brackets are NET assembly women.

only. The SC and NET have acted as agents of political socialization to members in their adulthood, many of whom did not have any prior political experiences or interest. Both organizations have provided avenues for women to channel their energy and creativity in meaningful activities especially in the field of politics.

The bane of Japanese politics is the pervasiveness of money politics. The unabashed pursuit of slush money alienates many Japanese, who respond by boycotting the polls.[51] The decline in voter turnout and voter disenchantment with the established parties are phenomena not unique to Japan. Voters in advanced industrial countries have become better educated and informed, and are less tolerant of the political parties' shortcomings. If the decline in voter turnout is undesirable, then the SC and NET's attempts to mobilize women to vote and be involved in other political activities ought to be viewed favorably. NET's clean and green image also shows that politics is not inevitably dirty or disconnected with various aspects of daily life. Its contribution to the political system is the induction of women who might otherwise abstain from politics. Although the party itself cannot arrest declining voter turnout in the wards where it competes, voter turnout might have been worse if there was no NET to attract women into politics.

NET has already enlivened the local political scene by injecting greater competition in metropolitan areas where it offers a candidate. Hitherto, choices at the local level were restricted to conservative politicians distinguishable only in terms of personalities, JCP's ideologically bound, party employees, union-dependent JSP and DSP contenders and the religious-based Kōmeitō candidates. At the mayoral and governorship elections, real competition often does not exist. There is the prevailing practice of *ainori* (riding together) where all local non-communist parties, despite the national parties' outward differences in policies, ideologies and values, jump on board the bandwagon and form a grand coalition or more accurately, a grand collusion in a duel against an out-gunned communist candidate. The outcome is virtually settled prior to the local elections and voters are presented with a *fait accompli* by the established parties. The lack of choice, a predictable outcome, and the contradiction of both ruling and opposition parties co-operating at the local level while maintaining the posture of confrontation at the national level are conditions which are not conducive to high voter turnout at the local elections. This grand collusion is also made possible because divisive issues, especially defense policies, are beyond the local government's jurisdiction and there are fewer bones of contention at the local level.

NET's involvement in electoral politics provides voters with more options. In small cities and villages, elections are sometimes not held because the number of candidates is identical to the number of seats available at the local assembly. Residents do not even have an opportunity to cast a protest vote. When the party runs a candidate in a district with such a cosy arrangement for incumbents, an election must be held and voters can express their voice through the ballot box. An example of its creation of a more competitive environment is the 1992 Local Election of Zama city in Kanagawa prefecture when 29 candidates including one NET hopeful competed for 28 seats.[53] If the party had not competed in Zama's city elections, the result would have been an extra term for incumbents without their having to face voters at the polls. That surely would have been any incumbent's paradise. In the local elections, NET has displaced candidates from the established parties. If increased competition especially by amateurs is considered desirable in a democratic polity, its participation ought to be appreciated.

Another contribution is the introduction of new issues into the political agenda of various local governments. While major established parties are interested in large construction projects of roads, bridges, and other facilities for their constituencies, NET has introduced new topics such as the separation and the recycling of rubbish, better child care centers, safer school food for children, water and food free from chemical contamination, and the use of environmentally friendly, natural soap. Issues which have not previously been considered political or important have been politicized by NET and certain themes like the separation of rubbish have even been absorbed by the political mainstream. Thus, it has tried to redefine and broaden the concept of what is political and has given renewed meaning to the saying, "The Personal is the Political."

Since 1987, Yokohama NET has pursued a distinctive set of policies in the city assembly and has attained various degrees of successes. When Yokohama NET first proposed the separation of rubbish to facilitate recycling, male assembly members joked that the volume of rubbish has increased because NET women activists are involved in politics and are not staying at home to clear the rubbish.[54] Eventually, the mayor and the city bureaucracy agreed to establish Midori and Asahi as experimental wards to test the feasibility of separating rubbish.[55] (Two of the NET assembly women come from both wards.) By 1992, Yokohama city decided to extend the system to all the wards. Finally, in March 1996, this waste sorting system was implemented in all of Yokohama's wards.[56] NET has also persuaded most schools in Yokohama to use biodegradable soap instead of synthetic soap. Through its urging, the city also set aside a budget to study the effects of synthetic soap.[57]

NET was a member of ruling coalitions in the cities of Kamakura, Fujisawa, Kawasaki, Zushi, and Machida. It has not remained merely an opposition for opposition's sake but when given the opportunity, became a responsible and constructive coalition partner in local government. Since the numbers of its assembly women are small within ruling coalitions, there is a danger that as a junior partner it may be dragged along by senior partners and forced to compromise on policies it would otherwise not have supported. One critic pointed out the case of Tokyo NET's sole prefectural member who was caught in a bind when her socialist coalition partners decided to support Governor Suzuki Shunichi's plans to develop Tokyo Bay. This project may harm the coastal environment.[58] However, such an outcome is but one possibility in a coalition arrangement. If NET can increase its strength and improve its bargaining position, it is less likely to be held hostage by more powerful coalition partners.[59]

Yokota and Ikeda, founding fathers of Kanagawa and Chiba SC respectively, have offered different visions of NET as a coalition partner. Yokota, because of his experiences in the labor movement and his attachment to the JSP as a long-time member and advisor, advocated a Red–Green coalition to counter the LDP.[60] To Yokota, Red included labor and the JSP while Green symbolized NET at the core of the environmental movement. Conceptually, this was similar to Germany's Red–Green coalition at the local level between the SPD and the Green Party against the conservatives, the Christian Democrats. However the Red–Green alignment was problematic in Japan because the JSP could not arrest its inexorable decline. Given the disintegration of the JSP, it is unrealistic to expect that a Red–Green coalition can provide sufficient numbers to check the conservatives. Moreover, the supporters of both parties came from different social composition. The JSP was backed by unions comprising mostly white- and blue-collar male workers while NET was supported by SC women members whose husbands belong to the white-collar managerial class. Backed by different social groups with their particular interests, it would not be easy for Red and Green organizations to harmonize their interests and strategies. As an alternative to the moribund JSP, Kanagawa, Tokyo, and Hokkaidō NET endorsed the Minshutō in the 1996 Lower House Election to prevent a conservative landslide by the LDP and Shinshintō. However, it is doubtful whether NET can significantly influence a much larger national party which has its own agenda. If the Minshutō were to sink eventually into oblivion after initial media publicity over its formation, it would be difficult for NET to play even an indirect role in national politics.

Being a well-intentioned underdog in local politics, NET has been treated by the Japanese press with kid gloves.[61] If the party were to expand, the press might subject it to closer and more critical scrutiny. Will it become a shooting star in Japanese politics, nothing more than an interesting footnote about a failed Green party? Even in the worst scenario where NET fizzles out, the ushering in of an unprecedented number of assembly women in local politics may be a source of inspiration to other women's organizations and candidates in the years ahead. If women can make a mark in Japan's local politics in increasing numbers, perhaps other women may be inspired to believe that they can stake a claim for equality not only in the political realm but also in social and economic spheres of Japanese society.

10 Conclusion

Advanced industrial democracies have experienced a significant shift in their values and social structures. According to the theory of value change, this transformation underpins the rise of social movements and Green parties as the political mode of social change. This hypothesis is supported in varying degrees by the experiences of certain West European countries. Japan has also experienced substantial changes to its values and social structures; various Japanese social movements and political parties have also adopted certain principles and practices that are associated with the West European Greens. But no significant Green parties have arisen in Japan. NET, the "Greenest" party in that nation, lacks certain characteristics that qualify it as a full-fledged Green party; it appears to be more hierarchical than most European Greens. Moreover, unlike the Greens in certain West European countries, no Japanese New Politics party has won elections at the national level.

If activists from the German Green Party were to examine NET, they would superficially discover many recognizable features of the New Politics party: the pursuit of ecological protection, pacifism, an alternative economy, the desire for a participatory culture, a rotation system to limit the terms of its assembly women, the party's control of its representative's salary, an organization populated by women, and amateurs who are not primarily motivated by material incentives. There are, however, glaring differences between NET and the West European Green Parties (Figure 10.1). These include: affluent housewife activists who are led by males; the narrow emphasis on motherhood, soap, and rubbish instead of feminism and other larger societal issues; and narrow social support from housewives rather than students, youths, male and female white-collar professionals. NET even adopts *kōenkai* and depends on an external sponsor, the SC, which offers goods and services to local residents.

A defining characteristic of the New Politics party is an anti-hierarchical orientation in principle and practice. Despite the idealism of the West

Table 10.1 A comparison between NET and the West European Green parties

	Western Europe	*Japan*
Grassroots organization	Party	a) Party b) *Kōenkai*
Top leaders	Male and female	Male
Social base	Youth, highly educated, white-collar professionals (male and female)	Urban, upper-middle-class housewives
Motivation of activists	Purposive (primary) Solidaristic (secondary)	Solidaristic (primary)
Issues	Ecology, human rights, direct participation, anti-nuclear energy, pacifism, feminism	Similar except: feminism Frame of reference: motherhood Emphasis: soap and rubbish, safe food
External Sponsor		Seikatsu Club/Green Co-op North Block

European Greens to promote direct participation by ordinary members in their decision-making processes and organization, they have succumbed to oligarchic tendencies. But these tendencies are even more pronounced in NET because of the male-led origins of the Seikatsu Club and the social norms of male leadership in Japanese society. Men spearheaded both parent and child organizations, their ideology, and grand strategy while women tended the day-to-day grassroots activities. The founding fathers and the SC male professional staff continue to wield an influence greatly disproportionate to their actual numbers. Male dominance is not an aberration; it is common among many Japanese social movements. Margaret McKean writes:

> Japanese observers often note the predominance of women in the anti-pollution movement. It may be that the majority of the rank and file members of citizens' movements in Japan were in fact women, but because our sample also tapped leadership levels it included more men. Indeed, except for all-women groups, the leadership of anti-pollution groups in our sample was entirely male. [I]n groups that also contain men, leadership activities in such groups tend to be performed by male members whenever traditional beliefs about female roles in voluntary organizations is greater, with women accepting decisions made by men, the women acting only in their own neighborhoods, and the men conducting communication outside of the group.[1]

Despite the rise of ecological consciousness among many affluent, well-educated, urban Japanese, they also continue to retain the "traditional" values of deference to male leadership, motherhood, and group loyalties. Thus, voters with a concern for ecology do not necessarily support a party that espouses environmental protection. Their behavior, therefore, is influenced by profound "traditional" values which have overriding importance over their interests in ecology. Although the SC and NET pursue ecological themes similar to those of the European Greens, there are also differences in nuances. While organic food, a ban on synthetic soap, and the separation of rubbish fall within the rubric of ecology, these are also issues which fall within the purview of traditional motherhood in Japan. European and Japanese Greens may champion similar ecology issues but the frame of reference is different. The former are feminists while the latter are "worrying mothers." Single women in Japan are unlikely to respond to the appeals of motherhood, and it is necessary for Japanese social movements to broaden their appeal beyond the prism of maternity.

The New Politics issues of Western Europe such as ecology, concern over nuclear power, stations and pacifism are not always interpreted as New Politics issues in a different national context. While NET has claimed them as its own, these are also issues which have been associated with the Old Left in Japan. To some voters, NET's platform may have little novelty appeal; they are also associated with the Old Politics of the moribund JSP and JCP. Moreover, the established parties from the Center and Right also support some aspects of environmental protection. Thus, NET obviously does not monopolize ecological issues in Japan.

From our study of NET organizations, we discovered that many NET assembly women have adopted *kōenkai*, a type of organization associated with Old Politics in Japan. A formal personal candidate support organization distinct from the party organization is not apparent among the European Greens. Instead of relying solely on a policy-oriented party organization, NET has adopted *kōenkai*, a time-tested organizational approach in Japan, to maximize its votes. This approach conforms to social norms that stress interpersonal relations and small group loyalties even in urban Japan. Rather than the Green ideal of an egalitarian, policy-oriented organization as a tool to change society, NET, instead, has been changed by the electoral imperative to have personality-oriented organization to win elections.

Why are the Greens exceptionally weak in Japan? That no significant New Politics party has emerged can be attributed to a constellation of particular problems faced by them, to the persisting strength of the Old Politics parties, and to the less hospitable institutional and cultural climate in Japan. To survive under these conditions, NET has adapted to its environment despite its pretensions of promoting a new social and political order. These compromises include acquiring *kōenkai* and other oligarchic practices. The SC and NET have benefited from an open political system, urbanization that created a larger pool of potential recruits, and value change among the Japanese. Ironically, an open political system also permits the entry of new challengers especially the "new" parties, the Nihonshintō, Shinseitō, Sakigake, Shinshintō and Minshutō, that propose reforms in Japanese politics. This proliferation of "new" parties that have greater media exposure, resources, and strong local support creates an additional barrier to NET's aspirations to play a role beyond local politics. In the case of the German Greens, they also compete in a less crowded party system. Changing patterns of urbanization have also created new difficulties for the SC and NET. The SC thrived in an urbanizing milieu where housewives sought safe food and companionship, but a slowdown in Japan's urbanization has reduced this pool of new recruits. The emergence of new urban communities also has permitted political parties including the conservatives to tap these social networks for support.

SC and NET members are affluent, well-educated and have the leisure to engage in various activities. Moreover, NET has also taken root in many cities and wards whose electorate exhibits some post-material characteristics such as affluence, high levels of education, and a growing concern for ecology. But it is unlikely to expand by riding on the back of rising environmental concern. A desire for greater environmental protection among some voters is merely one dimension of value change. It appears that even its supporters of ecological protection continue to embrace values associated with Old Politics such as group loyalties, male leadership, and motherhood. Rising post-material values in mass attitudes that place less emphasis on money and greater emphasis on ecology are juxtaposed with a profound belief in other lingering "traditional" values. If the "post-material" elements in Japanese society continue to harbor deep "traditional values," it will be difficult for Green Parties to flourish in Japan.

The weaknesses of both parent and child organizations can be traced back to their origins. The die was cast at the SC's founding moment. Its members were essentially limited to a singular group of urban housewives who were organized into the *han*. Their subsequent mobilization into social movement activities was not motivated purely by a desire to seek social change but based upon the feelings of solidarity within the *han*. By restricting itself to a social composition of housewives, the co-op had concomitantly limited itself to a narrow range of issues that appeal to them. Narrow issues of motherhood, soap, and rubbish have limited appeal to groups outside its social web. Social norms of group loyalties and interpersonal ties are impediments to social movements that try to appeal to groups outside the movements' social networks purely on the basis of Green issues. The prospects for the SC and NET are not rosy, especially when confronted by the relative decline in the numbers of the urban housewives. In contrast, the West European Greens seem to have a broader support base beyond the urban housewives, motivated more by purposive rather than solidaristic incentive, and a wider range of policy appeals. They also do not embrace Marxism or its Gramscian variant, have more women in leadership positions, and inhabit a cultural terrain that does not always place group loyalties above self and policies.

The relative weakness of NET is due, in part, to the persistent strength of the Old Politics parties.[2] Large sections of the agrarian and industrial sectors continue to embrace values and behavior associated with "traditional" rather than "modern" values. Old Politics parties, especially the LDP and the JCP, have succeeded in organizing an impressive percentage of the urban voters even in a post-industrial society. Their political machines continue to tap the "traditional" sentiments of group loyalties in the "former villages," neighborhood associations, newly emerging urban communities, and other social networks in the most urbanized areas. Moreover, the JCP has shown remarkable resilience unlike most of its counterparts in Western Europe.

Epilogue

The theory of value change has limited applicability to Japanese politics. There is a correlation between the rise of some aspects of post-materialism and the emergence of social movements. However, the study of the SC demonstrates that any direct linkage between value change and its emergence is tenuous. Its birth and growth depend on the mobilization efforts of leaders, planning, organization building, targeting mobilizing issues, and the enlistment of urban housewives with the resources of affluence, education, and leisure. The steady growth of the SC has by no means been assured by the rise of post-materialism in Japan. It required strong leadership, organization building, and membership recruitment before it emerged as one of the largest Japanese social movement with an electoral arm.

The role of individuals looms large in the study of the SC and NET. The founding fathers, Iwane and Yokota, were indispensable to these enterprises. Is the strong leadership demonstrated in the case of the SC also present in various social movements and Green Parties of Western Europe? We should avoid making an *a priori* assumption: since Green parties are reputed to be egalitarian in spirit, they are unlikely to yield domineering leaders. Whether or not the Green parties are established and led by strong individuals or not is an empirical question to be verified. The Japanese case study proves that, despite the rhetoric of an ecology party, strong leaders do exercise great influence on the organization. Future research on Green parties should examine more closely the roles of founding members, top parliamentary and non-parliamentary leaders. Do women exercise real influence as top leaders in the Green parties? If they do not, then there is an enormous gap between the ideals and the realities of the Green parties.

More impressive than "value change" is the profound continuity of various aspects of Japanese values and behavior. Supporters of urban parties ranging from NET to LDP are influenced by the deep values of small group loyalties that transcend "materialism" and "post-materialism." Thus, "value persistence" is an underlying factor in influencing the behavior of the Japanese political parties, social movements, and voters. This does not deny that value change has taken place. It merely recognizes the fact that "value persistence" exerts a profound impact on actors regardless of their ideological hues and social bases of political support. Regardless of their "premodern," "modern," and "post-modern" bases, all political parties in Japan engage in the provision of goods and services. The organizational vehicle is *kōenkai*. Even the JCP and NET have adopted this approach to mobilize political support. In addition, its parent organization, the SC, provides food and other services to local residents. Given the Japanese focus on personality, the bond of the small group, and tangible goods and services, ideology *per se*, whether Red or Green, will have limited efficacy in Japan.

The Greens are caught in an electoral dilemma. In order to promote change, they must join the electoral process. To win elections, they cannot dispense with leadership, organization, and attractive candidates; organizations and hierarchy are as necessary in a post-industrial society as in an industrial one. Hence any political parties or social movements that are naive enough to forsake organizations are unlikely to be politically effective. To avoid being a fringe party, they also need to broaden their social bases and dilute their radicalism in order to make the party more acceptable to a wider electorate. But when they do, they are co-opted by the political process, contravene Green ideals, alienate some of the Green idealists, and they risk losing their core supporters. It is difficult to see how Green parties can break out of this contradiction and emerge as a major force in advanced democracies.

Urban political organizations and political mobilization in Japan depend on social networks whose cohesion comes from personal ties, group loyalties, and reciprocal obligations rather than a purely ideological approach. In Japan, solidarity goals even among social movement activities are just as important if not more so than purposive incentives. Because of the pervasive social reality of "groupishness" in that country, the social network approach has been applied to the study of Japanese voting behavior.[3] A reviewer of this approach writes:

> [T]he authors [Flanagan *et. al.*] develop a social network model that owes its heritage primarily to Japanese studies. Though derived from Japanese studies, the social model is also a comparative model, supported by evidence from Europe and North America and meant to be applied to voting behavior in any industrial democracy.[4]

This approach can also be applied to the comparative study of social movements and Green parties.

To what extent do Green parties in Western Europe rely on social networks? Do they rely more on campaign and media technology by appealing to post-materialists through television, advertisements, and direct mail rather than person-to-person contacts? An emphasis on the circles of human relationships between leaders, activists, supporters, and voters may provide us with an explanation of how people with post-material values ended up campaigning and voting for Green parties rather than seeking *non*-political, post-material pursuits. Recent research on social movements in Western Europe suggests that such activities are also based on social networks.[5] However, it is unclear whether these networks are based primarily on policy or personal ties. This study has highlighted the importance of social networks for political parties and social movement activities in urban Japan. Similarly, New Politics in Western Europe may be better understood by examining their social networks, the underlying social glue, the building of new networks, and the limits to their growth. The inability to cast their social nets wider and further to pull in more diverse supporters contributes to the marginal position of the Greens in Western Europe and especially Japan.

Notes

1 Introduction

1 On the importance of class cleavages which structured political alignments in Western Europe, see Seymour Martin Lipset and Stein Rokkan, eds., *Party Systems and Voter Alignments* (New York: Free Press, 1967); Ronald Inglehart, *Culture Shift in Advanced Industrial Society* (Princeton, NJ: Princeton University Press, 1990); and Frances Fox Piven, ed., *Labor Parties in Post Industrial Societies* (Cambridge: Polity Press, 1991).
2 Maurice Duverger, *Political Parties* (London: Methuen, 1959).
3 Arend Lijphart, *Democracy in Plural Societies* (New Haven, CN and London: Yale University Press, 1977). For a summary of social cleavages and politics, see Jan-Erik Lane and Svante O. Ersson, *Politics and Society in Western Europe*, second edition (London: Sage, 1991), pp. 22–25, 52–100.
4 For a comprehensive explanation of the decomposition of electoral alignments in Western countries, see Russell J. Dalton, Paul Allen Beck, and Scott C. Flanagan, eds., *Electoral Changes in Advanced Democracies: Realignment or Dealignment?* (Princeton, NJ: Princeton University Press, 1984).
5 Piven, *Labor Parties in Post Industrial Societies*, p. 1. This observation is correct even though the Labour Party of Britain and the French Socialist Party won their national elections in 1997. Both parties, despite retaining their party labels, have shifted to the Center, sought support from the middle class and are no longer predominantly working-class parties.
6 Kitschelt identified eight countries as "clear" cases of countries with "significant Left-Libertarian Parties." They are: Austria, Belgium, Denmark, the Netherlands, Norway, West Germany, Iceland, and Luxembourg. See Herbert P. Kitschelt, "Left-Libertarian Parties: Explaining Innovation in Competitive Party Systems," *World Politics*, Vol. XL, No. 2, January 1988. For a summary of Green parties in the world, see Ferdinand Müller-Rommel, "Green Parties and Alternative Lists under Cross-national Perspective" in Ferdinand Müller-Rommel, ed., *New Politics in Western Europe: The Rise and Success of Green Parties and Alternative Lists* (Boulder, CO: Westview Press, 1989).
7 Malthias Kaelberer, "The Emergence of Green Parties in Western Europe," *Comparative Politics*, Vol. 25, No. 2, January 1993, p. 229.
8 Robert Michels, *Political Parties: A Sociological Study of the Oligarchical Tendencies of Modern Democracy* (London: Macmillan, 1962).
9 Kitschelt, "Left-Libertarian Parties: Explaining Innovation in Competitive Party Systems."

10 Thomas Poguntke, "New Politics and Party Systems: The Emergence of a New Type of Party?," *West European Politics*, Vol. 10, No. 1, January 1987.

11 *Ibid.* See also Ferdinand Müller-Rommel, "New Political Movements and 'New Politics' Parties in Western Europe" in Russell J. Dalton and Manfred Kuechler, eds., *Challenging the Political Order: New Social and Political Movements in Western Democracies* (New York: Oxford University Press, 1990).

12 This seemingly contradictory term is used to describe the German Green Party. See E. Gene Frankland, "Federal Republic of Germany: 'Die Grünen'" in Müller-Rommel, *New Politics in Western Europe*, p. 61.

13 Manfred Kuechler and Russell J. Dalton, "New Social Movements and the Political Order: Inducing Change for Long-term Stability" in Dalton and Kuechler, *Challenging the Political Order*. A summary of the various interchangeable terms is found in Thomas Poguntke, "Between Ideology and Empirical Research: The Literature on the German Green Party," *European Journal of Political Research*, Vol. 21, No. 4, June 1992.

14 For a good discussion on the overlapping features of social movements and political parties, see Gordon Smith, "Social Movements and Party Systems in Western Europe" in Martin Kolinsky and William E. Paterson, eds., *Social and Political Movements in Western Europe* (London: Croom Helm, 1976).

15 Sidney Tarrow, "Social Movements" in Adam Kuper and Jessica Kuper, eds., *The Social Science Encyclopaedia* (London: Routledge and Kegan Paul, 1985), p. 78.

16 Leon D. Epstein, "Political Parties" in Fred I. Greenstein and Nelson W. Polsby, eds., *Handbook of Political Science*, Volume 4 (Reading, Massachusetts: Addison-Wesley, 1975), p. 230.

17 For summaries of Green parties' participation in coalition government, see the various country studies in Müller-Rommel, *New Politics in Western Europe*.

18 On the issues of New Politics and electoral realignment, see Dalton, Flanagan, and Beck, *Electoral Change in Advanced Industrial Democracies*.

19 The term "post-industrial society" is often associated with Daniel Bell. See Daniel Bell, *The Coming of Post Industrial Society* (New York: Basic Books, 1973). For a list of indicators of post-industrial society, see Samuel P. Huntington, "Postindustrial Politics: How Benign Will It Be?," *Comparative Politics*, Vol. 6, No. 2, January 1974, pp. 163–166.

20 For a good summary of various theories that seek to explain the decline of class voting, see Dalton, Flanagan, and Beck, *Electoral Change in Advanced Industrial Democracies*, pp. 15–22.

21 Ronald Inglehart, *The Silent Revolution: Changing Values and Political Styles Among Western Publics* (Princeton, NJ: Princeton University Press, 1977). Inglehart is obviously not the only scholar who wrote on value change. Scott C. Flanagan, among others, has also worked on value change with Japan as a case study. Despite differences in nuances, conceptualization, and measurement of value change between Inglehart and Flanagan, both agree that there is greater emphasis on self-actualization and better quality of life issues among the masses of advanced industrialized democracies. For the debate on value change between Inglehart and Flanagan, see their two separate articles listed under the same heading of "Value Change in Industrial Societies," *American Political Science Review*, Vol. 81, No. 4, December 1987, pp. 1,289–1,318. See also Samuel H. Barnes, Max Kaase, *et al.*, *Political Actions: Mass Participation in Five Western Democracies* (Beverly Hills, CA: Sage, 1979).

22 Inglehart's theory of value change is based on Maslow's "hierarchy of needs." See

Inglehart, *The Silent Revolution*, pp. 22–23, 41–42, 137–138. According to Maslow, once basic or physiological needs are met, it is human nature to desire quality of life issues such as self actualization. See Abraham H. Maslow's Chapter 5, "A Theory of Human Motivation," in *Motivation and Personality* (New York: Harper, 1954), pp. 80–106.

23 This is a key theme in Inglehart, *Culture Shift in Advanced Industrial Society.*

24 See for example, Martin Kolinsky and William E. Paterson, *Social and Political Movements in Western Europe* (London: Croom Helm, 1976); Russell J. Dalton, *Citizen Politics in Western Democracies* (Chatham, NJ: Chatham House Publishers, 1988); Müller-Rommel, *New Politics in Western Europe*; and Dalton and Kuechler, *Challenging the Political Order.* Inglehart's *Culture Shift in Advanced Industrial Society* includes Japan in its comprehensive sweep, but it deals primarily with value change and has nothing to say about social movements and Green parties in Japan.

25 Robert Harmel, "On the Study of New Parties," *International Political Science Review*, Vol. 6, No. 4, 1985, p. 415.

26 Huntington, "Postindustrial Politics: How Benign Will it Be?," p. 163. A rough rule of thumb to indicate a post-industrial society is a country whose tertiary sector exceeds 50 percent of the whole economy in terms of occupational structures.

27 See for example, Taketsugu Tsurutani, *Political Change in Japan: Response to Post Industrial Challenge* (New York: David McKay, 1977) and Roger Benjamin and Kan Ori, *Tradition and Change in Postindustrial Japan: The Role of the Political Parties* (New York: Praeger, 1981).

28 The argument that Japan is experiencing a value change which places a greater premium on participation, individuality, and ecological issues among its citizens is also found in the following works: Scott C. Flanagan, "Changing Values in Advanced Industrial Societies: Inglehart's Silent Revolution from the Perspective of Japanese Findings," *Comparative Political Studies*, Vol. 14, No. 4, January 1982; Flanagan, "Electoral Change in Japan: A Study of Secular Realignment" in Dalton, Beck and Flanagan, *Electoral Change in Advanced Industrial Democracies*; Donald J. Calista, "Postmaterialism and Value Convergence: Value Priorities of Japanese Compared with Their Perceptions of American Values," *Comparative Political Studies*, Vol. 16, No. 4, January 1984; Ronald Inglehart, "Changing Values in Japan and the West," *Comparative Political Studies*, Vol. 14, No. 4, January 1982; and Inglehart, *Culture Shift in Advanced Industrial Society*, pp. 72–74, 144–153. Inglehart and Abramson also note:

> More strikingly still, the overall pattern [postmaterialism] that emerges in Japan and South Korea is the same as we find in Western Europe and Latin America. Although these two East Asian societies started with profoundly different cultural traditions from those of the West, they have both become advanced industrial societies – and their publics respond in a fashion that is almost indistinguishable from those of Western respondents. . . . The two East Asian countries not only conform to theoretical expectations, they actually show a slightly better fit than do most Western countries. The evidence indicates that the emergence of a polarization between Materialists goals and Postmaterialist goals is not a uniquely Western phenomenon. It is a phenomenon of advanced industrial society.
>
> (Paul R. Abramson and Ronald Inglehart, *Value Change in Global Perspective* (Ann Arbor, MI: University of Michigan Press, 1995), pp. 110–111)

29 In January 1994, a new electoral system in the Lower House was introduced in

Japan. It has two components: a first-past-the-post system coupled with proportional representation by party list.

30 Masumi believes that the environmental movement will not be able to sustain an electoral challenge in Japan. He writes: "[I]t is quite inconceivable that such an organization would develop into a political party with parliamentary representation, as in the case of the Greens in West Germany." See Junnosuke Masumi, "The 1955 System in Japan and Its Subsequent Development," *Asian Survey*, Vol. 28, No. 3, March 1988, p. 297.

Flanagan also writes: "It should be pointed out that there is no "New Party" per se in Japan and the Communists and center parties imperfectly represent the emerging New Politics agenda of interests and issues." See Flanagan, "Electoral Change in Japan: A study of Secular Realignment" in Dalton, Flanagan, and Beck, *Electoral Change in Advanced Industrial Democracies*, p. 182.

Kitschelt in his survey of New Politics parties in the world did not consider Japan to have even a marginal Green Party. See Kitschelt, "Left-Libertarian Parties: Explaining Innovation in Competitive Party Systems," pp. 198–199. An organization called the "Green Party" was founded in Kochi prefecture in 1982 but it did not make any electoral impact. See Ronald J. Hrebenar, *The Japanese Party System* (Boulder: Westview Press, 1986), p. 226.

31 In Japanese it is called *Nettowāku undō*.

32 See for example, *Mainichi shinbun*, April 23, 1991, p. 28 and *Asahi shinbun*, April 10, 1991, p. 27.

33 *Yomiuri shinbun*, evening edition, April 25, 1991, p. 9.

34 *Dairinin Undō*, No. 14, September 1996, p. 1.

35 For overlapping typologies of Old and New Politics, see Claus Offe, "New Social Movements: Challenging the Boundaries of Institutional Politics," *Social Research*, Vol. 52, No. 4, Winter 1985, p. 832 and Herbert Kitschelt, "Organization and Strategy of Belgian and West German Ecology Parties: New Dynamic of Party Politics in Western Europe?," *Comparative Politics*, Vol. 20, No. 2, January 1988, p. 131.

36 Some of these issues that are associated with the Greens had also been dealt with by movements before the advent of the post-industrial society. For example, the suffragette movement, the consumer co-operative movement, and the peace movement were prominent even in the early twentieth century. Obviously, while post-materialism may create conducive conditions for social movements and Green parties, it is not even a necessary condition for social movements when we consider the historical evidence. However, there is a correlation between the rise of post-industrialism and the advent of Green parties. One fascinating characteristic is their presence in different advanced industrial democracies at around the same time and advocating a wide range of similar issues.

37 Offe, "New Social Movements," p. 833.

38 See Michels, *Political Parties*.

39 Daniel Bell, "The Old War," *New Republic*, August 23 and 30, 1993, p. 18.

40 See Kitschelt, "Organization and Strategy of Belgian and West German Ecology Parties."

41 The terms "post-industrial," "advanced industrial," and "post-modern" are used interchangeably in this book.

42 This is also the case in other post-industrial societies, but the exclusion of women from top leadership positions in the political economy appears to be more acute in Japan.

43 Inglehart writes:

> Industrialization, urbanization, the attainment of prosperity, and other aspects of modernization have taken place so rapidly that even while Japan is taking a leading role among advanced industrial nations, some segments of the population are still undergoing the retreat from preindustrial values. The transition from preindustrial values to industrial values has been superimposed on the shift from Materialism to Postmaterialist priorities.
> (Inglehart, *Culture Shift in Advanced Industrial Society*, p. 146)

44 Harmel, "On the Study of New Parties," p. 416. A similar opinion by another reviewer of the New Politics literature prescribes:

> [W]hat is largely absent from the literature about green parties is an evaluation of the interaction between old and new left. The authors treat the greens more or less in isolation. Moreover it is largely unclear what kind of role communist parties play in the interaction between old and new left.
> (Kaelberer, "The Emergence of Green Parties in Western Europe," pp. 240–241)

45 See Joji Watanuki, "Social Structure and Voting Behavior" in Scott C. Flanagan, *et al.*, *The Japanese Voter* (New Haven, CN and London: Yale University Press, 1991).

46 See Joji Watanuki, "Patterns of Politics in Present-day Japan" in Seymour Martin Lipset and Stein Rokkan, eds., *Party Systems and Voter Alignments* (New York: Free Press, 1967).

47 The Kōmeitō depends on a proselytising Buddhist organization, Soka Gakkai, for support while the DSP relies on labor unions for its survival.

48 Kaelberer, "The Emergence of Green Parties in Western Europe," p. 236.

49 This approach is inspired by Charles Tilly, *From Mobilization to Revolution* (Reading, MA: Addison-Wesley, 1978). See also Mayer N. Zald and John D. McCarthy, *Social Movement in an Organizational Society* (New Brunswick, NJ and Oxford: Transaction Books, 1987) and J. Craig Jenkins, "Resource Mobilization Theory and the Study of Social Movements," *Annual Review of Sociology*, Vol. 9, 1983, pp. 527–550.

50 "Japan, in its fairly long history, has produced few, if any, dictatorial or charismatic leaders of the caliber of Napoleon, Hitler or Peter the Great. Japanese groupism does not permit any individual to shine or stand out." Kanji Haitani, "The Paradox of Japan's Groupism: Threat to Future Competitiveness," *Asian Survey*, Vol. 30, No. 3, March 1990, p. 241.

51 See Dalton and Kuechler, *Challenging the Political Order*.

52 Angelo Panebianco, *Political Parties: Organization and Power* (Cambridge: Cambridge University Press, 1988), p. xiii.

2 The Liberal Democratic Party and urban political machines

1 Among the largest cities of Tokyo, Yokohama, Osaka, Nagoya, Sapporo, Kyoto, Kobe, Fukuoka, Kawasaki, and Kita-Kyushu, Yokohama has consistently been

among the top three cities that chalked up the highest rate of population increase between 1970 and 1988. See Yokohama shiritsu daigaku keizai kenkyūsha, *Yokohama no keizai to shakai 1990* [Yokohama's Economy and Society] (Yokohama: Yokohama shiritsu daigaku, 1991), p. 30.

2 Yokohama was founded as a city port only in 1859, a consequence of American gunboat diplomacy and pressure on the Tokugawa Shogunate to provide the U.S. with trading rights and port facilities. From its beginning, Yokohama has been exposed to foreign influence and was the first city to publish a Japanese-language newspaper in 1864. Few cities in Japan can claim to be more international, modern, and open than Yokohama. The brief historical description of Yokohama is based on Yokohama City University, *Yokohama Past and Present* (Yokohama: Yokohama City University, 1990).

3 *Ibid.*, pp. 190–191.

4 The classic account of the *kōenkai* is found in Gerald L. Curtis, *Election Campaigning Japanese Style* (Tokyo: Kodansha International, 1983) first paperback edition. For other references to *kōenkai* in pre-war Japan, see Abe Hitoshi, Shindō Muneyuki, and Kawato Sadafumi, *Gaisetsu: gendai nihon no seiji* [An Outline: The Politics of Contemporary Japan] (Tokyo: Tokyo daigaku shuppankai, 1990), p. 152 and Masumi Junnosuke, *Nihon seiji shi* [The History of Japanese Politics] (Tokyo: Tokyo daigaku shuppankai, 1988), Vol. 3, p. 90.

5 The first four factors are mentioned in Curtis, *Election Campaigning Japanese Style*.

6 Positive evaluations of the U.S. urban machines are found in Richard Hofstadter, "The Citizen and the Machine" and Robert Merton, "Some Functions of the Political Machine" both in Jeffrey K. Hadden *et al.*, *Metropolis in Crisis* (Itasca, IL: F.E. Peacock, 1967). For recent evaluation of U.S. urban machines see Steven P. Erie, "Bringing the Bosses Back in: The Irish Political Machines and Urban Policy Making," in *Studies in American Political Development*, Volume 4 (New Haven, CN and London: Yale University Press, 1990) and Terrence J. McDonald, "The Burdens of Urban History: The Theory of the State in Recent American Social History," *Studies in American Political Development*, Volume 3 (New Haven, CN and London: Yale University Press, 1989).

7 Inoguchi Takashi and Iwai Tomoaki, *Zoku giin no kenkyū* [A Study of Policy Tribes] (Tokyo: Nihon keizai shinbun, 1987), p. 69. According to their survey, 16.6 percent of the national electorate and 14.7 percent of the voters in Mito city (their case study) believed that there are politicians who offer collective benefits to them.

8 Maurice Duverger, *Political Parties*, p. xxvii quoted by Leon D. Epstein, "Political Parties" in Fred I. Greenstein and Nelson W. Polsby, eds., *Handbook of Political Science* (Reading, MA: Addison-Wesley, 1975), p. 249.

9 Masumi, *Nihon seiji shi*, p. 341.

10 Miki Takeo, later Prime Minister, advised in October 1963, "Though we cannot ban personal *kōenkai* at present, they pose not a little problem for party activity due to their singular concentration on personal interest. We must think of ways to absorb them into the party organization in the future." See Masumi, "The 1955 System in Japan and its Subsequent Development," p. 292.

11 See also, *ibid.*, p. 376 and Curtis, *Election Campaigning Japanese Style*, pp. 138–140.

12 *Ibid.*, Curtis, pp. 136–137.

13 *Ibid.*, pp. 40–43, 126–178.

14 *Ibid.*, p. 137.

15 *Ibid.*

16 Information from Diet Member Suzuki Tsuneo (Kanagawa District One) who was a former political secretary of Kōno Yōhei. Interview on June 13, 1991.

17 Diet Member Kamei Yoshiyuki, interview on March 15, 1993.

18 Ukishima Toshio, Office Manager, LDP Kanagawa Prefectural Chapter, interview on March 1, 1991.

19 Yajima Mitsuhiro, *Kochira ishihara shintarō jimusho desu* [Hello, This is Ishihara Shintarō's Office] (Tokyo: Nihon bungeisha, 1991), pp. 68–71.

20 Tsurutani, *Political Change in Japan*, p. 87.

21 Statistics are taken from various years of ASSK.

22 Curtis, *The Japanese Way of Politics*, p. 200.

23 Miyake Ichirō, "Types of Partisanship, Partisan Attitudes, and Voting Choices" in Flanagan *et al.*, *The Japanese Voter* (New Haven, CN and London: Yale University Press, 1991), p. 258.

24 *Ibid.* Although Miyake did not say that *kōenkai* members are "loyal partisans", it is obvious that *kōenkai* participants fit best into this analytical category.

25 According to one survey, only 8.5 percent of LDP candidates' *kōenkai* supporters paid membership fees. *ASSK*, 1996, p. 377.

26 An example of obligation and human relationship as ties that bind the candidate and his or her supporter is my experience of gaining access to Umezawa Kenji. When I was studying Japanese at the Inter-University Center in Yokohama, I met Hiramoto Masao, host father to a classmate at the Center. Hiramoto turned out to be a close supporter and family friend of Umezawa. I was told that Hiramoto's father supported Umezawa with a religious fervor (*shūkyōteki*). The father was once hospitalized during an election campaign and Umezawa took time off from the campaign to visit him in hospital. Hiramoto senior was so touched by Umezawa's gesture of concern despite the ongoing campaign that he burst into tears. From that point in time, the Hiramoto family became staunch supporters of Umezawa. Because of an act of compassion by the candidate toward his father, Hiramoto has also imbibed the sense of gratitude, trust, and friendship toward Umezawa that transcends material benefits.

27 *ASSK*, 1996, pp. 373. Another 36.8 percent claimed that they joined the *kōenkai* because they liked the personality and the outlook of the conservative candidate.

28 For an account of "former village" mentality among residents of a small town in Kyushu Island in the 1960s, see Curtis, *Election Campaigning Japanese Style*, pp. 58–59.

29 Yokohama shi midori ku yakusho, *Midori: midori-ku kusei gaiyō* [An Outline of Midori ward's Administration], 1990, p. 7. Booklet published by Yokohama city in 1991. The names of the five "former villages" are Nihari, Tsuda, Yamanouchi, Nakazato, and Tana.

30 This information was repeated by all four LDP city assembly members from Midori ward whom I interviewed. The four are Shimamura Masao (Tsuda "former village"), interview on December 2, 1991; Kobayashi Syōzaburō (Tana "former village"), interview on December 4, 1991; Yoshimura Yoneju (Yamanouchi "former village"), interview on January 10, 1992; and Yajima Seiji (Nihari "former village"), interview on November 22, 1991.

In the 1991 Local Election, LDP candidates captured four out of 11 city assembly seats in Midori ward. In previous elections the conservatives usually captured five seats. In the 1991 Elections, the fifth LDP city assembly member from Nakazato "former village" retired from politics. That locality did not reach a consensus to support a particular successor. It was believed that in the 1991

Election, conservative voters from that "former village" split their support among the four remaining LDP candidates from the neigboring "former villages."

31 Ichikawa Taiichi, *"Seshū" daigishi no kenkyū* [A Study of Hereditary Diet Members] (Tokyo: Nihon keizai shinbunsha, 1990), p. 14.

32 Only 10.3 percent of Midori's residents were born in the same ward. In the 1991 Local Election, LDP city assembly members won 36.4 percent of the votes in Midori ward. Thus, a substantial percentage of the conservatives' votes came from migrants. Despite the very high level of voters' concern for ecological issues in that ward, NET captured only 11.7 percent of the votes in Midori ward in 1991. Statistics are from Yokohama shi senkyo kanri iinkai, *Yokohama shimin no tōhyō sanka jōkyō chōsa* [Survey on the Voting Conditions of Yokohama Residents] (Yokohama: 1991), p. 10 and Mainichi shinbunsha, *1991 Tōitsu chihō senkyo* [1991 Local Elections] (Tokyo: Mainichi shinbunsha, 1991), p. 316.

33 Miyoshi Yoshikiyo, interview on December 5, 1991; Kojima Yukiyasu, interview on March 18, 1993.

34 *Chōnai* is translated as town, street, or neighborhood depending on the context. *Jichikai* literally means self-governing association. This term is used more often in *danchi* areas and has a less traditional flavor. Despite the differences in terminology between *chōnaikai* and *jichikai* they are essentially the same.

35 Iwaseki Nobuhiko, *Chōnaikai no kenkyū* [Research on the Neighborhood Association] (Tokyo: Ocha no mizu shobo, 1989), p. 442.

36 Yokohama shi shiminkyoku, *Jūmin soshiki no genjō to katsudō* [The Activities and Present Conditions of Residents' Organizations and Local Groups] (Yokohama: Yokohama shi shiminkyoku, 1991), pp. 1, 3.

37 Kurasawa Susumu and Akimoto Ritsuo, eds., *Chōnaikai to chiiki shudan* [Neighborhood Associations and Local Groups] (Tokyo: Minerubia shobo, 1990), pp. 1, 3.

38 For other recent articles on the *chōnaikai*, see Endō Fumio, "Jichikai, chōnaikai nado no jūmin jichi soshiki to shichōson gyōsei to no kankei" [The Relationship Between Neighborhood Association and City-Village Local Administrations], *Jichi kenkyū*, Part 1, Vol. 819, No. 5, May 1992, pp. 3–17, Part 2, Vol. 820, No. 6, June 1992, pp. 3–14, and Nakagawa Go, "Chōnaikai no kaifuku" [The Revival of Neighborhood Associations], *Toshi Mondai Kenkyū*, Vol. 45, No. 5, May 1993, pp. 18–29.

39 Yokohama shi shiminkyoku, *Jūmin soshiki no genjō to katsudō*, pp. 22–24.

40 *Ibid.*, p. 62.

41 *Ibid.*, p. 37.

42 Sōmukyoku jimu kanribu tōkeika, *Yokohama shi no nōgyō* [The Agriculture of Yokohama City] (Yokohama: 1990), p. 31.

43 *Ibid.*, p. 62.

44 Yokohama shikai jimukyoku, *Yokohama shikai shi* [The History of Yokohama City Assembly] Volume 5 (Yokohama: 1985), pp. 1414–1417.

45 This is a slight modification of the various patterns of the involvement of neighborhood associations in election campaigning. See Iwaseki, *Chōnaikai no kenkyū*, p. 461.

46 In another survey, a comparison among Kyoto city, other smaller cities, and villages in Kyoto prefecture was made to discover the extent to which neighborhood associations and their affiliates act as support organizations for local politicians. The results indicate that slightly less than one-fifth of the neighborhood associations in Kyoto city provided organizational support to local politicians. In the villages, about two-thirds of *chōnaikai* extended organizational

backing to candidates. See Yoda Hiroshi, "Chihō giin to hoshu shihai no kiban" [Local Assemblymen and the Base of Conservative Rule] quoted in Aiba Juichi, ed., *Chiiki seiji no shaikaigaku* [The Sociology of Local Politics] (Tokyo: Seikai sisōsha, 1983), p. 69.

47 Miyake Ichirō, *Tōhyō kōdō* [Voting Behavior] (Tokyo: Tokyo daigaku shuppansha, 1989), p. 43.

48 *ASSK*, 1996, p. 362.

49 One of them, Yajima Seiji, was a former head of a *chōnaikai* federation. The author obtained a name list of all the *chōnaikai* federations from Midori ward's Election Management Committee in the ward office and gave a copy to each of the four assembly members to mark down the federations of neighborhood associations which supported them. In total, all four received support from 13 out of 24 federations of neighborhood associations in Midori ward.

50 Tano Sadako, JSP city assembly member (female), interview on February 24, 1992.

51 Ninagawa Shōichi, city assembly member and champion of anti-highway movement in Sakae ward, interview on February 6, 1992.

52 Matsumoto Kumiko, NET assembly member (female), Kōhoku ward, interview on March 25, 1992.

53 Aokage Takako, city assembly member (female), Asahi ward, Yokohama, interview on April 7, 1992.

54 Yokohama shi shiminkyoku, *Jūmin sosiki no genjō to katsudō*, p. 80.

55 Ishikawa Masumi and Hirose Mitsugu, *Jimintō chōki shihai no kōzō* [LDP: The Structure of Long-Term Dominance] (Tokyo: Iwanami shoten, 1989), p. 138.

56 Fukuda Susumu, interview on February 7, 1992.

57 For an account of the incident, see *Kanagawa shinbun*, April 23, 1983, p. 19.

58 Curtis, *Election Campaigning Japanese Style*, p. 111.

59 The campaign strategist (*sanbō*) is a *chōnaikai* head. One lieutenant of the campaign took particular pride in calling himself the boss of his neighborhood association.

60 The name of the complex is Nishi Terao Danchi in Kanagawa ward, Yokohama city.

61 Theodore C. Bestor gives a vivid account of the *mikosi* in the festival of a local community in Tokyo. However, his case study takes place in a *shitamachi* or traditional-like quarters of Tokyo. Festivals which include the portable shrines are found in relatively new *danchi* complexes too within the Tokyo metropolitan areas. For Bestor's account, see *Neighborhood Tokyo* (Stanford, CN: Stanford University Press, 1989). On the utility of festivals to foster a sense of community in metropolitan Japan, see also Jennifer Robertson, *Native and Newcomer: Making and Remaking a Japanese City* (Berkeley: University of California Press, 1991).

For an account of the mikoshi-carrying festival in a *danchi* complex in Yokohama city, see for example, *Kanagawa shinbun*, July 12, 1992, p. 18.

62 Curtis made a similar point:

> The settling down of the urban population has resulted in the growth of urban neighborhoods that are relatively stable in terms of population and that are increasingly characterized by the kinds of extended networks of personal relations, school and family ties, and active neighborhood associations (*chōnaikai*) that traditionally have provided major channels for LDP politician access to the electorate in small towns in the countryside.
>
> (Quote from *The Japanese Way of Politics*, p. 208)

For empirical studies on the emergence of a sense of community among urban residents, see Okuda Michihiro, *Toshi komyuniti no riron* [The Theory of Urban Community] (Tokyo: Tokyo daigaku shuppansha, 1983), pp. 24–67 and Morioka Kiyoshi, *et al.*, *Toshi shakaigaku no furontia* [The Frontiers of Urban Sociology] (Tokyo: Nihon hyōronsha, 1992).

63 Miyoshi Yoshikiyo, prefectural assembly member, Midori ward, Yokohama, interview on December 5, 1991.

64 Although Umezawa Kenji is extremely busy as the General Secretary of the LDP Kanagawa Prefectural Chapter, he made time to travel with his supporters on overseas trips to maintain the close personal ties between the candidate and his *kōenkai* members.

65 Information from Umezawa Kenji's *kōenkai* supporters who went on overseas vacation.

66 Suga Yoshihide, Nishi ward, Yokohama city, interview on April 9, 1993.

67 Iijima Tadayoshi of Sakae ward, a suburb of Yokohama, is a graduate of the prestigious Waseda University. He approaches the juniors and seniors from Waseda who reside in Sakae ward to support him. On the basis of a common school tie, new residents in Sakae ward who graduated from Waseda often give him their support. Iijima Tadayoshi, city assembly member, Sakae ward, Yokohama City, interview on March 30, 1993.

68 Ishikawa and Hirose, *Jimintō: chōki shihai no kōzō*, pp. 144–145.

69 Observation by Tano Sadako, JSP city assembly member (female), interview on February 27, 1992.

70 According to the police, there were 88,259 *yakuza* in 1990. *Nihon kokusei zue: 1992*, p. 555.

71 *Kanagawa Shinbun*, May 27, 1992, p. 19.

72 For a fascinating account of Fujiki, the LDP and the *yakuza* connection, see the four day series of the *Asahi shinbun*, June 16–19, 1992. The following account of Fujiki is based on the *Asahi shinbun*'s report.

Information on Fujiki's top post in the LDP assembly members' organization in Yokohama is taken from the membership directory kindly provided by a source who chooses to remain anonymous. Documents on Fujiki's position as chairman of Umezawa's fund raising organization is provided by the Kanagawa Prefecture Election Management Committee. Fujiki's chairmanship in Takeshita's fund raising organization in Kanagawa is found in the *Asahi shinbun*'s serialization on Fujiki.

73 *Ibid.*, June 16, 1992.

74 Satō Seizaburō and Matsuzaki Tetsuhisa, *Jimintō seiken* [LDP Rule] (Tokyo: Chūō kōronsha, 1986), pp. 114–116. *Min i* has a nuance close to general will (*sō i*).

75 Kamishima Jirō, ed., *Gendai nihon no seiji kōzō* [The Political Structure of Contemporary Japan] (Tokyo: Hōritsu bunkasha, 1985), p. 63.

76 See for example, Ichikawa, *"Seshū" daigishi no kenkyū* and Matsuzaki Tetsuhisa, *Nihongata demokurashi no gyakusetsu: nisei giin wa naze umareru no ka* [The Paradox of the Japanese Model of Democracy: Why have Second Generation Assembly Members Emerged?] (Tokyo: Tōjusha, 1991).

77 Curtis, *The Japanese Way of Politics*, p. 177.

78 For excellent accounts on the decline of the U.S. political machines, see David R. Mayhew, *Placing Parties in American Politics* (Princeton: Princeton University Press, 1986) and Alan Ware, *The Breakdown of Democratic Party Organization: 1940–1980* (Oxford: Oxford University Press, 1985).

79 Curtis, *Election Campaigning Japanese Style*, pp. 253–256.
80 See *Asahi shinbun*, June 29, 1993, p. 9.

3 The Liberal Democratic Party's quest for local policy-making party organization

1 A 1986 poll conducted by the *Asahi shinbun* quoted by Curtis, *The Japanese Way of Politics*, p. 50.
2 *Ibid.*
3 *Nihon kokusei zue*, 1992, p. 89.
4 *The Economist*, June 1, 1991, p. 28. The article commented:

> The LDP owes its majority in the Lower House to the loyalty of the over-represented farmers. However, with as many as three out of five LDP members being elected by voters who are literally dying out, party officials know it cannot be much longer before they have to dump the farmers in favor of the wage-earning city dwellers.

5 The Supreme Court ruled once again in January 1993 that the 1990 General Election was unconstitutional because of the disparity in the weightage of votes between urban and rural districts. See *Asahi shinbun*, Evening Edition, January 20, 1993, p. 1.
6 In Chiba District Four, a Diet Member has to serve 464,139 people while a Diet Member from Tokyo District Eight has to deal with only 136,330 people. Tokyo District Eight is of course not a rural district but, like most rural districts, it is suffering from depopulation. *Kanagawa shinbun*, August 15, 1992, p. 1.
7 *Kanagawa shinbun*, December 4, 1992, p. 1.
8 Initially 4 percent of market share was allotted to foreign rice. This will be increased gradually to 8 percent. Thereafter, tariffs may be introduced. *Asahi shinbun*, November 26, 1993, p. 2.
9 For the best summary on the various usage of the term "1955 system" see Miyake Ichirō *et.al.*, *Nihon seiji no zahyō* [The Co-ordinates of Japanese Politics] (Tokyo: Yūhikaku sensho, 1985), pp. 83–87, 117–124. See also Masumi, "The 1955 System in Japan and Its Subsequent Development" and Abe, Shindo, and Kawatō, *Gaisetsu: gendai nihon no seiji*, pp. 136–141.
10 *Jiyūminshu henshyūbu*, "1985 nen taisei e no tenbō" [Perspectives for the 1985 System] in *Jiyū minshu*, January 1982, pp. 224–229.
11 In 1980, the LDP won an absolute majority of 286 out of 511 seats. *Asahi nenkan*, 1981.
12 The LDP won only 250 out of 511 seats in the 1983 Lower House Election. *Asahi nenkan*, 1984, p. 75.
13 Tanaka represented the best and the worst of LDP politics. A dynamic leader who inaugurated Japan's welfare state with panache, he is also notorious for his money and machine politics. Tanaka's personal *kōenkai*, the Etsuzankai (Etsu Mountain Association) is usually cited as the model of the *kōenkai* approach. See for example, Igarashi Akio, "Daigishi kōenkai no seishinteki soshikiteki kōzō: moderu toshite no Etsuzankai" [The Spirit and the Organization of the Diet Members's *Kōenkai: Etsuzankai* as a Model] *Shisō*, May 1989, pp. 79–99. Fukuoka Masayuki, *Nihon no seiji fūdo: niigata sanku ni miru nihon seiji no genkei* [The Political

Culture of Japan: The Model of Japanese Politics as Seen in Niigata District Three] (Tokyo: Gakuyō shobō, 1985). See also Chalmers Johnson, "Tanaka Kakuei, Structural Corruption and the Advent of Machine Politics in Japan," *The Journal of Japanese Studies*, Vol. 12, No. 1, Winter 1986.

14 *Asahi nenkan*, 1987, p. 101.

15 Nakasone Yasuhiro, "Shinjidai o kizuku Jimintō no shimei: 1986 nen taisei no stāto" [The LDP's Mission to Constructing a New Era: The Start of the 1986 System], *Jiyū minshu*, October 1986, pp. 38–51.

16 Kent E. Calder, *Crisis and Compensation: Public Policy and Political Stability in Japan, 1949–1986* (Princeton: Princeton University Press, 1988), p. 115.

The most interesting piece on the LDP's 1986 system comes from the Japanese communists. See Kihara Satoru, "86 nen taisei ron no jitsuzō" [The Real Image of the 1986 System Debate], *Akahata hyōron toku shuppan*, July 27, 1987, pp. 12–18. It makes the interesting point that middle-class consciousness and conservatism toward livelihood issues are different from political conservatism among the masses. The article implies that livelihood conservatism among the Japanese will not be automatically translated into political support for the LDP.

17 Nakasone Yasuhiro, "Sengo seiji no sōkessan to wa nani ka" [What is the Comprehensive Settling of Accounts of Post-War Politics?] *Jiyū minshu*, November 1987, pp. 77–78.

18 Masumi, "The 1955 System in Japan and Its Subsequent Development," p. 305.

19 Matsuzaki Tetsuhisa, "86 nen taisei wa shinazu" [The 1986 System is not Dead], *Chūō kōron*, June 1987, pp. 142–154.

20 In the 1989 Upper House Election, the LDP won only 21 out of 76 local constituencies or 30.70 percent of the votes. In the proportional party listing, national constituency the LDP obtained 15 out of 50 seats or 27.32 percent of the total votes cast. *Asahi nenkan*, 1990, pp. 94–95. The defeat was due to the introduction of an unpopular consumption tax, the shares-for-favor Recruit scandal, which incriminated many LDP politicians, and the extra marital dalliances of Prime Minister Uno Sosuke.

21 The LDP obtained only 223 out of 511 Lower House Seats in 1993; it captured 300 out of 512 seats in 1986.

22 See for example, Inoguchi and Iwai, *Zoku giin no kenkyū*.

23 LDP Diet Members who are concerned with ecological issues are identified in *Asahi shinbun Weekly AERA*, March 3, 1992, pp. 6–9 and June 2, 1992, p. 7.

24 *Kanagawa shinbun*, April 7, 1990, p. 20.

25 The figure "21" signifies the twenty-first century. The LDP wanted to project the image that it is a far-sighted, future-oriented party.

26 Shinbori Toyohiko, interview on April 1, 1993.

27 Umezawa Kenji, Secretary General, LDP Kanagawa Chapter, interview on March 2, 1993.

28 Kojima Yukiyasu, Midori ward, Yokohama, interview on March 18, 1993.

29 Kanagawa prefecture had a population of 7.98 million in 1990. *Nihon kokusei zue* 1992, p. 70.

30 *Asahi nenkan*, 1987, p. 107.

31 Even the Chairman of the LDP Kanagawa Chapter, Diet Member Kamei Yoshiyuki, gave credit to Umezawa as the initiator of KF 21. Interview on March 15, 1993.

32 Saruda Katsumi, Head, Environmental Division, KF 21, interview on April 12, 1993.
33 *Kanagawa shinbun*, October 17, 1991.
34 Kanagawa Forum 21, *Kankyōkyōiku sinpojūmu hōkokusho* (Yokahama: Jimintō kanagawa kenren jimukyoku, 1992), p. 5.
35 *Kanagawa shinbun*, October 17, 1991.
36 Kanagawa Forum 21, *Kankyōkyōiku sinpojūmu hōkokusho*, p. 4.
37 *Ibid.*, pp. 47 and 58.
38 Kanagawa Forum 21, *Kanagawa kensei e no teigen* [Proposals to Kanagawa Prefectural Government] (Yokohama: Jimintō seisakukyoku, 1991). The second and third proposals were published in 1993 and 1995 respectively.
39 Umezawa Kenji told me with pride that the LDP seeks to preserve the legacy of the Shōwa Emperor by protecting Sagami Bay. Protecting the ecology has often been singled out as a hallmark of New Politics. Besides appealing to urban residents, there is a genuine attachment to the Emperor system among some conservatives. Arguably, this is a reflection of traditional values among many conservatives rather than post-material values. Nevertheless, the Kanagawa LDP chapter has cleverly used the Emperor system to legitimize its concerns for ecological issues among conservative supporters. The LDP's advocacy for the protection of Sagami Bay can therefore appeal to both the traditionalists who revere the Emperor and the post-materialists who support ecological protection for its own sake.
40 Kanagawa Forum 21, *Kanagawa kensei e no teigen*, 1991 Proposal, pp. 45–50.
41 Shinbori Toyohiko, interview on April 1, 1993.
42 Iijima Tadayoshi, Sakae ward, Yokohama, interview on March 30, 1993.
43 Suga Yoshihide, Nishi ward, Yokohama, interview on April 9, 1993.
44 Iijima Tadayoshi, Sakae ward, Yokohama, interview on March 30, 1993.
45 Shinbori Toyohiko, the office manager of KF 21, intimated that differences between the environment division and the pro-development divisions are inevitable, but that, thus far, serious clashes have been avoided.
46 For media coverage on other symposiums held by KF 21, see the following issues from the *Kanagawa shinbun*, February 17, 1992, p. 6, November 20, 1992 and December 2, 1992, p. 18.

4 The Japanese Communist Party: organization and resilience

1 The estimated party membership of the top three non-ruling communist parties in advanced industrial democracies in 1990 were: 1.3 million (Italy), 500,000 (Japan) and 200,00 (France). See statistics in Richard F. Starr, ed., *Yearbook on International Communist Affairs 1991* (Stanford, CN: Hoover Institution Press, 1991), pp. 174, 555, 601.
2 Peter Berton's speculation about the JCP's fate may well turn out to be prescient: "When monarchies were falling right and left after the end of World War I, it was said that if there would remain one king, it would be the king of England. Should we paraphrase it and say that if there will remain but one nonruling Communist party in the world, it will be the JCP?" Peter Berton, "The Japan Communist Party: The 'Lovable' Party," in Hrebenar, *The Japanese Party System*, p. 142.
3 On the JCP's anxiety about the introduction of a first-past-the-post system, see

Akahata [Red Flag], January 24, 1993, p. 1 and editorial of *Akahata*, April 3, 1993, p. 1. Shortly after the 1996 Lower House Elections, the party claimed that if the multi-member electoral system had been retained, it would have captured at least 40 to 50 seats rather than merely 26 seats. See *Asahi shinbun*, October 30, 1996, p. 2.

4 For the JCP's evaluation of its October 1996 Lower House success, see Fuwa Tetsuzō, "70 nendai o mo agemawaru rekishitekina yakushin" [Historical victory that superseded the 1970s], *Akahata hyōron tokushūban* [Red Flag Special Publication Edition], No. 1028, October 28, 1996, p. 3.

5 *Asahi shinbun*, July 7, 1997.

6 Kotsuka Hisao, the former chairman of the Kanagawa SC, and Andō Jinbei, top SC advisor, were ex-communists. The JCP had identified other SC activists who had Red backgrounds. See Yonekura Makoto, "Seikatsu kurabu seikyō to kanagawa nettowāku undō no senkyo" [The Election Campaigning of the Seikatsu Club and the Network Movement], *Akahata hyōron tokushūban*, No. 522, March 30, 1987, p. 18.

7 *Akahata*, March 23, 1990 cited in John F. Cooper, "Japan" in Richard F. Staar, ed., *Yearbook on International Communist Affairs, 1991*, p. 176. According to another survey, 20 to 30 percent of voters who supported the JCP in the previous election said that they would vote for its rival on the left, the JSP, because of events in Eastern Europe.

8 According to the 1995 exit polls, the JCP, besides firming up its traditional support, also gave a good fight by winning votes from previous non-party partisans and former supporters from other parties. According to another poll in the heavily populated prefecture of Osaka, the profile of JCP voters was as follows: 55 percent had supported the JCP in the 1993 General Election, 17 percent were non-party partisans, 10 percent were ex-JSP supporters, and 8 percent came from the JNP. See *Asahi shinbun*, July 24, 1995. The JCP benefited from the JSP's inexorable decline. According to a March 1995 survey, out of those who supported the JSP in the 1993 General Election, only 33 percent continued to support the Socialists. 51 percent became non-party partisans and the remaining 17 percent supported other parties. Since the JCP has become the only party of the Left, some of the erstwhile JSP supporters would switch their support to the communists.

9 Understandably the JCP denies that it is under the charismatic dominance of Miyamoto. See Fuwa Tetsuzō, "Nihon kyōsantō nimo iiwasetehoshii" [Let the JCP Speak Also], *Bungei shunju*, January 1996, No. 774, pp. 153–154.

10 Paul Langer notes that the JCP has undergone "political naturalization" by maintaining its independence from foreign influence and adapting to the Japanese environment. Paul F. Langer, *Communism in Japan: A Case of Political Naturalization* (Stanford, CN: Hoover Institution Press, 1972).

11 For an account of the JCP's shift to a parliamentary path, see George O. Totten, "The People's Parliamentary Path of the Japanese Communist Party, Part I: Agrarian Policies," *Pacific Affairs*, Vol. 46, No. 2, Summer 1973 and "Part II: Local Level Tactics," *Pacific Affairs*, Vol. 46, No. 3, Fall 1973. See also Hong N. Kim, "Deradicalization of the Japanese Communist Party under Kenji Miyamoto," *World Politics*, Vol. XXVIII, No. 2, January 1976. Fuwa Tetsuzō, the Chairman of the Presidium, affirmed: "What the JCP is aiming for is to change the national administration in the interests of the people, a change which can be carried out even within the framework of capitalism." *Japan Press Weekly*, No. 1801, July 11, 1992, p. 3.

Miyamoto pointed out that

> achievements by Marx and Lenin are historical products, and not golden rules which we must adhere to under all circumstances. For example, the "Manifesto of the Communist Party" includes the view that violent revolution is inevitable. But it is necessary to understand that this view is limited by its historical context because at the time there were no circumstances in which the people had taken power through voting.
>
> (*Akahata*, September 19, 1992 in *Bulletin*, No. 701, October 1992, p. 12)

12 Zenrōren, the labor union, which supports the JCP, has only 840,000 or 6.8 percent of the unionized labor force. *Nihon kokusei zue 1992*, p. 106.

13 For an account of the JCP's initial successes and subsequent failures in capturing the labor unions, see Masumi Junnosuke, *Postwar Politics in Japan: 1945–1955*, Japan Research Monograph No. 6 (Berkeley: University of California Center for Japanese Studies, 1985), pp. 260–267.

14 There were 37 million Japanese co-op members in 1992. *Ekonomisuto*, February 9, 1993, p. 18.

15 See for example, Odagiri Makoto, *Dokyumento seikyō* [A Document of the Consumer Co-operatives] (Tokyo: Shakai shisōsha, 1992), pp. 156–159.

16 Co-op Kanagawa has a membership of 811,823 members as of March 20, 1991. JCCU, *Co-op Facts and Figures 1990*. An English pamphlet from JCCU.

17 *Shin kanagawa* [New Kanagawa], April 20, 1980, p. 4.

18 Inokawa Hiroshi, Special Director, Co-op Kanagawa, interview on April 20, 1992. Inokawa also provided the information on the ties between his co-op and the LDP.

19 Nihon kyōsantō kanagawa ken iinkai, *Heiwa to kakushin o mezashite: nihon kyōsantō kanagawa kentō no ayumi* [Aiming for Peace and Progress: The Path of the Kanagawa JCP] (Yokohama: Shin kanagawasha, 1985), p. 72.

20 Information from Takahashi Kiyoko, JCP city female assembly member from Totsuka ward, Yokohama. Interview on December 21, 1991.

21 Odagiri, *Dokyumento seikyō*, p. 295.

22 "Kyōsantō no senkyo sakusen o sōkatsusuru" [A Comprehensive Study of the JCP's Election Strategy] in *Jiyū minshu* [Liberal Democrat], Vol. 233, September 1974, p. 115.

23 *Ibid.*, p. 118. See also "Nikkyō iryō orugu no anyaku" [The Secret Maneuvering of JCP Medical Co-Op Organizers], *Jiyū minshu*, Vol. 244, May 1976.

24 *Akahata*, January 18, 1993, p. 1.

25 *Japan Press Weekly*, No.1773, December 14, 1991, p. 12.

26 For an account of the JCP united front strategy, see Fuwa Tetsuzō, "Tōitsu sensen seisaku no tokuchō" [The Characteristics of the United Front Policy] in *Nihon kyōsantō kōryō to rekishi no kenshō* [The JCP's General Principles and Historical Verification] (Tokyo: Shin nihon shuppansha, 1991).

27 Yonekura, "Seikatsu kurabu seikyō to kanagawa nettowāku undō no senkyo," pp. 16–17.

28 *Ibid.*, p. 19.

29 *Akahata*, May 19, 1991 in *Japan Press Weekly*, No. 1746, June 1, 1991, pp. 24–25.

30 *Akahata*, May 19 and 20, 1991 in *Japan Press Weekly*, No. 1749, June 22, 1991, pp. 22–23.

31 Toba Kazuko, "Yatō dainitō o mezasu manshon-danchi katsudō no kyōka o" [Strengthen Mansion and Danchi Activities to become the Number Two Opposition Party], *Akahata hyōron tokushūban*, No. 784, December 30, 1991, pp. 15–16, 19–20.

32 *Ibid.*, p. 20. See also advertisements for JCP booklets on recycling, rubbish, and other environmental issues in *Akahata*, March 6, 1993, p. 10.

33 Fuwa's "Presidium Report," *Akahata*, May 19 and 20, 1991 in *Japan Press Weekly*, No. 1749, June 22, 1991, p. 24.

34 Japanese Communist Party, Central Committee, *Sixty Year History of Japanese Communist Party: 1922–1982* (Tokyo: Japan Press Service, 1984), p. 499.

35 Suzuki Kenji, "Nihon kyōsantō kōenkai o dō kakuritsu kyōkasuru Ka" [How Do We Establish and Strengthen JCP *kōenkai*?], *Akahata hyōron tokushūban*, Part 2, January 18, 1993, p. 34.

36 Iwaseki Hiroshi, Vice Chairman, JCP Kanagawa Prefecture, interview on January 10, 1993. Besides socio-cultural norms, the single-ballot, multi-member electoral district system in the Lower House forced politicians from the same party to compete against each other along personality and patronage lines because they could not do so in terms of policies.

37 Statistic was given by Fuwa in "Presidium Report," *Japan Press Weekly*, No. 1749, July 22, 1991, p. 28. According to another party source, its *kōenkai* membership comprises 65.37 percent of the Sunday *Akahata* readership. See Suzuki Kenji, "Nihon kyōsantō kōenkai no kakudai kyōka ni zenryoku o" [All Out Effort to Strengthen and Expand the JCP *Kōenkai*], in *Akahata hyōron tokushūban*, January 30, 1995, No. 939, p. 16.

38 Wabara Nobuo, "kōenkai katsudō no kihon mondai" [The Basic Problems of *Kōenkai* Activities], *Zenei* [Vanguard], No.599, December 1990, p. 164.

39 This approach is adopted by a number of JCP local assembly members in metropolitan Japan. In the case of Takahashi Kiyoko (Totsuka ward, Yokohama city), there was no JCP branch and only three JCP members in her neighborhood when she first ran under the JCP ticket. She intimated that her electoral organization then was a "family" *kōenkai*. Interview on December 21, 1991. Miyashita Izumi (Tsurumi ward, Yokohama city) originally came from Nagano Prefecture. As an electoral strategy, he would approach all the Tsurumi residents whose original hometown was also from Nagano. He would appeal: "We are from the same birthplace [*furusato*]. Please vote for me." Miyashita had a "neighborhood" (*jimoto*) *kōenkai* whose members supported him on the basis of personal friendship and not ideology. Interview, March 27, 1992. Another JCP local assembly woman, Uchihori Yaeko (Hodogaya ward, Yokohama city) intimated that her *jimoto kōenkai* included members who disliked the JCP. Interview, March 27, 1992.

40 See Suzuki, "Nihon kyōsantō kōenkai no kakudai kyōka ni zenryoku o," p. 18.

41 For case studies of successful JCP *kōenkai*, see "Kōenkai katsudō" [*Kōenkai* Activities] in *Akahata hyōron tokushūban*, 19 June, 1995, No. 960, pp. 25–30. Almost 20 years earlier, the *kōenkai* of a JCP assembly member had similar activities: baseball, table tennis, lessons on women's makeup and health, sports, skating, golf, hiking, barbecue, movies, and End of the Year parties. It reveals the persistence of service-oriented mobilization techniques adopted by the JCP and other political parties in Japan. See *Zenei*, No. 411, June 1977, pp. 156–157.

In February 1992, the author followed a Yokohama JCP *kōenkai* excursion trip to the hotsprings. Except for a brief reminder to support the JCP in the Upper

House Elections of 1992, the two-day affair revolved around sightseeing, dining, and singing.

42 Wabara, "Kōenkai katsudō no kihon mondai," p. 160.

43 In the 1992 Upper House Elections, the JCP's ratio of votes won in the national proportional representation constituency to the total votes won in the local constituencies was only 73.3 percent. *Akahata*, 19 September 1992 in *Bulletin*, No. 702, December 1992, pp. 47–48.

44 *Zenei*, No. 580, September 1989, p. 69.

45 *Asahi shinbun*, December 9, 1990, p. 2. See also *AERA*, July 21, 1992, p. 17. For the JCP's bitter denunciation of those who deserted the party, see *Akahata*, May 19 and 20, 1991 in *Japan Press Weekly*, No. 1749, June 22, 1991, p. 21.

46 Information from an anonymous JCP assembly member. In 1995, the party noted that around 50 JCP party members including 13 assembly members had deserted the party recently and stood as independents in elections. One of the reason cited was the fear of some assembly members that they could not win their re-elections if they were to stand on a JCP ticket. See Kobayashi Eezo, "Tōkiristsu to kojin no jiyū mondai: mushozoku rikkōho no shisōteki mondai nimo kanren shite" [Party Principles and the Issue of Personal Autonomy: Concerning the Thought Problem of Running as an Independent Candidate], in *Akahata hyōron tokushūban*, July 17, 1995, No. 964.

47 For a detailed coverage of the conference, see *Zenei*, No. 473, December 1981, Special Edition.

48 Shii's Report in *Nihon kyōsantō chūō iinkai kettei shū* [Compilation of the JCP Central Committee's Decision], October 9–11, 1991, p. 37. A party pamphlet.

Even in 1995, the JCP continued to make plaintive calls to replace personal *kōenkai* with party *kōenkai*. One report noted that certain *kōenkai* still retain the name of the candidate while another observed that in the case of some *kōenkai*, it is in actuality a personal *kōenkai* even though the signboard claims to be a JCP *kōenkai*. See Suzuki, "Nihon kyōsantō kōenkai no kakudai kyōka ni zenryoku o," p. 22 and Sotō Shizuko, "Tō kōenkai katsudō no kyōka nituite" [Concerning the Strengthening of JCP *Kōenkai* Activities], *Akahata hyōron toku shūban*, No. 944, March 6, 1995, No. 944, p. 87.

49 Akarui senkyo suishin kyōkai [Association To Promote Clean Elections], *Tōitsu chihō senkyo no jittai: dai jūsan kai* [The Actual Condition of the Thirteenth Local Election] (Tokyo: Akarui Senkyo Suishin Kyōkai, 1996), p. 366. According to the same authoritative survey, the percentages of party supporters who joined *kōenkai* in 1995 were: Sakigake (53.8), Shinshintō (33.8), JSP (33.8), LDP (36.4), Kōmeitō (28.6) and JCP (23.1). See p. 369.

50 See Preamble of the JCP's Constitution in Japanese Communist Party, *Program and Constitution* (Tokyo: Japan Press Service, 1986), p. 26.

51 Lenin's strategy for a party with a centralized and disciplined organization of leaders and professional revolutionaries is found in "What Is to Be Done?" (1902). For more explicit references to democratic centralism, see Lenin's "Freedom of Criticism and Unity of Action" (1906). Both articles are available in Robert V. Daniels, *A Documentary History of Communism*, Volume One (London: I. B. Tauris, 1985).

52 The JCP asserts that the party's adherence to democratic centralism is not due to the Leninist period alone but also from its experiences from the "1950 problem." In that year, the JCP split and the official history claimed that the schism occurred

because democratic centralism was not observed. *Akahata hyōron tokushūban*, No. 696, June 18, 1990, pp. 16–18.

53 Miyamoto referred to a 1991 NHK survey which indicated that 42.1 percent of voters would never support the JCP, another 35.2 percent prefers not to support the party and only 22.7 percent of voters are not against voting for the JCP. *Japan Press Weekly*, No. 1746, June 1, 1991, p. 23.

54 See Fabio Luca Cavazza, "The Italian Paradox: An Exit from Communism," *Daedalus*, Vol. 121, No. 2, Spring 1992; Martin J. Bull and Philip Daniels, "The 'New Beginning': The Italian Communist Party under the Leadership of Achille Occhetto," *The Journal of Communist Studies*, Vol. 6, No. 3, September 1990; and Martin J. Bull, "Whatever Happened to Italian Communism?," *West European Politics*, Vol. 14, No. 4, October 1991.

55 For JCP's criticisms of the PCI, see "The Significance of the Trend of the Italian Communist Party To Integrate Itself into the Socialist International," *Akahata hyōron tokushūban*, May 22, 1989, translated in Japanese Communist Party, *Important International Issues* 1989, Vol. 17 (Tokyo: Japan Press Service, 1993) and *Zenei*, No. 584, December 1989. Special issue on the world communist movement. See pp. 8–25.

> Some also argue that the JCP should be structured on the pluralist concept; that the JCP is a failure because, unlike the Italian Communist Party (PCI), its structure is not pluralist and in the fabric of party life there is no freedom to form factions. . . . They (PCI) approved military blocs on the grounds that the military equilibrium would be upset if Italy left NATO. The result is that the PCI is now much the same as a social democratic party. They are applying for membership of the Socialist International, and as they have done away with democratic centralism, the PCI is now facing extreme factional activity and conflict . . .
>
> (Japan Communist Party, *The 19th Congress of the Japanese Communist Party*, p. 29)

56 Comments by Fuwa heard by author when he attended a 15,000 member communist rally on June 9, 1992 in Yokohama. See *Shin kanagawa*, May 17, 1992, p. 1. See also Fuwa, "Nihon kyōsantō nimo iiwasetehoshii," pp. 154–155.

5 Social Movements and the Seikatsu Club

1 In the literature on Japanese social movements, the term "social movements" is often used interchangeably with "citizens' movements" (*shimin undō*) and "residents' movements" (*jūmin undō*).

The best English account of Japanese social movements is Margaret A. McKean, *Environmental Protest and Citizen Politics in Japan* (Berkeley and Los Angeles: University of California Press, 1981). Articles in English include: Yasunasa Kuroda, "Protest Movements in Japan: A New Politics," *Asian Survey*, Vol. 12, No. 11, November 1972 and *Japan Quarterly*, "Citizens Movements," *Japan Quarterly*, Vol. 20, No. 4, October–December 1973; Matsushita Keiichi, "Politics of Citizen Participation," *The Japan Interpreter*, Vol. 9, No. 4, Spring 1975; Maurice A. Kirkpatrick, "Consumerism and Japan's New Citizen Politics," *Asian Survey*, Vol. 13, No. 3, March 1975; and Takabatake Michitoshi, "Citizen's Movements: Organizing the Spontaneous," *The Japan Interpreter*, Vol. 9, No. 3,

Winter 1975. For recent Japanese sources on social movements, see Shakai undō ron kenkyūkai, *Shakai undō ron no tōgō o mezashite: riron to bunseki* [Aiming at an Integration of Social Movement Theory: Theory and Analysis] (Tokyo: Seibundo, 1990); Kurihara Akira and Shōji Kōkichi, eds., *Shakai undō to bunka keisei* [Social Movements and the Formation of Culture] (Tokyo: Tokyo daigaku shuppankai, 1987); Muta Kazue, "Seiji to shakai undō: nihon ni okeru atarashii shakai undō no tenkai" [Politics and Social Movements: The Development of a New Social Movement in Japan] in Aaoki Yasuhiro and Nakamichi Minoru, eds., *Gendai nihon seiji no shakai gaku* [The Sociology of Contemporary Japanese Politics] (Kyoto: Showado, 1991); and Hasegawa Koichi, "Han genshiryoku undō ni okeru josei no ichi: posuto cherunoburi no 'atarashii shakai undō'" [Women of the Anti-Nuclear Energy Movement: A Post-Chernobyl New Social Movement in Japan] in *Lebaisan*, No. 8, Spring 1991. For other good summaries of Japanese social movements, see "Shakai undō" in *Asahi nenkan*, 1993, pp. 187–190 and Jūmin toshokan, *Minikomi sō mokuroku* [A Catalogue of Social Movement Newsletters] (Tokyo: Heibonsha, 1992). The latter gives a comprehensive list of Japanese social movement organizations and their activities. A special issue on residents' movements appeared in *Toshi mondai*, Vol. 87, No. 10, October 1996.

2 ASSK, *Senkyo ni kansuru zenkoku ishiki chōsa* [National Survey on Attitudes Towards Elections], No. 2, 1991, p. 24. Matsushita Keiichi, a well-known scholar on social movements in Japan told me that an accurate measurement of social movement activities is almost impossible, especially when they are often small, localized, and unknown to researchers. Even though a bean counting of social movements to examine their scope and intensity is difficult, Matsushita claims that it is his impression that social movements in Japan have indeed grown in scope and intensity. Interview on May 19, 1993. An appeal to authority is less than satisfactory. Perhaps an accumulation of empirical studies of individual movements such as the SC may verify the proposition that social movements have indeed expanded in Japan.

3 See for example, "Seikatsu teiangata shimin undō no atarashii nami" [The New Wave of Citizen Movements with Livelihood Proposals] in *Asahi jānaru*, August 1986, pp. 16–21.

4 The most prominent protest movements in the 1960s were the 1960 anti-Security Treaty demonstrations and the anti-Vietnam War Movement (Beheiren). To say that the Greens subscribe to pacifism in the post-industrial era does not imply that other political movements in the industrial era did not adhere to such values. Pacifism is just one of the many issues on the Greens' agenda.

5 *Asahi nenkan 1993*, p. 187.

6 The rape of a 13-year-old Okinawan schoolgirl by three U.S. marines stationed in that prefecture triggered off mass protests in Okinawa and other parts of Japan and threatened to undermine public opinion support for the Alliance.

7 See Far East Information Service (FBIS), *Daily Report: East Asia*, 96–075, April 17, 1996, FBIS, 96–101, May 23, 1996 and FBIS, 96–114, June 12, 1996.

8 The malfunction of the Monju experimental fast-breeder nuclear station at Tsuruga in December 1995, the Tokaimura plant in Ibaraki prefecture in March 1997, and the Fugen reactor in Fukui prefecture in April 1997 generated increasing concern among the Japanese about the potential danger of nuclear power. In 1996, the town of Maki conducted a referendum that rejected the siting of a nuclear station in its vicinity. The central government and the nuclear power corporations are increasingly concerned that other localities may also catch the

"Maki allergy" to nuclear power and disrupt the country's ambitious nuclear power program. See Jon Choy, "Japanese Town Vote Jolts Tokyo's Nuclear Plans," Japan Economic Institute, *JEI Report*, No. 31B, August 16, 1996. Choy also writes:

> The plebiscite itself gained national prominence as an unusual exercise of constitutional protected local democracy. Central government policymakers immediately began to mourn that, if such behavior spread to other towns and other issues, their carefully laid long-term plans for the nation could be jeopardized. Since at least four other towns have passed ordinances allowing referenda on nuclear plants planned for their neighborhoods, the fears of the bureaucracy in Tokyo will be realized to some extent.
>
> (Jon Choy, "Local Government in Japan: The Next People-power Revolution," *JEI Report*, No. 43A, November 15, 1996, p. 20)

9 *The Economist* notes: "Japan gets a third of its electricity from nuclear power. Some 50 reactors have been built over the past 30 years. Another half a dozen or so are being built or planned." *The Economist*, April 19, 1997, p. 20.

10 Muta, "Seiji to shakai undō," p. 238. For another view that the SC is a social movement organization, see Amano Masako, "Seikatsusha undō no keisei ni mukete: seikatsu kurabu seikyō o jirei toshite" [Towards the Formation of a Social Movement: The Case of the Seikatsu Club], *Toshi mondai*, Vol. 87, No. 10, October 1996.

11 By 1997, plans were made to establish another SC in Aomori prefecture.

12 See for example, McKean, *Environmental Protest and Citizen Politics in Japan*, pp. 256–257.

13 Jūmin toshokan, *Minikomi sō mokuroku*, p. 35.

14 See for example, Hasegawa, "Han genshiryoku undō ni okeru josei no ichi."

15 *Seikatsu kurabu 1997*, p. 4. An SC annual booklet.

16 According to Zald and McCarthy: "A social movement organization (SMO) is a complex, or formal organization that identifies its goals with the preferences of a social movement or a counter movement and attempts to implement those goals." See Zald and McCarthy, *Social Movements In An Organizational Society*, p. 20.

17 For statistics and organizational maps of SC's facilities, see Maruyama Yoshio, "Seikatsu kurabu seikyō no jigyō soshiki" [The Economic Organization of the SC] in Satō Yoshiyuki, ed., *Joseitachi no seikatsu nettowāku* [The Livelihood Network of Women] (Tokyo: Bunshindo, 1988), pp. 30–78. Details of the SC's facilities are also found in Seikatsu kurabu rengōkai, *Seikatsu kurabu gurūpu 1996*.

18 The SC also relies on the voluntarism of its women members. See *ibid.*, Seikatsu kurabu gurūpu 1997, p. 4.

19 Besides McKean's *Environmental Protest and Citizen Politics in Japan*, see also Kurt Steiner, Ellis S. Krauss, and Scott C. Flanagan, eds, *Political Opposition and Local Politics in Japan* (Princeton: Princeton University Press, 1980).

In recent years, the city of Zushi is often cited as a case study of citizens' movements' involvement in electoral politics. See Purnendra C. Jain, "Green Politics and Citizen Power in Japan: The Zushi Movement," *Asian Survey*, Vol. 31, No. 6, June 1991; Kiichiro Tomino, "The Role of Citizen Movements in Japanese Politics," *Institute Reports*, East Asian Institute, Columbia University, March 1991; Watanabe Noboru, "Seikatsu jichigata jūmin undō no tenkai: Ikego beigun jūtaku kensetsu hantai undō o jirei toshite" [The Development of Citizens' Movements Based on Livelihood and Autonomy: The Case of the Anti-U.S. Military Ikego Housing Construction Resistance Movement] in Shakai undō kenkyūkai, *Shakai undō ron no tōgō o mezashite*. Although the SC and NET are also actively involved in the anti-military housing movement in Zushi, their activities are not confined to a single locality. See Yokoyama Keiichi, "Seikatsu kurabu seikyō ni miru seiji ishiki nokeisei" [The Formation of Political Consciousness in the SC], *Asahi Jānaru*, May 16, 1986, pp. 100–103.

20 *Seikatsu kurabu 1997*, p. 7.

21 Yokota Katsumi, *Sankagata shimin shakai ron* [The Theory of a Participatory Civil Society] (Tokyo: Gendai no rironsha, 1992), pp. 130–133.

22 *Shakai undō*, No. 150, September 15, 1992, p. 4.

23 The Right Livelihood Award was also awarded to Petra Kelly, the prominent founding member of the German Green Party in 1982. The SC's achievement is also recorded in Iwadare Hiroshi, "Consumer Co-operatives in the Spotlight," *Japan Quarterly*, Vol. 18, No. 4, October–December 1991, p. 434.

24 The speech is reproduced in Iwami Takashi, *Raito riburihuddo awōdo* [Right Livelihood Award]. A 1990 pamphlet from Chiba Seikatsu Club, p. 30.

25 The paradigms we will consider are obviously not exhaustive. For a good summary of the different approaches adopted in the study of social movements, see Russell J. Dalton, Manfred Kuechler, and William Bürklin, "The Challenge of New Move-ments" in Dalton and Kuechler, *Challenging the Political Order*, pp. 3–20.

26 The two leading scholars associated with this perspective are Robert Dahl and Charles E. Lindblom. See Robert Dahl, *Who Governs* (New Haven, CN: Yale University Press, 1961) and Charles E. Lindblom, *Politics and Markets* (New York: Basic Books, 1977). For a critique of pluralism, see John Manley, "Neopluralism: A Class Analysis of Pluralism I and Pluralism II," *American Political Science Review*, Vol. 77, No. 2, June 1983, pp. 368–383. See also, Grant Jordan, "The Pluralism of Pluralism: An Anti-theory?," *Political Studies*, Vol. 18, No. 2, June 1990, pp. 286–301.

27 Robert A. Dahl and Edward R. Tufte, *Size and Democracy* (Stanford, CN: Stanford University Press, 1971).

28 See for example, Hong N. Kim, "Urbanization and Changing Voting Patterns in Japan: 1958–1979," *Keio Journal of Politics*, No. 4, 1983 and Flanagan, "National and Local Voting Trends: Cross-level Linkages and Correlates of Change" in Steiner, Krauss and Flanagan, *Political Opposition and Local Politics in Japan*, pp. 131–133. See also Scott C. Flanagan, "Electoral Change in Japan: A Study of Secular Realignment" in Dalton, Flanagan and Beck, *Electoral Change in Advanced Industrial Democracies*, pp. 166, 171–172.

29 Sidney Verba, Norman Nie, and Kim Jae-On, *Participation and Political Equality* (Cambridge: Cambridge University Press, 1973), p. 100.

30 Seikatsu kurabu seikatsu kyōdō kumiai kanagawa, *Tsūjō sōtaikai giansho* [General Meeting Report of SC Kanagawa], No. 22, 1993 Annual Report, p. 77.

31 Iwane Kunio, *Atarashii shakai undō no shihan seiki* [The New Social Movements' Last Quarter of the 20th Century] (Tokyo: Kyōdō tosho sābisu, 1993), pp. 27–29.

32 For accounts of early protest movements, see William W. Kelly, *Deference and Defiance in Nineteenth-century Japan* (Princeton, NJ: Princeton University Press, 1985) and Herbert P. Bix, *Peasant Protest in Japan, 1590–1884* (New Haven, CN and London: Yale University Press, 1986).

33 Institute of Statistical Mathematics, *A Study of the Japanese National Character: The Ninth Nation Wide Survey*, Research Memorandum No. 572 (Tokyo, 1995) p. 7.

34 Inglehart also examined data from the Institute of Statistical Mathematics, Tokyo. He argues that:

as the leading example of economic growth in the post-war era, Japan constitutes a crucial case for testing our hypotheses. The time series data are unambiguous, clearly indicating that from 1953 to 1983, there was an intergenerational shift away from materialism among the Japanese public.

See Inglehart, *Culture Shift in Advanced Society*, p. 74.

35 Institute of Statistical Mathematics, *A Study of the Japanese National Character*, p. 7.
36 The latest survey by the Institute of Statistical Mathematics revealed the following: 79 percent of the respondents supported the statement that "each of us must do his part to protect the world environment even if our lives become somewhat less convenient than they are now" while only 17 percent agreed with the opposing view that "even now we still must think of making our own lives more convenient." Institute of Statistical Mathematics, *A Study of the Japanese National Character*, p. 31. In 1983, in response to the question "How serious an issue do you consider the protection of the environment to be?," 37 percent claimed that it was extremely serious while another 50 percent believed that it was serious. Ten years later, a subsequent survey showed that environmental consciousness has deepened among many Japanese. In the 1993 survey, 50 percent claimed that it was extremely serious while another 43 percent affirmed that it is indeed serious. Institute of Statistical Mathematics, *A Study of the Japanese National Character*, p. 25.
37 According to two surveys conducted by Yokohama city, 29.7 percent of the households in the northern portion of Midori ward have an annual income of more than 10 million yen. In contrast, only 16.6 percent of Yokohama's households have similar income. See Yokohama shi sōmu gyōsei ku chōsa shitsu, *Kōhoku ku to midori ku no chiiki seikatsu to gyōsei ni kansuru kuminishiki chōsa* [Survey On the Outlook of Ward Residents Concerning City Administration and Local Livelihood of Kohoku and Midori Ward] (Yokohama: Yokohama kōhō insatsu, 1991), p. 20 and Yokohama shi kikaku zaisei kyoku toshi kagaku kenkyū shitsu, *Yokohama shimin ishiki chōsa* [Survey on the Outlook of Yokohama Residents] (Yokohama: yokohama kōhō insatsu, 1991), p. 24.
38 According to a 1984 survey of Tokyo SC members, 83 percent of the members' husbands are salary men. 65 percent of the husbands are university graduates and 54 percent are *kakarichō* (assistant section chief) and above. Yamasaki Tetsuya, "Shufu no seikyō undō no ishiki henyō: seikatsu kurabu seikyō no kumiai chōsa kara" [The Housewives' Co-Op Movement and Changes in Consciousness: From the Survey of the Seikatsu Club], *Toshi mondai*, Vol. 79, No. 6, June 1988, p. 34.
39 See for example, Dorothy Robins-Mowry, *The Hidden Sun: Women of Modern Japan* (Boulder, CO: Westview Press, 1983), p. 127.
40 Itō Hiromi, Chief of Organization Division, Nagano SC, interview on August 27, 1992.
41 Sumiko Iwao, *The Japanese Woman: Traditional Image and Changing Reality* (New York: Free Press, 1993), pp. 28–29, 33.

6 Origins of the Seikatsu Club

1 Iwane was born in 1932 in Kyoto. For an autobiographical account, see Iwane Kunio, *Seikatsu kurabu to tomoni* [Along with Seikatsu Club] (Tokyo: Shinjidaisha, 1979).

2 The Green Co-op North Block of Fukuoka succeeded in sponsoring its first candidate in 1989. The Green Co-op's participation in electoral politics was inspired by the precedent of the SC. Yoshida Toshio, founding father of Green Co-op North Block, interview on September 23, 1992.

3 Kobayashi Shigenobu, interview on July 22, 1992.

4 See for example, Robins-Mowry, *The Hidden Sun: Women of Modern Japan*, p. 223. Mary Goebel Noguchi, "The Rise of the Housewife Activist," *Japan Quarterly*, Vol. 39, No. 3, July–September 1992, pp. 351–352. Noguchi's article gives the impression that housewife activists including those from the SC have captured leadership positions in Japanese social movements. For another piece of mis-information, see Iwami Takashi, *Seikatsu Club Consumers' Co-operative: On the Practice* (Tokyo: Institute of Japanese Renaissance, 1988), p. 1. Booklet in English. Iwami wrote: "Seikatsu Club originated in 1965 when a housewife appealed to her neighborhood to get milk of reasonable price. Two hundrad (sic.) housewives responded to her and assembled at Setagaya in Tokyo." For the opposing view that the SC and NET are led by men, see Sasakura Naoko, Kanajima Satomi, and Sugawara Kazuko, *Josei ga seiji o kaeru* [Women Who Change Politics] (Tokyo: Shinsensha, 1990), p. 118.

5 Iwane, *Seikatsu kurabu to tomoni*, pp. 55–56. For other autobiographical accounts of the origins of the SC by Iwane, see "Seikatsu kurabu ni totte 'dairinin undō' to wa nani ka" [What is the Agent Movement to SC?], *Shakai undō*, No. 162, September 1992, pp. 20–29 and Iwane, *Atarashii shakai undō no shihan seiki*, pp. 9–25. Other accounts in the SC's newsletter, *Seikatsu to jichi* appeared on the following issues: No. 86, March 15, 1975, a five-part series stretching from No. 93, March 15, 1976 to No. 98, November 1, 1976 and No. 191, March 1, 1985.

6 *Ibid.*, Iwane, *Seikatsu kurabu to tomoni*, p. 63.

7 *Ibid.*, p. 89.

8 *Ibid.*, p. 81. Iwane repeated later the cliché that Japanese men only return home to sleep during the weekdays and play golf on Sunday. The implication is that it is almost impossible to organize the salary man since he is not physically present in the neighborhood. See Iwane Kunio, "Seikatsu kurabu no mezasumono to dairinin undō" [The Goal of Seikatsu Club and the Agents Movement] in *Shakai undō bukkuletto* [Social Movement Booklet], No. 1, 1989, p. 41.

9 Iwane, *Seikatsu kurabu to tomoni*, p. 76.

10 *Ibid.*, p. 14.

11 The Shufuren (Federation of Housewives) were successful in promoting a cheap and safe milk movement. A pack of milk was sold for only ¥10 then by the group. Another incident which aroused fear among housewives for their families' health was the Morinaga Company which sold contaminated milk. Satō Yoshiyuki, ed., *Josei tachi no seikatsu nettowāku* [The Livelihood Network of Women] (Tokyo: Bunshindo, 1988), pp. 165, 261.

12 Iwane, "Seikatsu kurabu no mezasu mono to dairinin," p. 34. Dogged by suspicions that the SC was an instrument of the JSP, the SC leaders tried to assure SC members that although some of its top leaders were JSP members, "the SC is not the JSP." See *Seikatsu to jichi*, No. 73, January 15, 1972, p. 4.

13 Iwane, *Seikatsu kurabu to tomoni*, p. 16.

14 Iwane, Interview on May 13, 1992.

15 Iwane, *Seikatsu kurabu to tomoni*, p. 93. Confirmation by *Mainichi shinbun*, March 1981, p. 23.

16 See for example *Seikatsu Shinpō* [Livelihood Newsletter], No. 21, February 1, 1967.

17 Kōno Teruaki, Saitama SC founding father, interview on October 26, 1992.

18 According to a Kanagawa SC staff member who had conducted research on the frequency of food purchases through the *han*, one-third of the members meet once a month, another third do so in less than a month while the remainder may take longer than a month before they meet again for food purchases. However, the women may meet more often for other SC activities or just for social interaction. Information from Ishii Akira, an SC staff member despatched to Singapore to learn English and conduct research on social movements in South-East Asia. Conversation in Singapore, February, 1994.

19 In October 1982, Kanagawa SC opened its first depot or store. Seikatsu kurabu seikatsu kyōdō kumiai, *Arutanatibu: seikatsu kurabu kanagawa 20 nen no ayumi* [The Alternative: The 20 years of Kanagawa Seikatsu Club] (Yokohama, 1991), p. 66.

20 Ministry of Health and Welfare, *Consumers' Livelihood Co-operative Society Law* (Tokyo: Japan Consumers' Co-operative Union, 1989), p. 1.

21 Chapter 1, Article 5 of the Co-op Law, *ibid.*, p. 2.

22 *Seikatsu to jichi*, No. 101, March 1, 1977, p. 1.

23 The leader of the NLC was Kōno Yōhei, the son of LDP faction leader, Kōno Ichirō. The NLC's power base was in Kanagawa prefecture due to two factors: Kōno Yōhei inherited the political mantle from his father who was the top political boss in Kanagawa and support from the large number of urban floating voters in that prefecture. Kōno Yōhei returned to the LDP's fold in 1986, became the cabinet spokesman in the LDP Miyazawa government and finally the President of the LDP in opposition after its defeat in the July 1993 Lower House Election.

24 Iwane, *Seikatsu kurabu to tomoni*, pp. 65 and 207.

25 Togliatti was the leader of the Italian Communist Party (PCI) which sought a different road from the USSR to socialism.

26 For a good summary of structural reform theory in Japan, see Curtis, *The Japanese Way of Politics* (New York: Columbia University Press, 1988), pp. 138–148.

27 Ironically, an early proponent of structural reform within the JCP is Fuwa Tetsuzō. Fuwa, despite his flirtation with structural reform, adhered to party discipline, returned to the party's orthodox fold and avoided being booted out of the JCP. Besides Curtis' account of structural reform, see also Kijima Masamichi, *Kōzō kaikaku ha: sono kako to mirai* [The Structural Reform Faction: Past and Future] (Tokyo: Gendai no rironsha, 1977) and Andō Jinbei, *Sengo nihon kyōsantō shiki* [An Autobiographical Account of the Postwar Japan Communist Party] (Tokyo: Gendai no rironsha, 1976), pp. 220–222.

For the JCP's critique of structural reform, see Miyamoto Kenji, *Nihon kakumei no tenbō* [The Development of Japan's Revolution] (Tokyo: Shin nihonsho, 1967), No. 41, pp. 90–93, 138–142.

28 Andō Jinbei, interview on April 2, 1993.

29 Kotsuka Hisao, interview on April 19, 1993.

30 *Ibid.*, p. 215.

31 *Ibid.*, p. 219.

32 The Social Citizens League was subsequently renamed Social Democratic League (Shakai Minshu Rengō) or Shaminren for short. Its leader was Eda Saburō's son, Eda Satsuki, who became a cabinet minister after the July 1993 Lower

House Election because Shaminren was part of the ruling coalition. Eda Satsuki maintained warm relations with NET and personally campaigned for Kanagawa NET candidates in their abortive attempts to secure Lower House seats in the 1993 Election.

33 *Seikatsu to jichi*, No. 103, June 1, 1977, p. 2 and No. 104, August 1, 1977, p. 2.

34 *Seikatsu to jichi*, No. 122, June 1, 1979, pp. 1–2.

35 Iwane, *Atarashii shakai undō no shihan seiki*, p. 169.

36 Ikeda Tōru, interview on August 12, 1992.

37 Interviews with the founding fathers of SC and NET women leaders of regional SCs in Hokkaidō, Nagano, Chiba, and Saitama revealed a similar pattern: regional SCs were invariably established by males who were inspired by Iwane's social movement experiment in Tokyo. The regional founding fathers who were interviewed are: Kobayashi Shigenobu (Hokkaidō SC), July 22, 1992; Momose Hiromichi (Nagano SC), August 27, 1992; Ikeda Tōru (Chiba SC), August 12, 1992; and Kōno Teruaki (Saitama SC), October 26, 1992.

38 Yokota Katsumi, interview on May 7, 1992. Yokota was born in 1939 in Ibaraki prefecture. For an autobiographical account, see Yokota Katsumi, *Orutanatibu shimin shakai sengen: mō hitotsu no shakaishugi* [The Declaration of an Alternative Civil Society: Another Socialism] (Tokyo: Gendai no rironsha, 1989).

39 *Ibid.*, pp. 36–38.

40 *Ibid.*, pp. 39–40.

41 *Ibid.*, pp. 42–43. See also *Seikatsu to jichi* (Kanagawa edition), No. 43, January 20, 1975, pp. 2–3 and No. 46, January 1, 1976, p. 1. Both articles referred to the strife as an ordeal for the Kanagawa SC.

42 Seikatsu kurabu seikatsu kyōdō kumiai, *Orutanatibu: seikatsu kurabu kanagawa 20 nen no ayumi*, p. 12.

43 Seikatsu kurabu jibunshi henshū iinkai [Editorial Committee of Seikatsu Club's History], *Ikikata o kaeru onna tachi* [Women who Change the way of Living] (Tokyo: Shinsensha, 1981), pp. 58–63, 88–90.

44 Yokota, *Orutanatibu shimin shakai sengen*, pp. 42–43.

45 Seikatsu kurabu kanagawa, *Nē kiite kiite* [Hear, Hear] (Tokyo: Shin jidaisha, 1989), pp. 40–46.

46 Terada Etsuko, interview on July 7, 1992.

47 *Mainichi shinbun* (Tokyo edition), March 6, 1981, p. 23.

48 The Social Movement Center publishes the monthly *Shakai undō* which functions as NET's national voicepiece. It holds a library which contains information on local NETs and periodically organizes seminars and conferences. From 1992, it also acts as a liaison office to link the NET movement in nine prefectures.

49 Iwane was also invited by Hokkaidō SC and Fukuoka's Green Co-op North Block to explain the foundation of NET. At the first National NET Movement Seminar held in Atami, Shizuoka Prefecture on October 3 and 4, 1992, Iwane gave the opening keynote address. The session was attended by the author. Iwane continues to lecture Tokyo SC professional staff when they first join the organization on the meaning and purpose of the SC.

50 The SC group began advocating safe soap in 1974. See *Seikatsu to jichi*, No. 85, August 20, 1974, pp. 4–5.

51 Yokota, *Orutanatibu shimin shakai sengen*, pp. 46–47. For an analysis and chronology of Japan's experience with synthetic soap and the subsequent anti-synthetic soap movement between 1937 and 1996, see *Shakai undō*, No. 205, April 1997, pp. 2–25.

52 Japan Tobacco (JT) estimated that there are 33.49 million smokers in Japan.

JT calculated that 26.1 percent of the total population are smokers. 60.4 percent of men and 13.3 percent of women are smokers. *Japan Times*, December 9, 1992, p. 2. Arguably, cigarette smoking is as damaging if not even more harmful to the health of human beings than synthetic soap. An anti-tobacco, clean air campaign would have been beneficial to the health of SC members' family and the general public, but an anti-tobacco campaign was likely to arouse resistance from many of the members' husbands, male workers of the SC group, and smokers, both male and female. Some of the regional SCs' top leaders were chain-smokers. Given the high rate of smoking in Japan, an anti-tobacco campaign was unlikely to generate widespread voter support.

53 *Seikatsu to jichi*, No. 134, June 1, 1980, p. 2.
54 *Seikatsu to jichi*, No. 169, May 1, 1983, p. 11.
55 Terada Etsuko, interview on July 7, 1992.

7 Seikatsu Club: ideology and organization

1 See for example, SC leaders' praises of "Gramsci's farsightedness" in Iwane Kunio, *Shakai undō toshite no Seikatsu Kurabu o kataru* [Discuss Seikatsu Club as a Social Movement] (Tokyo: Shakai undō kenkyū sentā setsuritsu junbikai, 1979), pp. 32–35. In my interviews with some of the SC founders, Gramscian terminologies, especially "hegemony," were frequently used. Yokota Katsumi also recommended the following book to me: Katagiri Kaoru, *Guramushi* [Gramsci] (Tokyo: Riburopoto, 1991).

  SC leaders have written extensively on the relevance of Gramscian ideology to social movements in Japan. See for example, the three articles in Fōramu 90's, ed., *Guramushi no shisō kūkan* [Gramsci's Ideas] (Tokyo: Shakai hyōronsha, 1992). They are Yokota Katsumi, "Guramushi to shakai sanka" [Gramsci and Social Participation], pp. 154–158; Maruyama Shigeki, Guramushi no sisō hōhō to konnichi no "atarashii shakai undō" [The Method of Gramscian Thought and New Social Movement], pp. 221–225; and Kotsuka Hisao, "Konichi no shimin shakai to Guramushi" [Civil Society Today and Gramsci], pp. 232–236.

  See also Ishidō Kiyotomo, Iidamomo, and Katagiri Kaoru, eds., *Ikiteiru Guramushi* [Gramsci Alive] (Tokyo: Shakai hyōronsha, 1989). Articles by the above SC leaders in this book are Kotsuka Hisao, "Ima Guramushi ni kodawaru Guramushi botsugo gojūnen sinpojūmu kara kyujū nendai e" [From the Fiftieth Anniversary Symposium Which Adheres to Gramsci to the 1990s], pp. 194–201; Yokota Katsumi, "Guramushi to nihon no seikatsusha undō no keiken kara" [Gramsci and the Experience of Japan's Consumer Movement], pp. 319–326; and Maruyama Shigeki, "Guramushi to wākāzu korekutibu" [Gramsci and Workers Collectives], pp. 327–336. See also Yokota, "Guramushi to Nihon shakai undō no keiken kara" [From the Experience of Japanese Social Movements], pp. 16–22 and Kotsuka Hisao, "Ima Guramushi ni Kodawaru" [Adhering to Gramsci] in *Gendai no riron*, No. 240, August 1987, pp. 5–9.

2 Iwane, *Seikatsu kurabu to tomoni*, p. 65.
3 "Foreword" by Iwami Takashi in Yokota Katsumi, *I Among Others: An Introspective Look at the Theory and Practice of the Seikatsu Club Movement* (Yokohama: Seikatsu Club Seikyo Kanagawa, 1991), preface xiii. This is an abridged version in English of Yokota's *Orutanatibu: shimin shakai sengen*.
4 Kotsuka Hisao, "Seikatsusha no jidai" [The Era of Citizens that are concerned with Livelihood Issues], *Bunka shiirizu*, No. 9, 1984, pp. 1–18.

5   Yokota, *Sanka gata shimin shakai ron*, p. 125.

6   Satō, *Josei tachi no seikatsu netto wāku*, p. 61.

7   For a succinct summary of the Japanese co-op movement, see Iwadare, *Consumer Co-operatives in the Spotlight*. See also Nihon hōsō shuppan kyōkai, *Nihon no shōhisha-undō* [The Consumer Movement of Japan] (Tokyo: Nihon hōsō shuppan kyōkai, 1980); Noruma Hidekazu, ed., *Seikyō 21 seiki e no chōsen: nihongata moderu no jikken* [Co-Ops: The Challenge Towards the 21st Century: The Experiment of the Japanese Model] (Tokyo: Ōtsuki shoren, 1992); and Seikyō sōgō kenkyūsho, *Kyōdō kumiai no shin seiki* [Co-Ops and the New Century] (Tokyo: Co-opu shuppan, 1992). For a cover story of the Japanese co-op movement, see *Ekonomisuto*, February 9, 1993. See also Muto Ichiyo, "The Alternative Livelihood Movement," *AMPO Japan–Asia Quarterly Review*, Vol. 24, No. 2, 1993, pp. 4–11, for a summary of Japan's co-op movement, the Green Co-op and the SC. For an account of the historical development of Japan's co-op movement from the viewpoint of a top SC leader, see Kotuska Hisao, *Musubitsuki shakai: kyōdō kumiai sono rekishi to riron* [A Network Society: The History and Theory of the Co-op Movement] (Tokyo: Daiichi shorin, 1994).

8   *Ibid.*, Iwadare, *Consumer Co-operatives in the Spotlight*, p. 431.

9   Yamamoto Aki, *Nihon seikatsu kyōdō kumiai undō shi* [The History of Japanese Co-operative Union] (Tokyo: Nihon hyōronsha, 1982).

10 An indication of its mission is its staunch refusal to sell mayonnaise even though it is profitable to do so. The organization believes that members should, as far as possible, be self-reliant and produce their mayonnaise which is "made by mixing egg yolks, vinegar, oil and seasoning and can be produced easily at home." See Yokota, *Orutanitibu shimin shakai sengen*, p. 60.

11 Seikatsu kurabu seikatsu kyōdō kumiai, *Orutanatibu: seikatsu kurabu kanagawa 20 nen no ayumi*, pp. 156–157.

12 According to one survey, 92.4 percent of members claimed that their initial motive to join the SC was the desire to obtain good-quality food. Only 11.6 percent cited interest in social movements as the impetus to join the SC. See Seikatsu kurabu rengō shōhi iinkai, *Shōhi seikatsu kenkyūkai hōkokusho*, p. 16.

13 Yokota, *Orutanatibu shimin shakai sengen*, pp. 161–168.

14 *Ibid.*, p. 168.

15 The Green Co-op North Block, an allied co-op which sponsors NET in Fukuoka prefecture, offers funeral services to its members. Yoshida Toshio, interview on September 23, 1992.

16 Explanation by Hamada Hiroko, Section Chief, Chiba SC and Liaison Officer for Chiba NET, conversation on August 12, 1992.

17 Fujimura Kisako, NET assembly woman, Fujisawa city, Kanagawa, interview on July 29, 1992.

18 Ordinary SC member, Midori ward, Yokohama, conversation on July 6, 1992.

19 Yokota, *Sankagata shimin shakai ron*, p. 82. See also Yokota, *Orutanatibu shimin shakai sengen*, pp. 50–57.

20 Iwao Sumiko translated the term *"dairinin"* as "proxy." See Iwao, *The Japanese Woman*, p. 249. Iwao has a short chapter on the Kanagawa NET. See pp. 246–264.

21 *Seikatsu to jichi*, No. 101, March 1, 1977, p. 1.

22 The SC's special term for such citizens is *seikatsusha* or literally a being who engages in livelihood.

23 This is a variation of Yamasaki Tetsuya's argument that NET's electoral success

was not an ephemeral boom, but the outcome of more than 20 years of social movement. See Yamasaki, "Shufu no seikyō undō no ishiki henyō: seikatsu kurabu seikyō no kumiai chōsa kara," p. 31.

24 Japanese Consumers' Co-operative Union, *Co-op Facts and Figures: 1990*. A 1991 pamphlet.

25 Statistics calculated from Seikatsu kurabu rengō kai, *Seikatsu kurabu gurūpu 1992*, p. 2. An annual booklet.

26 Kōno Eiji, Director, Tokyo SC, interview on October 27, 1992. See also Yokota, *Orutanatibu shimin shakai sengen*, p. 16. See also early SC newsletter, *Koe*, No. 59, August 5, 1970, p. 6. The organization target was to organize 10 percent of Setagaya ward's households.

27 *Ibid.*, Yokota, p. 16. See also Kotsuka, *Musubitsuki shakai*, pp. 104–106. According to Kotsuka, in the best case, the rate of organization around an SC depot is slightly more than 30 percent of the local residents (within a radius of 700 meters) but the the average rate of organization for the depot is between 20 and 25 percent.

28 Katō Kōichi, Special Director, Community Club, SC, interview on May 14, 1992.

29 Information from Ōnishi Yōko, NET candidate, Totsuka ward, 1992 Local Election, interview on June 5, 1992. Also related by Makishima Sayoko, NET candidate, Minami ward, 1987 Local Elections and Chairwoman, Southern Yokohama Block, Kanagawa SC, interview on November 20, 1992.

30 Yokota, *Orutanitibu shimin shakai sengen*, p. 52.

31 Comyuniti kurabu, *Sōritsu sōkai giansho* [Proposals of Inaugural General Meeting], 1991 booklet, p. 35.

32 Seikatsu kurabu seikatsu kyōdō kumiai, *Orutanatibu: seikatsu kurabu kanagawa 20 nen no ayumi*, pp. 274–275. For the media's coverage of SC's Workers' Collective, see for example the following articles from the *Kanagawa shinbun*, June 12, 1991, February 5, 1992, p. 14 and March 26, 1992, p. 17.

33 Seikatsu kurabu seikatsu kyōdō kumiai, *Orutanatibu: seikatsu kurabu kanagawa 20 nen no Ayumi*, pp. 266–268.

34 *Ibid.*, pp. 129–132. The Kanagawa SC had 12 Livelihood halls and 15 delivery centers in 1995. Seikatsu kurabu rengō kai, *Seikatsu kurabu 1996*, p. 17.

35 *Ibid.*, pp. 279–281.

8 The Network Movement: a Japanese Green party?

1 A New Politics party must be led by women and men; there should be gender equality in theory and practice. Since NET's membership comprises only women, it should not be led by men.

2 For an alternative view that NET is indeed a New Politics party, see Fuji Atsushi, "Nyū politikusu tekina undō seitō toshite no dairinin" [The Agent Movement as a New Politics movement party], *Shakai undō*, No. 192, March 1996.

3 Hokkaidō NET has not formally adopted the rotation system. It is still under consideration. *Shakai undō*, No. 152, November 15, 1992, pp. 10 and 21 and *Shakai undō*, No. 163, October 15, 1993, p. 12.

4 As a result of the revolution in international telecommunications, the SC and NET are able to obtain real-time information and draw inspiration from the German Greens. Ikeda Tōru, founding father of Chiba SC, visited the German Green Party for a fact-finding mission in 1986. Interview on August 12, 1992.

In 1989, Tokyo NET produced a Japanese translation of the German Green Party's policies and principles. See Seikatsu kurabu wakku bukku, *Dairinin undō: sono kanōsei* [The Agent's Movement: That Possibility], 1988 booklet, p. 18. There are also intermittent contacts between the German Greens and Kanagawa NET. See for example, Kanagawa nettowāku undō, *NET to nan channeru?* [What Channel is NET?] (Yokohama: Kanashin shuppan, 1990), p. 123. Between July and August 1985, Kanagawa NET studied and discussed the German Green Party. Kanagawa nettowāku undō, *Sōkai giansho dairoku gō* [General Assembly Proposals, Number 6], July 1989, p. 7.

5 Padgett and Paterson write: "The Green's organizational principle represents a very optimistic reading of human nature, and putting them into practice has proved difficult," in Stephen Padgett and William Paterson, "The Rise and Fall of the German Left," *New Left Review*, No. 186, February 1991, p. 67. The original two-year rule for Green assembly members in the Bundestag was modified after the first legislative term. The rules were bent by introducing a "diagonal rotation" where assembly members can subsequently serve in the Landstag or the European Parliament. Thomas Poguntke, "Unconventional Participation in Party Politics: The Experience of the German Greens," *Political Studies*, Vol. XL, No. 2, June 1992, p. 243.

6 NET assembly women receive a third of what they have contributed to the party. In the case of Kanagawa NET, their salaries are controlled by the prefectural party HQ. In other prefectures, the NETs at the ward level administer the funds. Kanagawa NET assembly women from Yokohama and Kawasaki receive ¥26,000 every month. Those from the smaller cities and villages receive ¥24,000 and ¥22,000 respectively. Even though the salary of an assembly woman from the special designated cities may be twice that of an assembly woman from a small city, Kanagawa NET gives them a similar amount for their expenses on the principle of equality. This is a source of dissatisfaction among some NET assembly women from the specially designated cities who have to put in much more work than their counterparts from small cities and villages.

7 The first national symposium for delegates from regional NET was held in Atami, Shizuoka prefecture in 1992. The liaison office, known as the Social Movement Center, is located in Setagaya ward, Tokyo. It publishes the magazines *Shakai undō* [Social Movement] and *Dairinin undō* [NET Agent Movement].

8 Ikeda Tōru, interview on August 12, 1992.

9 Chiba NET consciously rejects any centralizing agency. Its liaison office is not even a separate organization with its own premises. The person responsible for maintaining the lines of communication between Chiba's independent NETs is an SC section chief whose desk is located in Chiba SC's main office. Hamada Hiroko, Chiba NET's liaison officer, interview on August 12, 1992.

10 At NET's Tenth Annual General Assembly in July 1993, 14 out of 18 management committee members are new faces. *Shakai undō*, No. 162, September 15, 1993, p. 61.

11 When speaking with peers in informal situations, the Japanese dispense with honorific language. Interestingly, when the assembly women interacted with the SC founding father, Iwane Kunio, they used honorific language when addressing him while Iwane did not reciprocate with the same level of polite language. Iwane also had the tendency of interjecting and cutting off the comments of the assembly women when they were speaking. A few assembly women were visibly annoyed by Iwane's regal style in the discussion group in which the author also

participated. Despite talk of egalitarianism on the part of Iwane and NET women, they did not escape from the hierarchical structure of Japanese society which they were supposed to change. The relationship between Iwane and the women was obviously not between equals judging from the tone and language adopted in the discourse. Observation by author in Atami, Shizuoka, October 3, 1992.

12 Aokage Takako, NET city assembly woman, Asahi ward, Yokohama, interview on April 7, 1992. For a description of Aaokage's *kōenkai* as a fan club, see Sasakura, Nakajima and Sugawara, *Josei ga seiji o kaeru*, p. 112.

13 *Ibid.*, interview.

14 Kanagawa NET advocated a complementary *kōenkai* approach at its second Annual General Meeting in 1985. This was in anticipation of the 1987 Local Elections where it was to run a large slate of candidates for the first time. Kanagawa nettowāku undō, *Dainikai sōkai giansho*, pp. 22–23. For Kanagawa SC's prescription of *kōenkai*, see the diagram in Seikatsu kurabu seikatsu kyōdō kumiai kanagawa, *Seikatsusha niyoru seiji* [Politics through People Concerned with Livelihood], a 1991 booklet on NET's policies. See p. 13.

In early 1992, Kanagawa NET promoted the *kōenkai* of its candidate to run in the Lower House Election of Kanagawa District Two. Kanagawa NET explained that since 120,000 votes are needed to win the election, it is necessary to transcend the SC-NET group by constructing a "Yokoyama Sumiko *Kōenkai*," a personal support organization named after the candidate. See *NET*, No. 93, April 1, 1992, p. 1. *NET* is Kanagawa NET's newsletter.

15 Yoshida Toshio, Special Director, Green Co-op North Block, interview on September 23, 1992 and Iwane Kunio, interview on May 13, 1992.

16 Argument put forward by Ide Sachio, Editor of *Shakai undō*. Interview on May 8, 1992.

17 For a breakdown of the number of votes needed to win a seat in different regions and electoral systems, see *Shakai undō*, No. 134, May 15, 1991, pp. 2–5 and *Shakai undō*, No. 182, May 1995, pp. 16–21.

18 *Shakai undō*, No. 157, April 15, 1993, p. 37. See also *NET*, No. 93, April 1, 1992, p. 3. It argued that party organization and *kōenkai* are "two wheels" which the candidate relies on to win her election. It noted that there are supporters who join a *kōenkai* but not the NET organization. NET called for the promotion of its beliefs among *kōenkai* supporters and that the organization should not be a "fan club" of the assembly woman. Iwane also warned that in the search for votes, NET should not degenerate into a personal election vehicle. Iwane, *Atarashii shakai undō no shihan seiki*, p. 172.

19 Eva Kolinsky wrote, "In 1988, the Greens had around 40,000 members: among the 13,000 women, no more than 3,000 can be expected to take an active role in the party . . . (there is) a shortage of women willing to hold an office in the party organization." "Women in the Green Party," in Eva Kolinsky, ed., *The Greens in West Germany: Organization and Policy Making* (Oxford: Berg, 1989), p. 204.

20 The nomination process of NET candidates is pieced together from numerous interviews with NET assembly women.

21 Terada Etsuko, interview on July 7, 1992.

22 Andō Jinbei, interview on April 22, 1993. Andō is a fascinating activist who was purged from the Japanese Communist Party for his support of structural reform theory. He joined the SC shortly after it was established in 1965. Andō is an advisor of the Kanagawa and Tokyo SC. He was the editor of *Gendai rironsha*

[Contemporary Theory Publishing Company] that commented on Gramscian theory, social movements and the Left in Japan. Andō also edited Yokota's books. Andō and many SC leaders are kindred spirits as a result of their interests in Gramscian ideology and commitment to social movements.

23 For the view that the SC is led by men, see Sasakura, Kanajima and Sugawara, *Josei ga seiji o kaeru*, p. 118 and *Ekonomisuto*, May 5, 1991, p. 89.

24 The emphasis on motherhood is not unique to NET. It is noted that "the contemporary women's movement in Japan continues to identify priorities in terms of traditional feminine roles, notably motherhood" in Linda L. Johnson, "The Feminist Politics of Takako Doi and the Social Democratic Party of Japan," *Women's Studies International Forum*, Vol. 15, No. 3, 1992, p. 393.

25 This bifurcation of interest is apparent in the special issue of *Shakai undō*, No. 152, November 15, 1992.

26 Taniguchi Tadashi, a male SC worker who is assigned to organize NET in Saitama prefecture told me this story:

> Some SC women members from Saitama once complained that the SC's professional staff is dominated by males. The women were then asked whether they will allow their daughters to be SC delivery workers in order to climb up the organization ladder. The women then kept quiet because none were willing to urge their daughters to embark on a tough physical job.
> (Interview on October 26, 1992)

27 For an account of Japanese women's lack of employment mobility, see Mary C. Brinton, Hang-Yue Ngo, and Shibuya Kumiko, "Gendered Mobility Patterns in Industrial Economies: The Case of Japan," *Social Science Quarterly*, Vol. 72, No. 4, December 1991, pp. 807–815.

28 There are 16 advisors to Kanagawa NET and they receive a stipend from the organization. Kotsuka Hisao, Director, Kanagawa SC, interview on April 19, 1993.

29 Katō Kōichi, Special Director, Community Club, SC. Interview on May 14, 1992. Katō intimated that he was ordered (*meirei*) by Yokota to become the campaign strategist of Yokoyama Sumiko, the first woman candidate from Kanagawa NET to contest in the Lower House Elections of 1990. In the 1991 Local Election, Kobayashi, the founding father of Hokkaidō SC, formally left the organization and became the *sanbō* of Hokkaidō NET. Kobayashi Shigenobu, Interview on July 22, 1992.

30 Yokoyama Keiji, interview on April 26, 1993. For a collection of Yokoyama's essays on social movements, see *Chiiki seiji to jichitai kakushin* [Local Politics and Reform of Local Government] (Tokyo: Kojinsha, 1990). Yokoyama is introduced as an advisor to Kanagawa NET in this book. He is also Emeritus Professor of Chūō University.

31 Inaba Mitsuru, interview on October 23, 1991.

32 For an edited volume of Inaba's articles for Kanagawa NET, see Inaba Mitsuru, *Kanagawa nettowākku undō no kanosei o motomete* [Seeking The Potential of the Kanagawa Network Movement] (Yokohama, Kanagawa nettowākku undō, 1994).

33 Kōno Eiji, Tokyo SC's Special Director, intimated that he negotiated with the JSP to obtain an endorsement for Tokyo NET's first prefectural candidate. Interview on October 27, 1992.

34 For a lengthy article on the conflict, see *Asahi shinbun*, evening edition (Tokyo), May 12, 1993, p. 27. The assembly woman also made available copies of various circulated memorandums indicting the "undemocratic leadership" of the SC and NET to the author.

35 Kōno Eiji, *Ima naze dairinin undō ka* [Why is there a NET Movement Today?] (Tokyo: Seikatsu kurabu seikatsu kyōdō kumiai, 1993), p. 13.

36 In this regard, NET's adoption of images of motherhood is similar to the style adopted by many housewives in politics. Sugiyama Lebra writes:

> As a professional housewife, (a woman) might offer some time for volunteer work. Furthermore her responsibility for monitoring the family health may induce her to be alert to health hazards like industrial pollution, food poisoning, medical malpractice, which may involve her in consumer movements and ultimately in politics. These steps are being taken by some urban women . . . .
>
> (See Sugiyama Lebra, *Japanese Women: Constraint and Fulfillment* (Hilo: University of Hawaii Press, 1984), pp. 311–312)

Hasegawa Kōichi makes a similar point by describing the typical participants in Japan's social movements as "worrying mothers" who use the symbolism of motherhood for their ends. See Hasegawa, "Han genshiryoku undō in okeru josei no ichi," p. 52.

37 For an account of a group of women civil servants who protested against their tea-making duties on the basis of gender, see Susan Pharr, "Shokujo ni okeru tōsō: ochakumi no hanran" [Struggle in the Work place: Rebellion against Tea making], *Lebaisan*, No. 8, Spring 1991. On the tradition of placing males before female students in class list, see for example Kanagawa NET's opposition to sexist roles in tea making in *Kanagawa shinbun*, March 16, 1993, p. 20. In 1993, Yokohama city permitted principals to decide whether they desire to mix the names of males and female students to avoid giving the impression that males are more valued than females. See *Kanagawa shinbun*, March 4, 1993, p. 18. On Hokkaidō NET's pursuit of the same issue in the local assembly, see *Shakai undō*, No. 170, May 1994, p. 37.

38 *Asahi shinbun*, (Sapporo edition), October 25, 1991, p. 27.

39 Kanagawa nettowākku undō, *1995 Tōitsu jichitaisen seisaku* [Policies for the 1995 Local Elections], booklet, pp. 35–37.

40 In a case study on NET's campaign spending in Yokohama's Kanagawa ward, the press noted that the NET campaign in that ward spent only ¥2.5 million, well below the permitted limit of ¥4.8 million prescribed for that ward. Political spending by the established parties were merely the tip of the iceberg; actual spending in Yokohama local elections ranged between ¥30 million and ¥50 million. See *Kanagawa shinbun*, April 19, 1987, p. 20. The average 1991 campaign spending of NET's 11 city assembly candidates was ¥1.35 million, a mere fraction of what the established parties splurged in their elections. The figures are calculated from statistics provided by Shi senkyo kanri iinkai, *Yokohama shihō* [Yokohama City Report], 1991. Kanagawa NET raised a reported ¥84.9 million while LDP gave an under-reported figure of ¥489 million in 1991. The JCP raised the most – ¥956.6 million in the same year. See *Kanagawa shinbun*, November 27, 1992, p. 1.

41 According to Yokohama's Election Management Committee, NET candidates raised funds exclusively from individuals while LDP candidates received funds mostly from small, medium and big businesses. Most of NET's contributors are

women whose small donations ranged from ¥10,000 to ¥30,000. The only male whose name appeared in most of Yokohama NET candidate's list of contributors is Yokota. He gave a token ¥10,000 to every NET candidate in Yokohama. His main contribution to NET is of course not financial. Figures are taken from Shi senkyo kanri iinkai, *Yokohama shihō*, 1991, various pages.

42 Kitschelt, "Organization and Strategy of Belgian and West German Ecology Parties: A New Dynamic of Party Politics in Western Europe?."

43 Iwane Kunio, interview on May 13, 1992. For Iwane's prescription of a Green–Gray alliance, see Iwane, *Atarashii shakai undō no shihan seki*, pp. 39–42. For his critique of a Green–Red alliance, see pp. 149–158. For a debate on Iwane's views on the same issues, see *Shakai undō*, No. 160, July 15, 1993, pp. 2–17.

44 Ikeda Tōru, interview on August 12, 1992. See *Shakai undō*, No. 150, September 15, 1992, p. 4.

45 Yokota Katsumi, Interview on May 7, 1992. Yokota was one of the 21 members of the JSP's national advisory council. See *Kanagawa shinbun*, November 13, 1991, p. 2. Yokota's role as a national advisor of *Jichirō* is garnered from an interview with Professor Yokoyama Keiji, May 22, 1993. Yokota's advocacy for a Green–Red alliance is found in Yokota, *Sankagata shimin shakai ron*, pp. 129–133.

46 Author's observation at Kanagawa NET's Annual Conference in Fujisawa city, Kanagawa on July 4, 1992. On the Kanagawa NET's endorsement of Chiba Keiko, a JSP Upper House Diet woman, see *NET*, No. 85, August 1, 1992, p. 1.

47 *Asahi shinbun* (Tokyo edition), June 28, 1993, p. 31.

48 *Mainichi shinbun*, June 24, 1993, p. 22.

49 On Eda Satsuki's endorsement of NET, see *NET*, No. 97, August 1, 1993, p. 4. Some SC and NET members have a soft spot for Eda Satsuki not only because of *Shaminren's* involvement in citizen-oriented politics, but also because of his father's involvement with Iwane to break away from the JSP to form an alternative party inspired by Gramscian ideology.

50 For a hint on the problem of *Zendentsu's* endorsement of NET despite mutually contradictory policies, see *NET*, No. 97, August 1, 1993, p. 2 and *Shakai undō*, No. 161, August 15, 1993, p. 44.

51 *Kanagawa shinbun*, June 15, 1995, p. 28.

52 The Kanagawa NET has formalized its alliance with Minshutō through forging a "political contract" with the national party. In the case of Tokyo NET and Hokkaidō NET, the relationship with Minshutō is less formal. See *Shakai undō*, No. 200, November 1996, pp. 39, 41, and No. 204, March 1997, p. 43.

53 Superficially, Sakigake and Minshutō have given lip-service to amateur-based politics. In reality, most of their politicians came from the established parties especially the LDP and JSP, adopt the *kōenkai* and a top-down approach to politics.

54 Helmut Fogt wrote: "The founding members from the Left have used the Greens to create lasting political careers for themselves. . . . In effect, key offices are always held by the same small party elite." See Fogt, "The Greens and the New Left: Influences of Left-Extremism on Green Party Organization and Policies," in Kolinsky, *The Greens in West Germany*, p. 119.

55 *Seikatsu to jichi*, No. 185, September 1, 1984, p. 9.

9 The Seikatsu Club and NET: problems and prospects

1 Seikatsu kurabu, *Seikatsu kurabu gurūpu 1992*, p. 3. The membership of Tokyo SC declined from 56,322 to 55,765 in 1991 from the previous year.

2 Interviews with Ikeda Tōru on August 1992 and Kōno Teruaki on October 26, 1992.

3 *Shakai undō*, No. 150, September 1992, p. 29. See also Iwane, *Atarashii shakai undō no shihan seiki*, pp. 27–28.

4 *Ekonomisuto*, May 21, 1991, p. 89.

5 A 1992 study by the MHW predicted that between 1990 and 2010, more than 90 percent of Japan's population growth will be concentrated in Saitama, Chiba, and Kanagawa. The projected increases within the next 20 years for these three prefectures are: 38.7 percent (Saitama), 31.2 percent (Chiba), and 26.1 percent (Kanagawa). When the populations of these three prefectures are added to Tokyo's, the capital metropolitan region will be home to 29 percent of Japan's population. *Kanagawa shinbun*, December 16, 1992, p. 1.

6 According to the Prime Minister's Office, "the number of Japanese women in the labor force reached 26,510,000 in 1991, accounting for 40.8 percent of Japan's total labor force. Compared to 1975, these figures represent increases of 6,640,000 women in the labor force and 3.5 percentage points." Office for Women's Affairs, Prime Minister's Office, *The Current Status of Women* (Tokyo, 1992).

7 In 1965, 58.6 percent of women are housewives but by 1987, only 49.0 percent are housewives. See Keizai keikakucho, *Kokumin seikatsu hakusho* [White Paper on Citizen's Livelihood] (Tokyo: Ōkurashō insatsukyoku, 1992), pp. 67–68.

8 Between 1985 and 1990, the price of land in the big six metropolitan areas consistently registered double digits rate of increase over the previous year. See statistics in *Nihon kokusei zue*, 1992, p. 508.

9 Iwane Kunio, "Shufu nakijidai no seikatsu kurabu undō" [The SC Movement in an Era when Houswives are in Decline], *Shakai undō*, No. 182, May 1995.

10 Ware, *The Breakdown of Democratic Party Organization: 1940–1980*, p. 189.

11 Makishima Sayoko, NET candidate, Minami ward, Yokohama city 1987 Local Election and Chairperson, Kanagawa SC from 1996, interview on November 20, 1992.

12 Inoguchi and Iwai, *Zoku giin no kenkyū*, pp. 226–230. See also the excellent account of the LDP's attempts to clamp down the co-op movement in *Asahi shinbun*, March 18, 1985, p. 3.

13 The tax payment of big stores is 37 percent of their profits. The SC pays only 27 percent of their profits to tax. Thus, big stores complain that co-ops have an unfair advantage over them because of their lower tax brackets.

14 Odagiri, *Dokyumento seikyō*, p. 283.

15 According to one account, LDP members who were critical of the co-ops pressured the MHW to examine whether the co-ops were breaking the law by participating in electoral politics. See *Asahi shinbun*, March 18, 1985, p. 3.

16 For a full reproduction of the MHW's notification dated June 30, 1987, see Seikatsu kurabu seikyō porojekuto chiimu, *Ima seikatsu shiminha kara no teigen* (Tokyo: Omiya no mizushobo, 1988), pp. 145–151.

17 *Jiyū shinpō*, July 5, 1987, p. 7.

18 Odagiri, *Dokyumento seikyo*, pp. 310–311. A copy of the pamphlet circulated by Kanagawa LDP Women's Bureau was given to the author by Odagiri Makoto.

19 *Ibid.*, p. 312.

20 See the article, "Seikyō e no seiji katsudō kisei kō kangaemasu" [Thinking about the Regulation of Political Activities of the Co-Ops] *Shōhisha repōto*, No. 656–657, August 27, 1987, pp. 6–7.

21 Yoshida Toshio was summoned by Fukuoka's Ken Shōhi Seikatsuka [Prefectural Comsumption and Livelihood Section] to receive a lecture on the necessity of the Green Co-op North Block to avoid political participation. Yoshida's reply to the MHW representative was that it is the constitutional right of a co-op to participate in politics. Therefore it rejects the MHW's interpretation of the Co-op Law. Interview on September 23, 1992.

The Fukuoka Green Co-op expressed concern about the appropriate relationship between the co-op and the NET movement after the MHW once again warned it against any political involvement in the 1996 Lower House Elections. See *Shakai undō*, No. 205, April 1997, p. 56.

22 Information from Yatagawa Katsuyoshi, section chief, Social Betterment Division, Social Welfare Bureau, MHW. Interview on November 12, 1992. Yatagawa also kindly gave me the cautionary letters which are sent to the co-ops' prefectural federation HQs. The Social Betterment Division within the MHW is responsible for the regulation of the co-ops.

23 *Ibid.*

24 Waseda daigaku daiichi bungakubu shakaigaku senshu, *Seikatsu kurabu seikyō ni kansuru chōsa to kōsatsu* [The Consideration and Survey on the Seikatsu Club] (Tokyo: Sanei iinsatsu, 1991), pp. 122 and 130.

25 The SC was fond of using mayonnaise as a prime example of its pristine motivation and unwillingness to compromise with members' demands for mayonnaise for the sake of profits. The co-op felt that it was better for members to exercise their creativity by producing their own mayonnaise. However, when members were denied mayonnaise, they simply joined another co-op to obtain mayonnaise or purchased it from the supermarket. There are limits to the SC's ability to transform the values and behavior of its members.

26 There was the "Greening" of SPD policy at the Nürnberg Congress of 1986. See Padgett and Paterson, "The Rise and the Fall of the West German Left," p. 57. However there are limits to the SPD's flexibility to co-opt certain policies such as the immediate shutting down of nuclear plants or leaving NATO. For the above comment and also the analysis of the SPD's ambivalence toward the Green Party as a rival and potential coalition partner, see Peter H. Markl, "The SPD After Brandt: Problems of Integration in a Changing Urban Society," *West European Politics*, Vol. 11, No. 1, January 1988.

27 For a comparison between the social democratic parties of Germany and Japan, see Takahashi Susumi and Hirashima Kenji, "Seikentō ka bannen yatō ka" [A Ruling Party? A Perennial Opposition Party?], *Lebaisan*, Summer 1990.

28 In the 1991 Local Elections, the LDP in Yokohama adopted the recycling of rubbish as a policy in its election platform. *Yomiuri shinbun*, April 5, 1991, p. 5.

29 On the vulnerability of Kanagawa NET to issue change, see *Kanagawa shinbun*, July 22, 1993. Kanagawa NET competed in three out of five electoral districts in that prefecture and obtained only 127,464 votes or 3.45 percent of total votes cast in Kanagawa.

30 See William M. Chandler, "Party System Transformation in the Federal Republic of Germany" in Steven B. Wolinetz, ed., *Parties and Party Systems In Liberal Democracies* (London: Routledge, 1988).

31 For a breakdown of local electoral systems and the number of votes needed to win by NET assembly women, see *Shakai undō*, No. 134, May 1991, pp. 2–5 and *Shakai undō*, No. 182, May 1995, pp. 16–21.

32 Besides a bias against smaller parties, the new electoral system may also be less

friendly to women candidates. See R. Darcy and David L. Nixon, "Women in the 1946 and 1993 Japanese House of Representatives Elections: The Role of the Election System," *Journal of Northeast Asian Studies*, Vol. 15, No. 1, Spring 1996 and Raymond V. Christensen, "The New Japanese Election System," *Pacific Affairs*, Vol. 69, No. 1, Spring 1996, pp. 61–62.

33 *Kanagawa shinbun*, October 5, 1992, p. 1.

34 Even the eight-party ruling coalition led by Prime Minister Hosokawa Morihiro between 1993 and 1994 retained a considerable conservative presence of ex-LDP renegades that include the JNP, JRP and Sakigake, although the JSP was the largest party in the coalition, it was not in the driver's seat.

35 Kanagawa NET had signed a "political contract" with the Minshutō to promote a common agenda while Tokyo NET's support for Minshutō is less formal. The latter supports some of the Minshutō candidates but not an explicit support for the Minshutō. See *Shakai undō*, No. 204, March 1997, p. 43.

36 In the 1997 Tokyo Metropolitan Election, the Minshutō won only 10.33 percent of the total votes cast while NET won only 2.53 percent. For an analysis of the Minshutō's disappointing results, see *Asahi shinbun* (Tokyo edition), July 7, 1997, p. 26.

37 Terada Etsuko, interview on July 7, 1992.

38 NET sent a delegation to Cambodia to study the situation. See *Kanagawa shinbun*, December 18, 1992, p. 21.

39 Kanagawa NET has belatedly begun to study and formulate national-level policies. Five policy areas have been identified for study: 1) the electoral system and political funding, 2) energy, 3) constitution, SDF and peace-keeping operations, 4) market liberalization of agricultural products, and 5) economic policies. See *Shakai undō*, No. 163, October 15, 1993, p. 45.

40 *Kanagawa shinbun*, November 9, 1992, p. 2.

41 Watanabe Noboru, "Chihō seiji ni okeru 'seikatsusha seiji' no kanōsei: 'dairinin' undō no bunseki o toshite" [The Possibility of Consumer Politics in Local Politics: Through the Analysis of the Agent Movement], *Toshi mondai*, Vol. 82, No. 10, October 1991, p. 85.

42 Utsuki Tomoko, Kanagawa NET's spokeswoman, commented that Kanagawa NET assembly women are concerned primarily with problems associated with the family. Interview on July 9, 1992. Inaba, the Kanagawa NET's manager, told me that: "There are many social problems in Japan. NET is not a philanthropic social institution. If it pursues these causes, there will be no time left for politics."

43 Tominaga Sagae, 1991 NET candidate, Tama ward, Kawasaki city, interview on July 20, 1992.

44 Nasu Hisashi, Yamasaki Tetsuya, and Watanabe Noboru, 1991 unpublished survey on Tokyo NET members.

45 Yazawa Sumiko, Kunihiro Yoko, and Ito Machiko, "Toshi josei to seiji sanka no nyuwabu: netto dairinin undō no chōsa kara" [A New Wave of Japanese Political Women: A Survey of Network Women], *Keizai to bōeki*, No. 161, November 1992, p. 23.

46 In a booklet prepared for the 1991 Local Election, Kanagawa NET gave rare lip-service to feminism as one of the many declaratory principles. See Kanagawa nettowāku undō, *'91 Tōitsu chijitaisen ni mukete* [Preparing for the 1991 Local Elections] 1991, p. 5. See also the booklet prepared for the 1995 Local Election, Kanagawa nettowāku undō, *Seisaku 95* [Policies 1995], pp. 35–37 for Kanagawa NET's formal position on women's rights.

47 Hrebenar, *The Japanese Party System*, pp. 222–223 and Robins-Mowry, *The Hidden Sun*, pp. 135–136, 227.
48 *Shakai undō*, No. 204, March 1997, p. 43.
49 Thus far, Hokkaidō NET is the only regional NET that had expressed support for greater indigenous rights for the Ainu.
50 Some of NET's policy omissions are mentioned in Watanabe, "Chihō seiji ni okeru seikatsusha seiji no kanōsei," p. 85.
51 According to a survey of 4,014 voters from Yokohama (polled by Yokohama City Election Management Committee), 58.2 percent of voters believed that the low voting rate was a result of voters' dissatisfaction and distrust of politics. This was the most common reason cited for low voter turnout. See the committee report, *Yokohama shimin no tōhyō sanka jōkyō chōsa* [A Survey on the Voting Patterns of Yokohama Residents], No. 5, November 1991, p. 57. The Kanagawa Prefecture Election Management Committee conducted a similar survey in 1991. Out of 1,547 respondents from the prefecture, 48 percent believed that abstention from voting is a consequence of voters' dissatisfaction and distrust of politics. Survey results were reported in *Kanagawa shinbun*, February, 1992, p. 20.
52 See for example Dalton, *Citizen Politics in Western Democracies*.
53 *Kanagawa shinbun*, September 21, 1992, p. 2.
54 The sarcasm was recorded in the *Yomiuri shinbun*, February 9, 1991, p. 27. The disposal of household rubbish is a woman's job in Japan regardless whether she is a housewife or a working woman. According to a survey by Yokohama city, 90.9 percent of the women claimed to dispose rubbish alone. Shisei monitā ankēto hōkusho, *Shimin seikatsu to gomi* [Citizen Livelihood and Rubbish], (Yokohama: Yokohama shi, 1991), p. 7.
55 *Ibid.*
56 *Yoke* (Yokohama), "The Active City Assemblywomen Focus Serious Attention on Daily Problems," *Yoke*, Vol. 13, No. 72, July 1995, p. 9.
57 *Kanagawa shinbun*, March 22, 1992, p. 18.
58 Ōtsu Hiroshi, "Shufu giin ga chihō seiji o kaeru" [Assembly women who Change Local Politics] in Kannai Yoshiko, ed., *Josei gaku to iu ibunka taiken* [Another World of Women's Studies], (Tokyo: Akashi shoten, 1992), pp. 196–197.
59 In the Tokyo metropolitan elections in June 1993, all three prefectural candidates from NET won seats in Suginami, Setagaya and North Tama Number Two ward. See *Asahi shinbun* (Tokyo edition), June 28, 1993, p. 21.
60 Yokota, *Sankagata shimin shakai ron*, pp. 130–133.
61 See for example, the favorable publicity given to NET by the editorial column of *Asahi shinbun*, a top newspaper with a circulation of 8.2 million readership. *Asahi shinbun*, April 22, 1991, p. 2.

10 Conclusion

1 McKean, *Environmental Protest and Citizen Politics in Japan*, pp. 127–128.
2 For an argument on the durability and strength of the Old Parties in Western Europe, see Peter Mair, "Myths of Electoral Change and the Survival of Traditional Parties," *European Journal of Political Research*, Vol. 24, No. 2, August 1993.
3 See Scott C. Flanagan, "Mechanisms of Social Network Influence in Japanese Voting Behavior" in Flanagan, *The Japanese Voter*.

4 See book review in *American Political Science Review,* Vol. 86, No. 3, September 1992, p. 825.
5 See for example, Alberto Melucci, *Nomads of the Present: Social Movements and Individual Needs In Contemporary Society* (London: Hutchinson Radius, 1989) and P. Bert Klandermans, "Linking the 'Old' and the 'New': Movement Networks in the Netherlands" in Dalton and Kuechler, *Challenging the Political Order.*

Bibliography

English-language sources

Abramson, Paul R., and Ronald Inglehart, *Value Change in Global Perspective* (Ann Arbor, MI: University of Michigan Press, 1995).

American Political Science Review.

Bank of Japan, *Comparative Economic and Financial Statistics: Japan and Other Major Countires* (Tokyo: Bank of Japan, 1996).

Barnes, Samuel and Max Kaase, *et al.*, *Political Actions: Mass Participation in Five Western Democracies* (Beverly Hills, CA: Sage, 1979).

Bell, Daniel, *The Coming of Post Industrial Society* (New York: Basic Books, 1973).

——, "The Old War," *New Republic*, August 23 and 30, 1993.

Benjamin, Roger and Kan Ori, *Tradition and Change in Postindustrial Japan: The Role of the Political Parties* (New York: Praeger, 1981).

Berton, Peter, "Japanese Eurocommunists: Running in Place," *Problems of Communism*, Vol. 35, No. 4, July–August 1986.

——, "The Japanese Communist Party: The 'Lovable' Party" in Hrebenar, *The Japanese Party System*.

Bestor, Theodore C., *Neighborhood Tokyo* (Stanford, CN: Stanford University Press, 1989).

Bix, Herbert P., *Peasant Protest in Japan, 1590–1884* (New Haven, CN and London: Yale University Press, 1986).

Brinton, Mary C., Hang-Yue Ngo, and Shibuya Kumiko, "Gendered Mobility Patterns in Industrial Economies: The Case of Japan," *Social Science Quarterly*, Vol. 72, No. 4, December 1991.

Bull, Martin J., "Whatever Happened to Italian Communism?," *West European Politics*, Vol. 14, No. 4, October 1991.

Bull, Martin J., and Philip Daniels, "The 'New Beginning': The Italian Communist Party under The Leadership of Achille Occhetto," *The Journal of Communist Studies*, Vol. 6, No. 3, September 1990.

Bulletin (Japanese Communist Party).

Calder, Kent E., *Crisis and Compensation: Public Policy and Political Stability in Japan, 1949–1986* (Princeton: Princeton University Press, 1988).

Calista, Donald J., "Postmaterialism and Value Convergence: Value Priorities of

Japanese Compared with Their Perceptions of American Values," *Comparative Political Studies*, Vol. 16, No. 4, January 1984.

Cavazza, Fabio Luca, "The Italian Paradox: An Exit from Communism," *Daedalus*, Vol. 121, No. 2, Spring 1992.

Chandler, William M., "Party System Transformation in the Federal Republic of Germany" in Steven B. Wolinetz, ed., *Parties and Party Systems In Liberal Democracies* (London: Routledge, 1988).

Choy, Jon, "Japanese Town Vote Jolts Tokyo's Nuclear Plans" in Japan Economic Institute, *JEI Report*, No. 31B, August 16, 1996.

———, "Local Government in Japan: The Next People-power Revolution" in Japan Economic Institute, *JEI Report*, No. 43A, November 15, 1996.

Christensen, Raymond V, "The New Japan Election System," *Pacific Affairs*, Vol. 69, No. 1, Spring 1996.

Cooper, John F., "Japan" in Starr, *Yearbook on International Communist Affairs 1991*.

Curtis, Gerald L., *Election Campaigning Japanese Style* (Tokyo: Kodansha International, 1983), first paperback edition.

———, *The Japanese Way of Politics* (New York: Columbia University Press, 1988).

Dahl, Robert, *Who Governs* (New Haven, CN: Yale University Press, 1961).

Dahl, Robert A. and Edward R. Tufte, *Size and Democracy* (Stanford, CN: Stanford University Press, 1971).

Dalton, Russell J., *Citizen Politics in Western Democracies* (Chatham, NJ: Chatham House Publishers, 1988).

Dalton, Russell J., Paul Allen Beck, and Scott C. Flanagan, eds., *Electoral Changes in Advanced democracies: Realignment or Dealignment?* (Princeton: Princeton University Press, 1984).

Dalton, Russell J. and Manfred Kuechler, eds., *Challenging the Political Order: New Social and Political Movements in Western Democracies* (New York: Oxford University Press, 1990).

Dalton, Russell J., Manfred Kuechler, and William Bürklin, "The Challenge of New Movements," in Dalton and Kuechler *Challenging the Political Order*.

Daniels, Robert V., *A Documentary History of Communism*, Volume 1 (London: I.B. Tauris, 1985).

Darcy, R and David L. Nixon, "Women in the 1946 and 1993 Japanese House of Representatives Elections: The Role of the Election System," *Journal of Northeast Asian Studies*, Vol. 15, No. 1, Spring 1996.

Duverger, Maurice, *Political Parties* (London: Methuen, 1959).

Economist, The.

Epstein, Leon D., "Political Parties" in Fred I. Greenstein and Nelson W. Polsby, eds., *Handbook of Political Science*, Volume 4 (Reading, MA: Addison-Wesley, 1975).

Erie, Steven P., "Bringing the Bosses Back in: The Irish Political Machines and Urban Policy Making," *Studies In American Political Development*, Volume 4 (New Haven, CN and London: Yale University Press, 1990).

Far East Information Service, *Daily Report, East Asia*.

Flanagan, Scott C., "Electoral Change in Japan: A Study of Secular Realignment" in Dalton, Beck, and Flanagan, *Electoral Change in Advanced Industrial Democracies*.

——, "Changing Values in Advanced Industrial Societies: Inglehart's Silent Revolution from the Perspective of Japanese Findings," *Comparative Political Studies*, Vol. 14, No. 4, January 1982.

——, "Value Change in Industrial Societies," *American Political Science Review*, Vol. 81, No. 4, December 1987.

——, "National and Local Voting Trends: Cross-level Linkages and Correlates of Change," in Steiner, Krauss, and Flanagan, *Political Opposition and Local Politics in Japan.*

Flanagan, Scott C. *et al*, eds., *The Japanese Voter* (New Haven, CN and London: Yale University Press, 1991).

Fogt, Helmut, "The Greens and the New Left: Influences of Left-extremism on Green Party Organization and Policies" in Kolinsky, *The Greens in West Germany.*

Frankland, E. Gene, "Federal Republic of Germany: 'Die Grünen'" in Müller-Rommel, *New Politics in Western Europe.*

Harmel, Robert, "On the Study of New Parties," *International Political Science Review*, Vol. 6, No. 4, 1985.

Hofstadter, Richard, "The Citizen and the Machine" in Jeffrey K. Hadden, *et al.*, *Metropolis in Crisis* (Ithaca, IL: F.E. Peacock, 1967).

Hrebenar, Ronald J., *The Japanese Party System* (Boulder: Westview Press, 1986).

Huntington, Samuel P., "Postindustrial Politics: How Benign Will It Be?," *Comparative Politics*, Vol. 6, No. 2, January 1974.

Inglehart, Ronald, *The Silent Revolution: Changing Values and Political Styles Among Western Publics* (Princeton, NJ: Princeton University Press, 1977).

——, "Changing Values in Japan and the West," *Comparative Political Studies*, Vol. 14, No. 4, January 1982.

——, "Value Change in Industrial Societies," *American Political Science Review*, Vol. 81, No. 4, December 1987.

——, *Culture Shift in Advanced Industrial Society* (Princeton, NJ: Princeton University Press, 1990).

Institute of Statistical Mathematics, *A Study of the Japanese National Character: The Ninth Nation Wide Survey*, Research Memorandum No. 572, (Tokyo, 1995).

Iwadare Hiroshi, "Consumer Co-operatives in the Spotlight," *Japan Quarterly*, Vol. 38, No. 4, October-December 1991.

Iwami Takashi, *Seikatsu Club Consumers' Co-operative: On the Practice* (Tokyo: Institute of Japanese Renaissance, 1988).

——, "Foreword," in Yokota, *I Among Others.*

Iwao, Sumiko, *The Japanese Woman: Traditional Image and Changing Reality* (New York: Free Press, 1993).

Jain, Purnendra C., "Green Politics and Citizen Power in Japan: The Zushi Movement," *Asian Survey*, Vol. 31, No. 6, June 1991.

Japan Press Weekly.

Japan Quarterly, "Citizens Movements," *Japan Quarterly*, Vol. 20, No. 4, October–December 1973.

Japan Times.

Japanese Communist Party, Central Committee, *Sixty Year History of Japanese Communist Party: 1922–1982* (Tokyo: Japan Press Service, 1984).

——, *Program and Constitution* (Tokyo: Japan Press Service, 1986).

——, *Manifesto on Freedom and Democracy* (Tokyo: Japan Press Service, 1989).

——, *The 19th Congress of the Japanese Communist Party* (Tokyo: Japan Press Service, 1990).

——, *Important International Issues 1989*, Volume 17 (Tokyo: Japan Press Service, 1993).

Japanese Consumers' Co-operative Union, *Co-op Facts and Figures: 1990*. A 1991 pamphlet.

Jenkins, J. Craig, "Resource Mobilization Theory and the Study of Social Movements," *Annual Review of Sociology*, Vol. 9, 1983.

Johnson, Chalmers, "Tanaka Kakuei, Structural Corruption and the Advent of Machine Politics in Japan," *The Journal of Japanese Studies*, Vol. 12, No. 1, Winter 1986.

Johnson, Linda L., "The Feminist Politics of Takako Doi and the Social Democratic Party of Japan," *Women's Studies International Forum*, Vol. 15, No. 3, 1992.

Jordan, Grant, "The Pluralism of Pluralism: An anti-theory?," *Political Studies*, Vol. XXXVIII, No. 2, June 1990.

Kaelberer, Malthias, "The Emergence of Green Parties in Western Europe," *Comparative Politics*, Vol. 25, No. 2, January 1993.

Kanji, Haitani, "The Paradox of Japan's Groupism: Threat to Future Competitiveness," *Asian Survey*, Vol. 30, No. 3, March 1990.

Kelly, William W., *Deference and Defiance in Nineteenth-century Japan* (Princeton, NJ: Princeton University Press, 1985).

Kiichiro Tomino, "The Role of Citizen Movements in Japanese Politics," *Institute Reports*, East Asian Institute, Columbia University, March 1991.

Kim, Hong N., "Deradicalization of the Japanese Communist Party under Kenji Miyamoto," *World Politics*, Vol. XXVIII, No. 2, January 1976.

——, "Urbanization and Changing Voting Patterns in Japan: 1958–1979," *Keio Journal of Politics*, No. 4, 1983.

Kirkpatrick, Maurice A., "Consumerism and Japan's New Citizen Politics," *Asian Survey*, Vol. 13, No. 3, March 1975.

Kitschelt, Herbert, "Organization and Strategy of Belgian and West German Ecology Parties: New Dynamic of Party Politics in Western Europe?," *Comparative Politics*, Vol. 20, No. 2, January 1988.

——, "Left-libertarian Parties: Explaining Innovation in Competitive Party Systems," *World Politics*, Vol. XL, No. 2, January 1988.

Klandermans, P. Bert, "Linking the 'Old' and the 'New': Movement Networks in the Netherlands" in Dalton and Kuechler, *Challenging the Political Order*.

Kolinsky, Eva, "Women in the Green Party" in Eva Kolinsky, ed., *The Greens in West Germany: Organization and Policy Making* (Oxford: Berg, 1989).

Kolinsky, Martin and William E. Paterson, *Social and Political Movements in Western Europe* (London: Croom Helm, 1976).

Krauss, Ellis S., "The Urban Strategy and Policy of the Japan Communist Party: Kyoto," *Studies in Comparative Communism*, Vol. XII, No. 4, Winter 1979.

Kuechler, Manfred and Russell J. Dalton, "New Social Movements and the Political Order: Inducing Change for Long-term Stability" in Dalton and Kuechler, *Challenging the Political Order.*

Lane, Jan-Erik and Svante O.Ersson, *Politics and Society in Western Europe*, second edition (London: Sage, 1991).

Langer, Paul F., *Communism in Japan: A Case of Political Naturalization* (Stanford, CN: Hoover Institution Press, 1972).

Lijphart, Arend, *Democracy in Plural Societies* (New Haven, CN and London: Yale University Press, 1977).

Lindblom, Charles E., *Politics and Markets* (New York: Basic Books, 1977).

Lipset, Seymour Martin and Stein Rokkan, eds., *Party Systems and Voter Alignments* (New York: Free Press, 1967).

McDonald, Terrence J., "The Burdens of Urban History: The Theory of the State in Recent American Social History," *Studies in American Political Development*, Volume 3 (New Haven, CN and London: Yale University Press, 1989).

McKean, Margaret A., *Environmental Protest and Citizen Politics in Japan* (Berkeley and Los Angeles: University of California Press, 1981).

Mair, Peter, "Myths of Electoral Change and the Survival of Traditional Parties," *European Journal of Political Research*, Vol. 24, No. 2, August 1993.

Manley, John, "Neopluralism: A Class Analysis of Pluralism I and Pluralism II," *American Political Science Review*, Vol. 77, No. 2, June 1983.

Markl, Peter H., "The SPD After Brandt: Problems of Integration in a Changing Urban Society," *West European Politics*, Vol. 11, No. 1, January 1988.

Maslow, Abraham H., *Motivation and Personality* (New York: Harper, 1954).

Masumi, Junnosuke, *Postwar Politics in Japan: 1945–1955*, Japan Research Monograph No. 6 (Berkeley: University of California Center for Japaneses Studies, 1985).

——, "The 1955 System in Japan and Its Subsequent Development," *Asian Survey*, Vol. XXVIII, No. 3, March 1988.

Matsushita, Keiichi, "Politics of Citizen Participation," *The Japan Interpreter*, Vol. 9, No. 4, Spring 1975.

Mayhew, David R., *Placing Parties in American Politics* (Princeton: Princeton University Press, 1986).

Melucci, Albert, *Nomads of the Present: Social Movements And Individual Needs In Contemporary Society* (London: Hutchinson Radius, 1989).

Merton, Robert, "Some Functions of the Political Machine" in Jeffrey K. Hadden, *et al.*, *Metropolis in Crisis* (Ithaca, IL: F. E. Peacock, 1967).

Michels, Robert, *Political Parties: A Sociological Study of the Oligarchical Tendencies of Modern Democracy*, reprint (London: MacMillan, 1962).

Ministry of Health and Welfare, *Consumers' Livelihood Co-operative Society Law* (Tokyo: Japan Consumers' Co-operative Union, 1989).

Miyake, Ichiro, "Types of Partisanship, Partisan Attitudes, and Voting Choices" in Scott C. Flanagan, ed., *The Japanese Voter.*

Müller-Rommel, Ferdinand, "Green Parties and Alternative Lists under Cross-national Perspective" in Ferdinand Müller-Rommel, ed., *New Politics in Western*

Europe: The Rise and Success of Green Parties and Alternative Lists (Boulder: Westview Press, 1989).

——, "New Political Movements and 'New Politics' Parties in Western Europe" in Dalton and Kuechler, *Challenging the Political Order.*

Muto, Ichiyo, "The Alternative Livelihood Movement," *AMPO Japan-Asia Quarterly Review,* Vol. 24, No. 2, 1993.

Noguchi, Mary Goebel, "The Rise of the Housewife Activist," *Japan Quarterly,* Vol. XXXIX, No. 3, July–September 1992.

Offe, Claus, "New Social Movements: Challenging the Boundaries of Institutional Politics," *Social Research,* Vol. 52, No. 4, Winter 1985.

Office for Women's Affairs, Prime Minister's Office, *The Current Status of Women,* (Tokyo, 1992).

Padgett, Steven and William Paterson, "The Rise and the Fall of the West German Left," *New Left Review,* No. 186, February 1991.

Panebianco, Angelo, *Political Parties: Organization and Power* (Cambridge: Cambridge University Press, 1988).

Piven, Frances Fox, ed., *Labor Parties in Post Industrial Societies* (Cambridge: Polity Press, 1991).

Poguntke, Thomas, "New Politics and Party Systems: The Emergence of a New Type of Party?," *West European Politics,* Vol. 10, No. 1, January 1987.

——, "Between Ideology and Empirical Research: The Literature on the German Green Party," *European Journal of Political Research,* Vol. 21, No. 4, June 1992.

——, "Unconventional Participation in Party Politics: The Experience of the German Greens," *Political Studies,* Vol. XL, No. 2, June 1992.

Robertson, Jennifer, *Native and Newcomer: Making and Remaking a Japanese City* (Berkeley: University of California Press, 1991).

Robins-Mowry, Dorothy, *The Hidden Sun: Women of Modern Japan* (Boulder, CO: Westview Press, 1983).

Smith, Gordon, "Social Movements and Party Systems in Western Europe" in Martin Kolinsky and William E. Paterson, eds., *Social and Political Movements in Western Europe* (London: Croom Helm, 1976).

Starr, Richard F., ed., *Yearbook on International Communist Affairs 1991* (Stanford, CN: Hoover Institution Press, 1992).

Steiner, Kurt, Ellis S. Krauss, and Scott C. Flanagan, eds., *Political Opposition and Local Politics in Japan* (Princeton: Princeton University Press, 1980).

Sugiyama, Lebra, *Japanese Women: Constraint and Fulfillment* (Hilo: University of Hawaii Press, 1984).

Takabatake, Michitoshi, "Citizens' Movements: Organizing the Spontaneous," *The Japan Interpreter,* Vol. 9, No. 3, Winter 1975.

Tarrow, Sidney, "Social Movements" in Adam Kuper and Jessica Kuper, eds, *The Social Science Encyclopaedia* (London: Routledge and Kegan Paul, 1985).

Tilly, Charles, *From Mobilization to Revolution* (Reading, MA: Addison-Wesley, 1978).

Totten, George O., "The People's Parliamentary Path of the Japanese Communist Party, Part I: Agrarian Policies," *Pacific Affairs,* Vol. 46, No. 2, Summer 1973.

——, "The People's Parilamentary Path of the Japanese Communist Party, Part II: Local Level Tactics," *Pacific Affiars*, Vol. 46, No. 3, Fall 1973.

Tsurutani, Taketsugu, *Political Change in Japan: Response to Post Industrial Challenge* (New York: David McKay, 1977)

Verba, Sidney, Norman Nie, and Kim Jae-On, *Participation and Political Equality* (Cambridge: Cambridge University Press, 1973).

Ware, Alan, *The Breakdown of Democratic Party Organization: 1940–1980* (Oxford: Oxford University Press, 1985).

Watanuki, Joji, "Patterns of Politics in Present-day Japan" in Seymour Martin Lipset and Stein Rokkan, eds., *Party Systems and Voter Alignments* (New York: Free Press, 1967).

——, "Social Structure and Voting Behavior" in Flanagan, *et al.*, *The Japanese Voter.*

Yasunasa Kuroda, "Protest Movements in Japan: A New Politics," *Asian Survey*, Vol. 12, No. 11, November 1972.

Yoke (Yokohama), "The Active City Assemblywomen Focus Serious Attention on Daily Problems," *Yoke*, Vol. 13, No. 72, July 1995.

Yokohama City University, *Yokohama Past and Present* (Yokohama: Yokohama City University, 1990).

Yokota Katsumi, *I Among Others: An Introspective Look at the Theory and Practice of the Seikatsu Club Movement*, (Yokohama: Seikatsu Club Seikyo Kanagawa, 1991).

Zald, Mayer N. and John D. McCarthy, *Social Movement in an Organizational Society* (New Brunswick, NJ and Oxford: Transaction Books, 1987).

Japanese-language sources

Abe Hitoshi, Shindō Muneyuki, and Kawato Sadafumi, *Gaisetsu: gendai nihon no seiji* (Tokyo: Tokyo daigaku shuppansha, 1990).

AERA.

Aika Juichi, ed., Chiiki seyï no shaikaigaku (Tokyo: Seikai sisōsha, 1983).

Akarui senkyo suishin kyōkai, *Senkyo ni kansuru zenkoku ishiki chōsa*, various years.

——, *Tōitsu chihō senkyo no jittai: dai jūsankai*, various years.

Amano Masako, "Seikatsusha undō no deisei no mukete: seikatsu kurabu seikyō o jirei toshite," *Toshi mondai*, Vol. 87, No. 10, October 1996.

Andō Jinbei, *Sengo nihon kyōsantō shiki* (Tokyo: Gendai no rironsha, 1976).

Asahi jānaru.

Asahi nenkan.

Asahi shinbun.

Comyuniti kurabu, *Sōritsu sōkai giansho*, 1991 booklet.

Dairinin undō.

Ekonomisuto.

Endō Fumio, "Jichikai, chōnaikai nado no jūmin jichi soshiki to shichōson gyōsei to no kankei", *Jichi kenkyū*, Part 1, Vol. 819, No. 5, May 1992; Part 2, Vol. 820, No. 6, June 1992.

Fōramu 90's, ed., *Guramushi no shisō kūkan* (Tokyo: Shakai hyōronsha, 1992).

Fuji Atsushi, "Nyū politikusu tekina undō seitō toshite no dairinin," *Shakai undō*, No. 192, March 1996.

Fukuoka Masayuki, *Nihon no seiji fūdo: niigata sanku ni miru nihon seiji no genkei* (Tokyo: Gakuyō shōbō, 1985).

Fuwa Tetsuzō, *Nihon kyōsantō kōryō to rekishi no kenshō* (Tokyo: shin nihon shuppansha, 1991).

——, "Nihon kyōsantō nimo iiwasetehoshii," *Bungei shunju*, No. 774, January 1996.

——, "70 nendai o mo agemawaru rekishitekina yakushin," *Akahata hyōron toku shūban*, No. 1028, October 28, 1996.

Hasegawa Kōichi, "Han genshiryoku undō ni okeru josei no ichi: posuto cheruno-buiri no 'atarashii shakai undō'" in *Lebaisan*, No. 8, Spring 1991.

Ichikawa Taiichi, *"Seshū" daigishi no kenkyū* (Tokyo: Nihon keizai shinbunsha, 1990).

Igarashi Akio, "Daigishi kōenkai no seishinteki soshikiteki kōzō: moderu toshite no etsuzankai," *Shisō*, May 1989.

Inaba Mitsuru, *Kanagawa nettowāku undō no kanosei o motomete* (Yokohama: Kanagawa nettowāku undō, 1994).

Inoguchi Takashi and Iwai Tomoaki, *Zoku giin no kenkyū* (Tokyo: Nihon keizai shinbunsha, 1987).

Ishidō Kiyotomo, Iidamomo, and Katagiri Kaoru, eds., *Ikiteiru Guramushi* (Tokyo: Shakai hyōronsha, 1989).

Ishikawa Masumi and Hirose Mitsugu, *Jimintō chōki shihai no kōzō* (Tokyo: Iwanami shoten, 1989).

Iwami Takashi, *Raito raiburifuddo awōdo*, a 1990 Chiba Seikatsu Club pamphlet.

Iwane Kunio, *Seikatsu kurabu to tomoni*, (Tokyo: Shinjidaisha, 1979).

——, *Shakai undō toshite no seikatsu kurabu o kataru* (Tokyo: Shakai undō kenkyū sentā setsuritsu junbikai, 1979).

——, "Seikatsu kurabu no mezasu mono to dairinin undō", *Shakai undō bukkuletto*, No. 1, 1989.

——, "Seikatsu kurabu ni totte 'dairinin undō' to wa nani ka", *Shakai undō*, No. 162, September 1992.

——, *Atarashii shakai undō no shihan seiki* (Tokyo: Kyōdō tosho sābisu, 1993).

——, "Shufu nakijidai no seikatsu kurabu undō," *Shakai undō*, No. 182, May 1995.

Iwaseki Nobuhiko, *Chōnaikai no kenkyū* (Tokyo: Ocha no mizu shobo, 1989).

Jiyū minshu.

Jiyū shinpō.

Jūmin toshokan, *Minikomi sō mokuroku* (Tokyo: Heibonsha, 1992).

Jiyūminshu kenshyūbu, "1985 nen taisei e no tenbō" *Jiyū Minshu*, January 1982.

Kamishima Jirō, ed., *Gendai nihon no seiji kōzō* (Tokyo: Hōritsu bunkasha, 1985).

Kanagawa Forum 21, *Kanagawa kensei e no teigen* (Yokohama: Jimintō seisakukyoku, 1991).

——, *Kankyōkyōiku sinpojūmu hōkokusho* (Yokohama: Jimintō kanagawa kenren jimukyoku, 1992).

Kanagawa Ken, *Gikai Jihō*, Vol. 43, 1991.

Kanagawa nettowāku undō, *Dainikai sōkai giansho*, September 1985.

——, *Dairoku sōkai giansho*, July 1989.

——, *NET to nan channeru?* (Yokohama: Kanashin shuppan, 1990).

——, *'91 tōitsu chijitaisen ni mukete*, 1991.

——, *Seisaku 95.*

——, *1995 Tōitsu jichitaisen seisaku*, booklet.

Kanagawa senkyo kanri iinkai, *Daijūichi tōitsu chihō senkyo*, 1991.

Kanagawa shinbun.

Katagiri Kaoru, *Guramushi* (Tokyo: Riburopoto, 1991).

Keizai keikakuchō, *Kokumin seikatsu hakusho* (Tokyo: Ōkurashō insatsukyoku, 1992).

Kihara Satoru, "86 nen taisei ron no jitsuzō," *Akahata hyōron toku shuppan*, July 27, 1987.

Kijima Masamichi, *Kōzō kaikaku ha: sono kako to mirai* (Tokyo: Gendai no rironsha, 1977).

Kobayashi Eezo, "Tōkiritsu to kojin no jiyū mondai: mushozoku rikkōho no shisōteki mondai nimo kanren shite," *Akahata hyōron toku shūban*, No. 964, July 17, 1995.

Koe.

Kōno Eiji, *Ima naze dairinin undō ka* (Tokyo: Seikatsu kurabu seikatsu kyōdō kumiai, 1993).

Kotsuka Hisao, "Seikatsusha no jidai", *Bunka shiirizu*, No. 9, 1984.

——, "Ima guramushi ni kodawaru" in *Gendai no riron*, No. 240, August 1987.

——, "Konichi no shimin shakai to guramushi" in Fōramu 90's, *Guramushi no shisō kūkan.*

——, "Ima guramushi ni kodawaru guramushi botsugo gojunen sinpojūmu kara kyuju nendai e" in Ishodō, Iidamomo, and Katagiri, *Ikiteiru Guramushi.*

——, *Musubitsuki Shakai: kyōdō kumiai sono rekishi to riron* (Tokyo: Daiichi shorin, 1994).

Kurasawa Susumu and Akimoto Ritsuo, eds., *Chōnaikai to chiiki shudan* (Tokyo: Minerubia shobo, 1990).

Kurihara Akira and Shōji Kokira, eds., *Shakai undō to bunka keisei* (Tokyo: Tokyo daigaku shuppankai, 1987).

Mainichi shinbun.

Mainichi shinbunsha, *1991 tōitsu chihō senkyo* (Tokyo: Mainichi shinbunsha, 1991).

Maruyama Shigeki, "Guramushi no sisō hōhō to konichi no 'atarashii shakai undō'" in Fōramu 90's, *Guramushi no shisō kūkan.*

——, "Guramushi to wākazu korekutibu" in Ishodō, Iidamomo, and Katagiri, *Ikiteiru Guramushi.*

Maruyama Yoshio, "Siekatsu kurabu seikyō no jigyō sasiki" in Yoshiyuki, *Joseitachi no seikatsau netlowāku.*

Masumi Junnosuke, *Nihon seiji shi* (Tokyo: Tokyo daigaku shuppansha, 1988) Vols. 3 and 4.

Matsuoka Hideo and Arita Yoshifu, eds., *Nihon kyōsantō e no tegami* (Tokyo: Kyōiku shiryō shuppansha, 1990).

Matsuzaki Tetsuhisa, "86 nen taisei wa shinazu," *Chūō kōron*, June 1987.

——, *Nihongata demokurashi no gyakusetsu: nisei giin wa naze umareru no ka* (Tokyo: Tōjuha, 1991).

Miyake Ichirō, *et al.*, *Nihon seiji no zahyō* (Tokyo: Yūhikaku sensho, 1985).

Miyamoto Kenji, *Nihon kakumei no tenbō* (Tokyo: Shin nihonsho, 1967), No. 41.

Morioka Kiyoshi, *et al.*, *Toshi shakai gaku no furontia* (Tokyo: Nihon hyōronsha, 1992).

Muruyama Shigeki, "Guramushi to wākāzu korekutibu," in Ishidō, Iidamomo, and Katagiri, *Ikiteiru Guramushi.*

Muta Kazue, "Seiji to shakai undō: nihon ni okeru atarashii shakai undō no tenkai" in Aaoki Yasuhiro and Nakamichi Minoru, eds., *Gendai nihon seiji no shakaigaku* (Kyoto: Showado, 1991).

Nakagawa Go, "Chōnaikai no kaifuku," *Toshi mondai kenkyū*, Vol. 45, No. 5, May 1993.

Nakasone Yasuhiro, "Shin jidai o kizuku jimintō no shimei: 1986 taisei no stāto," *Jiyū minshu*, October 1986.

——, "Sengo seiji no sōkessan to wa nani ka," *Jiyū minshu*, November 1987.

Nasu Hisashi, Yamasaki Tetsuya, and Watanabe Noboru, unpublished 1991 survey on Tokyo NET.

NET.
Nihon hōsō shuppan kyōkai, *Nihon no shōhisha undō* (Tokyo: Nihon hōsō shuppan kyōkai, 1980).

Nihon keizai shinbun.

Nihon kokuze zue.

Nihon kyōsantō kanagawa ken iinkai, *Heiwa to kakushin o mezashite: nihon kyōsantō kanagawa kentō no ayumi* (Yokohama: Shin kanagawasha, 1985).

Noruma Hidekazu, ed., *Seikyō 21 seiki e no chōsen: nihongata moderu no jikken* (Tokyo: Ōsuki shoren, 1992).

Odagiri Makoto, *Dokyumento seikyō* (Tokyo: Shakai shisōsha, 1992).

Okuda Michihiro, *Toshi komyuniti no riron* (Tokyo: Tokyo daigaku shuppansha, 1983).

Ōtsu Hiroshi, "Shufu giin ga chihō seiji o kaeru" in Kannai Yoshiko, ed., *Josei gaku to iu ibunka taiken* (Tokyo: Akashi shoten, 1992).

Pharr, Susan, "Shokujo ni okeru tōsō: ochakumi no hanran," *Lebaisan*, No. 8, Spring 1991.

Sasakura Naoko, Kanajima Satomi, and Sugawara Kazuko, *Josei ga seiji o kaeru* (Tokyo: Shinsensha, 1990).

Satō Seizaburō and Matsuzaki Tetsuhisa, *Jimintō seiken* (Tokyo: Chūō kōronsha, 1986).

Satō Yoshiyuki, ed., *Joseitachi no seikatsu nettowāku* (Tokyo: Bunshindo, 1988).

Seikatsu kurabu jibunshi henshū iinkai, *Ikikata o kaeru onna tachi* (Tokyo: Shinsensha, 1981).

Seikatsu kurabu kanagawa, *Nē kiite kiite* (Tokyo: Shin jidaisha, 1989).

Seikatsu kurabu rengōkai, *Seikatsu kurabu gurūpu.* Various years.

Seikatsu kurabu seikatsu kyōdō kumiai, *Arutanatibu: seikatsu kurabu kanagawa 20 nen no ayumi* (Yokohama, 1991).

Seikatsu kurabu seikatsu kyōdō kumiai kanagawa, *Seikatsusha niyoru seiji*, a 1991 booklet on NET's policies.

———, *Tsujō sōtaikai giansho*, No. 22, 1993.

Seikatsu kurabu seikyō porojekuto chiimu, *Ima seikatsu shiminha kara no teigen* (Tokyo: Omiya no mizushobo, 1988).

Seikatsu kurabu wakku bukku, *Dairinin undō: sono kanōsei*, a 1988 booklet.

Seikatsu shinpō.

Seikatsu to jichi.

Seikyō sōgō kenkyūsho, *Kyōdō kumiai no shin seiki* (Tokyo: Co-opu shuppan, 1992).

Shakai undō.

Shakai undō ron kenkyūkai, *Shakai undō ron no tōgō o mezashite: riron to bunseki* (Tokyo: Seibundo, 1990).

Shi senkyo kanri iinkai, *Yokohama shihō*, 1991.

Shin kanagawa.

Shisei monitā ankētō hokusho, *Shimin seikatsu to gomi* (Yokohama: Yokohama shi, 1991).

Shōhisha repōto.

Sōmukyoku jimu kanribu tōkeika, *Yokohama shi no nōgyō* (Yokohama: 1990).

Sotō Shizuko, "Tō kōenkai katsudō no kyōka nituite," *Akahata hyōron toku shūban*, No. 944, March 6, 1995.

Suzuki Kenji, "Nihon kyōsantō kōenkai o dō kakuritsu kyōka suru ka," *Akahata hyōron toku shūban*, Part 2, January 18, 1993.

———, "Nihon kyōsantō kōenkai no kakudai kyōka ni zenryoku o," *Akahata hyōron toku shūban*, January 30, 1995.

Tanaka Aiji, *Shiji seitō o motanai yūkensha no kansuru jishoteki kenkyū* (Yokohama: Toyo eiwa jogakuin daigaku nyubun gakubu, 1992).

Takahashi Susumu and Hirashima Kenji, "Seikentō ka bannen yatō ka," *Lebaisan*, Summer 1990.

Takata Minoru, "Chiiki shakai no hendō to chōnaikai jichikai," *Toshi mondai*, Vol. 83, No. 1, January 1992.

Toba Kazuko, "Yatō dainitō o mezasu manshon-danchi katsudō no kyōka o," *Akahata hyōron toku shūban*, No. 784, December 30, 1991.

Toshi mondai.

Wabara Nobuo, "Kōenkai katsudō no kihon mondai," *Zenei*, No.599, December 1990.

Waseda daigaku daiichi bungakubu shakaigaku senshū, *Seikatsu kurabu seikyō ni kansuru chōsa to kōsatsu* (Tokyo: Sanei iinsatsu, 1991).

Watanabe Noboru, "Seikatsu jichigata jūmin undō no tenkai: ikego beigun jūtaku kensetsu hantai undō o jirei toshite" in Shakai undō kenkyūkai, *Shakai undō ron no tōgō o mezashite.*

———, "Chihō seiji ni okeru 'seikatsusha seiji' no kanōsei: 'dairinin' undō no bunseki o toshite," *Toshi mondai*, Vol. 82, No.10, October 1991.

Yajima Mitsuhiro, *Kochira ishihara shintarō jimusho desu* (Tokyo: Nihon bungeisha, 1991).

Yamamoto Aki, *Nihon seikatsu kyōdō kumiai undō shi* (Tokyo: Nihon hyōronsha, 1982).

Yamasaki Tetsuya, "Shufu no seikyō undō no ishiki henyō: seikatsu kurabu seikyō no kumiai chōsa kara," *Toshi mondai*, Vol. 79, No. 6, June 1988.

Yazawa Sumiko, Kunihiro Yōko, and Ito Machiko, "Toshi josei to seiji sanka no nyuwabu: netto dairinin undō no chōsa kara," *Keizai to bōeki*, No. 161, November 1992.

Yokohama shi kikaku zaisei kyoku toshi kagaku kenkyū shitsu, *Yokohama shimin ishiki chōsa* (Yokohama: Yokohama kōhō insatsu, 1991).

Yokohama shi midori ku yakusho, *Midori: midori ku kusei gaiyō*, 1990.

Yokohama shi senkyo kanri iinkai, *Senkyo no ayumi*, Vol. 12, 1988–1991.

Yokohama shi shiminkyoku, *Jūmin soshiki no genjō to katsudō* (Yokohama: Yokohama shi shiminkyoku, 1991).

Yokohama shi sōmu gyōsei ku chōsa shitsu, *Kōhoku ku to midori ku no chiiki seikatsu to gyōsei ni kansuru kumin ishiki chōsa* (Yokohama: Yokohama kōhō insatsu, 1991).

Yokohama shikai jimukyoku, *Yokohama shikai shi*, Volume 5, (Yokohama: 1985).

Yokohama shimin no tōhyō sanka jōkyō chōsa, No. 5, November 1991.

Yokohama shiritsu daigaku keizai kenkȳsha, *Yokohama no keizai to shakai 1990* (Yokohama: Yokohama shiritsu daigaku, 1991).

Yokota Katsumi, "Guramushi to nihon shakai undō no keiken kara" in *Gendai no Riron*, No. 240, August 1987.

——, *Orutanatibu shimin shakai sengen: mō hitotsu no shakaishugi* (Tokyo: Gendai no rironsha, 1989).

——, *Sankagata shimin shakai ron* (Tokyo: Gendai no rironsha, 1992).

——, "Guramushi to shakai sanka" in Fōramu 90's, *Guramsi no sisō kūkan.*

——, "Guramushi to nihon no seikatsusha undō no keiken kara" in Ishidō, Iidamomo, and Katagiri, *Ikiteru Guramushi.*

Yokoyama Keiji, "Seikatsu kurabu seikyō ni miru seiji ishiki no keisei," *Asahi Jānaru,* May 16, 1986.

——, *Chiiki seiji to jijitai kakushin* (Tokyo: Kojinsha, 1990).

Yomiuri shinbun.

Yonekura Makoto, "Seikatsu kurabu seikyō to kanagawa nettowāku undō no senkyo," *Akahata hyōron tokushūban,* No. 522, March 30, 1987.

Zenei.

Interviews

Andō Jinbei, Kanagawa and Tokyo SC adviser (April 2, 1993).

Aokage Takako, NET city assembly woman, Asahi ward, Yokohama city (April 7, 1992).

Azuma Ritsuko, NET city assembly woman, Zushi City (July 9, 1992).

Chiba Misako, NET assembly woman, Saiwai ward, Kawasaki city (July 18, 1992).

Ejima Junko, NET candidate, 1991 Elections, Isogo ward, Yokohama city (June 12, 1992).

Fujimura Kisako, NET assembly woman, Fujisawa city, Kanagawa (July 29, 1992).

Fujisaki Yasuko, NET candidate, 1991 Local Elections, Hodogaya ward, Yokohama city (June 5, 1992).

Fukuda Susumu, LDP city assembly man, Kanagawa ward, Yokohama city (February 7, 1992).

Hamada Hiroko, Section Chief, Chiba SC and Liaison Officer for Chiba NET (August 12, 1992).

Hamada Michiyo, NET village assembly woman, Ishigarichō, Hokkaidō (July 24,1992).

Ide Sachio, Editor of *Shakai undō* (May 8, 1992).

Iijima Tadayoshi, LDP city assembly man, Sakae ward, Yokohama city (March 30, 1993).

Ikeda Tōru, founding father of Chiba SC (August 12, 1992).

Inaba Mitsuru, Office Manager, Kanagawa NET (October 23, 1991).

Inokawa Hiroshi, Special Director, Co-Op Kanagawa (April 20, 1992).

Inoue Kaoru, NET city assembly woman, Koshiya city, Saitama (October 26, 1992).

Ishii Akira, professional staff, Kanagawa SC (February 1994).

Ishii Motsumi, *Kōmeitō* city assembly man, Kanagawa ward, Yokohama city (January 21, 1992).

Ishii Yoshiaki, *Kōmeitō* city assembly man, Midori ward, Yokohama city (April 9, 1992).

Itō Hiromi, Chief of Organization Division, Nagano SC (August 27, 1992).

Iwadare Hiroshi, Asahi Shinbun's specialist on the co-op movement (March 17, 1992).

Iwahashi Yuri, NET city assembly woman, Chiba City (August 10, 1992).

Iwamoto Masao, DSP city assembly man, Kanagawa ward, Yokohama city (January 28, 1992).

Iwane Kunio, SC founding father (May 13, 1992).

Iwaseki Hiroshi, Vice Chairman, JCP Kanagawa prefecture (January 10, 1993).

Kamei Yoshiyuki, LDP Diet man, Kanagawa District Five (March 15, 1993).

Kanisawa Michiko, NET city assembly woman, Kanagawa ward, Yokohama city (January 8, 1992).

Katō Kōichi, Special Director, Community Club, Kanagawa SC (May 14, 1992).

Katō Naohiko, LDP city assembly man, Kanagawa ward, Yokohama city (February 10, 1992).

Katō Reiko, NET city assembly woman, Okaya city, Nagano (August 27,1992).

Kikukawa Chikako, NET assembly woman, Fukuoka city (September 24, 1992).

Kimura Kōji, Section Chief, General Affairs, Kanagawa SC (August 5, 1992).

Kishida Jin, Manager of General Affairs Division, Kanagawa SC (August 5, 1992).

Kiuchi Hiroshi, Mass Party (Dai Shūtō) assembly man, Kōhoku ward, Yokohama city (February 12, 1992).

Kobayashi Shigenobu, founding father, Hokkaido SC (July 22, 1992).

Kobayashi Shōzaburō, LDP city assembly man, Midori ward, Yokohama city (December 4, 1991).

Kojima Yukiyasu, LDP prefectural assembly man, Midori ward, Yokohama city (March 18, 1993).

Kōno Eiji, Special Director, Tokyo SC (October 27, 1992).

Kōno Teruaki, founding father of Saitama SC (October 26, 1992).

Kotsuka Hisao, Chairman, Kanagawa SC (April 19, 1993).

Kurimoto Akira, Head of International Division, JCCU (April 1, 1992).

Makishima Sayoko, NET candidate, Minami ward, Yokohama city 1987 Local Election and Chairwoman, Southern Yokohama Block, Kanagawa SC (November 20, 1992).

Maruyama Shigeki, Head, International Division, SC Federation (April 10, 1992).

Masumoto Masako, NET candidate, 1991 Local Elections, Tsurumi ward, Yokohama city (June 4, 1992).

Matsumoto Kumiko, NET assembly woman, Kōhoku ward, Yokohama city (March 25, 1992).

Matsushita Keiichi, Scholar on social movements (May 19, 1993).

Miyashita Izumi, JCP assembly man, Tsurumi ward, Yokohama city (March 27, 1992).

Miyoshi Yoshikiyo, LDP prefectural assembly man, Midori ward, Yokohama city (December 5, 1991).

Momose Hiromichi, founding father, Nagano SC (August 27, 1992).

Mukaeda Eiko, NET assembly woman, Midori ward, Yokohama city (November 2, 1991).

Nakagawa Shunsuke, JSP assembly man, Kanagawa ward, Yokohama city (January 23, 1992).

Nakajima Kazuko, NET city assembly woman, Chūō ward, Sapporo city (July 24, 1992).

Nakano Kunio, JCCU public relations officer (April 1, 1992).

Ninagawa Shōichi, city assembly member and champion of anti-highway movement in Sakae ward, Yokohama city (February 6, 1992).

Nishioka Masako, NET candidate, 1991 Local Elections, Sakae ward, Yokohama city (June 2, 1992).

Oda Reiko, NET city assembly woman, Zushi city (July 9, 1992).

Odagiri Makoto, analyst of co-op movement (April 27, 1993).

Ogata Yasuo, Head of International Bureau, JCP (May 24, 1993).

Ōnishi Yōko, NET candidate, Totsuka ward, Yokohama city, 1991 Local Elections (June 5, 1992).

Ōnuki Norio, JCP city assembly member, Midori ward, Yokohama city (December 10, 1991).

Saruda Katsumi, Head, Environmental Division, LDP Kanagawa Forum 21 (April 12, 1993).

Sasaki Hiroko, NET city assembly woman, Higashi ward, Sapporo city (July 24, 1992).

Sasakura Naoko, feminist and analyst on Japanese women in politics (April 25, 1992).

Satō Kazuko, NET candidate, 1991 Local Elections, Midori ward, Yokohama city (June 23, 1992).

Satō Yōko, NET assembly woman, Miyamae ward, Kawasaki city (July 18, 1992).

Shibata Toyokatsu, JCP city assembly man, Kanagawa ward, Yokohama city (December 10, 1991).

Shimamura Masao, LDP city assembly man, Midori ward, Yokohama city (December 2, 1991).

Shinbori Toyohiko, Office Manager, Kanagawa Forum 21 (April 1, 1993).

Suga Yoshihide, LDP city assembly man, Nishi ward, Yokohama city (April 9, 1993).

Sugiyama Sakae, Chairwoman, Hokkaido SC (July 22,1992).

Suzuki Tsuneo, LDP Diet man, Kanagawa District One (June 13, 1991).

Takahashi Kiyoko, JCP city assembly woman, Totsuka ward, Yokohama city (December 21, 1991).

Takano Akiko, JCP assembly woman, Kōhoku ward, Yokohama city (May 21, 1992).

Takeuchi Etsuko, NET city assembly woman, Chiba city (August 10, 1992).

Taniguchi Tadashi, SC worker, Saitama (October 26, 1992).

Tano Sadako, JSP city assembly woman, Midori ward, Yokohama city (February 24, 1992).

Terada Etsuko, ex-Kanagawa NET assembly woman (July 7, 1992).

Tominaga Sagae, 1991 NET candidate, Tama word, Kawasaki city (July 20, 1992).

Tsuboi Teruko, Representative, Tokyo NET (October 8, 1992).

Tsuda Shōko, Representative, Hokkaido NET (July 21, 1992).

Uchihori Yaeko, JCP city assembly woman, Hodogaya ward, Yokohama city (March 27, 1992).

Ueno Michiko, NET candidate, 1991 Local Elections, Kanazawa ward, Yokohama city (June 3, 1993).

Ukishima Toshio, Office Manager, LDP Prefectural Chapter (March 1, 1991).

Umezawa Kenji, Secretary General, LDP Kanagawa Chapter (March 2, 1993).

Utsuki Tomoko, Representative, Kanagawa NET and NET assembly woman, Yamato city (July 9, 1992).

Uwabu Reiko, Chairwoman, Chiba SC (August 12, 1992).

Watanabe Mitsuko, NET prefectural assembly woman, Midori ward, Kanagawa prefecture (May 26, 1993).

Yajima Seiji, LDP city assembly member, Midori ward, Yokohama city (November 22, 1991).

Yamaguchi Taka, NET city assembly woman, Sapporo city (July 24, 1992).

Yatagawa Katsuyoshi, section chief, Social Betterment Division, Social Welfare Bureau, Ministry of Health and Welfare (November 12, 1992).

Yokota Katsumi, founding father, Kanagawa SC (May 7, 1992).

Yokoyama Keiji, Kanagawa SC adviser (April 26, 1993).

Yokoyama Sumiko, NET candidate in 1990 and 1993 Lower House Elections (May 22, 1993).

Yoshida Toshio, founding father of Green Co-op North Block, Fukuoka city (September 23, 1992).

Yoshimura Yoneju, LDP city assembly member, Midori ward, Yokohama city (January 10, 1992).

Index

Page numbers in **bold** type refer to **figures**. Page numbers in *italic* type refer to *tables*. Page numbers followed by 'n' refer to notes.